You Must Remember This

Also by Lansing Lamont

Day of Trinity

Campus Shock

Breakup

No Twilight About Me
(Editor)

Friends So Different
(Co-Editor)

Letters of John Masefield
(Co-Editor)

YOU MUST REMEMBER THIS

A Reporter's Odyssey
From Camelot to Glasnost

Lansing Lamont

Beaufort Books
New York

Library of Congress Cataloging-in-Publication Data

Lamont, Lansing.
You must remember this :
a reporter's odyssey from Camelot to glasnost /
Lansing Lamont.
p. cm.
ISBN 978-0-8253-0583-2 (alk. paper)
1. Lamont, Lansing. 2. Journalists–United States–Biography.
I. Title.

PN4874.L22A3 2008
070.92–dc22
[B]
2007052199

Published in the United States by Beaufort Books, New York
www.beaufortbooks.com
Distributed by Midpoint Trade Books, New York
www.midpointtradebooks.com

2 4 6 8 10 9 7 5 3 1

PRINTED IN THE UNITED STATES OF AMERICA

Riccho son doro et riccho son di suono
No mi sonar si tu non hadel buono

I am rich in gold and rich in tone;
If you lack a good tune, leave me alone

— Sixteenth-century Venetian inscription on a harpsichord

"There are three things which are real — God, human folly, and laughter. The first two are beyond our comprehension, so we must do what we can with the third."

— Indian philosopher

To Ada, fifty-four years out and still my true love.
To all those friends who helped enrich this story along the way.
To my children and their families down the long line.

Contents

Introduction

I came to this story by the luck of genes and a wayward curiosity.

I was weaned on the rich clan history of my Scottish forebears, a number of whom were writers. From their annals I drew much of the material for the opening chapter of this book. For the rest, it's my own concoction, a correspondent's story set in the turbulent central decades of the twentieth century.

I grew up in a well-connected family of capitalist strivers, socialist rebels, and strong-willed women hell-bent on defying custom. It virtually assured I would not end up a gray-flannelled drone clipping coupons. Early on, threading my way through the confusion of battling aunts and cousins, I took to wondering why birds sing, boys fight, and grown-ups do hateful things to one another.

My parents read the *New York Times* and the reliably Republican *Herald Tribune*; in the kitchen, the help read the *Daily News* with its snappy prose and graphic photos of gangland killings. I smuggled the *News* into my bedroom and began nurturing my own secret fantasyland. It was a place peopled with hitmen like Icepick

Phil, with raffish jazzmen like Wild Bill Davison, dashing stars like Bogart and, best of all, the hard-bitten reporters with page-one bylines who covered them. Not an uplifting group of role models, but one that led to a dream.

Outside my bedroom window, far below on the avenue, there were car crashes and fire engines forever racing by in full clangor. I wanted to run to the crash scene or follow the engines. Something in my ancestral genes sparked a yen to be at the center of things. My people had fought in the American Revolution; my great-great grandfather talked politics with Abraham Lincoln; my grandfather reported for Horace Greeley's old *New York Tribune* and later advised presidents. I dreamed of one day eavesdropping on the world's events and players.

So in time I morphed from a boy with Mitty-like fantasies about Bogie, trenchcoated and on deadline, to a paid eavesdropper in the real world of political and foreign affairs. With a few detours along the way.

The opening chapters describe the detours—family tensions and tragedy; gloriously misspent school years; the toughening army experience—en route to becoming a Washington, then foreign, correspondent for *Time*. That career centers the memoir. It spanned the volcanic decade of the sixties and beyond.

I would not achieve the luster of my grandfather Thomas W. Lamont, the voice of the House of Morgan at its zenith, or the celebrity of my controversial uncle, Corliss. But my reporting, through the pages of *Time*, reached a vast audience they might have envied. I played on a fast and often slippery track potholed with violent events and the occasional epiphany. I supped with the great and recorded their triumphs and defeats. At transforming moments I was a Zelig with a press pass.

I was in the church when they carried John Kennedy's casket down the aisle; in the hotel pantry when Robert Kennedy lay dying on the blood-soaked floor. I sat at the widow's feet in Atlanta when they gathered to say good-bye to the martyred Martin Luther King Jr. I stood amid the exploding buildings as downtown Washington went up in flames following King's assassination. I ran with the cops and protesters in the Battle of Chicago at the 1968 Democratic convention. I ran in the mean streets of Belfast and Derry in Northern Ireland where sectarian wars raged and small children got blown away.

Everywhere I interviewed the key players, seeking answers to the madness, from the hapless Hubert Humphrey to the scarred Robert Oppenheimer, the man who gave birth to the atomic bomb. What I learned I either reported to *Time* or later embedded in my books. If I witnessed much of the world's disorder in this story through the cool eyes of a journalist, I made sure to embroider these pages with warmer reminiscences of a personal kind: family larks, the foibles of the famous I knew, tales of exotic characters—some gone off the deep end. I dwelled among eccentrics, high and low, balmy relatives (one of my forebears was a reputed witch), or high-flying politicos with reckless egos.

One of the coins of political journalism is informed gossip, and this memoir has its plentiful nuggets. Washington abounded in off-beat personalities and low-comedy follies during the Kennedy-Johnson years. Britain, a nation of eccentrics and high-voltage public scandals, was grist for the reporter's mill the years I worked the London beat. In both Washington and in London, where I was a senior correspondent in the magazine's premier foreign bureau, I had rare access to the salons of power. Inevitably some of those powerful sources became friends—but only as long as they and I continued to trust each other, trust being the other coin of political journalism.

So this memoir portrays a cast of achievers, charmers, rogues, people engaged for the most part in worthy, often great endeavors, despite their all too human lapses.

The Scot has a knack for making much out of little, but even he would be taxed to embroider the past century. There was nothing small about it and my generation saw most of it, from the dawning of the atomic age to the unspeakable terrors of the present.

Behind the tale of a boy's dreams fulfilled—to have reported a historic time with all its high drama—lies the backstory of a young man who tried with some success to escape the weight of a loving but demanding father and family. I never fully escaped; you never do. But I found a rewarding counterweight in the riches of a journalist's life.

L.L.
March 13, 2008
New York City

You Must Remember This

1

Curtain Up: A Whiff of Claymore

Midway through the first act, I started kicking on the applause lines, trying to get the attention of my very pregnant mother who had settled into the fifth row of Manhattan's Belasco Theatre on a winter evening in 1930.

She was absorbed in the words of De Lawd, the protagonist of *The Green Pastures*, the musical folktale evoking a black heaven, which had taken Broadway by storm that season. At some point she felt a particularly sharp poke in her belly. Ka-thump. She nudged my father next to her. When the intermission curtain fell, they left the theatre and raced by cab to Doctor's Hospital on the Upper East Side.

There in the wee hours of Thursday, March 13, my mother loosed me squalling on the world, her third son. She never returned to the Belasco to catch the second act. I was the second act, the whole show for that matter, or so I imagined for a long time afterward. Only years later did I learn my parents had been hoping for a daughter. "Poor little boy," my grandmother wrote, "nobody wants him."

I hadn't a clue. I could easily have presumed I was a unique creation induced by stage magic. For a good while I thought I had a birthright to some piece of the Great White Way, that De Lawd had specially favored me. Which, it turned out, he had. He'd arranged that I be not only the son of a Wall Street banker, but a scion of one of the heads of the legendary House of Morgan, whose wealth eclipsed King Midas's. Not a bad hand considering the rest of the landscape that year.

Lines of the jobless and dispossessed formed in front of failing banks and soup kitchens. Men fought over barrels of garbage. On Wall Street despairing men leaped from high ledges to their deaths; others in homburgs and fraying suits sold apples for a nickel apiece. In a lot of homes (mercifully not ours) few babies were heard crying; people were afraid to have them. The market crash had taken its toll. Prohibition was in its eleventh year. That August, Judge Crater disappeared.

It was in some ways almost as bleak a scene as that which my ancestors had encountered seven hundred years before.

Out of the freezing gales that sweep the North Atlantic triangle of Iceland, Norway, and the British Isles came the earliest Lamonts in the opening centuries of the last millennium.

They were Norsemen, as fierce as the storms that blew their crude ships from Iceland or the Faeroe Islands southward to the Hebrides and the northern tip of Ireland, or southeasterly to the base of Norway. From Norway they would have crossed the North Sea to the coast of Scotland and made their way west through the Firth of Forth, skirting the bottom of Loch Lomond, ending up in the gloomy wilds of Cowal and the Argyll peninsula.

At the dawn of Scotland's nationhood the Lamonts were lords

of all Cowal, dwelling in the medieval fastnesses and "sodden path-less valleys" of an unsubdued sliver of the western Highlands.

They were a small but compact clan commanding respect from their neighbors. They spoke the language of the Gaels, spoke it long after English had become the accepted speech of Scotland. Their earliest written record was a charter in 1235 deeding certain Cowal lands to the monks of Paisley Abbey. The charter was signed by one Laumon, grandson of the clan's progenitor; Sir Walter Scott referred to Laumon as "Lamon mor," the Great Lamont.

Insulated in mind and geography from the mainstream of Scotland's struggle for independence, the Lamonts were neither shrewd bettors nor inspired warriors. On the two occasions they chose sides and sallied forth to battle, they lost impressively: first, they backed the wrong claimant to the Scottish throne; then they backed an English king who ultimately got the chop.

During the fourteenth-century revolt against the English Crown and its surrogates in Scotland, the clan erred in affronting the family of Robert the Bruce, hero of Bannockburn; it sided with the failed effort of the rival of Bruce's grandson to win the Scottish throne. That was the beginning of the Lamonts' decline as a Highland force. Their Cowal lands were claimed by the neighboring Campbells who'd supported the victorious Bruce. These were "the sleekit Campbells," in historian Hector McKechnie's words, "who combined claymore and parchment as never Celts before" in their warring against other clans. By the end of the 1300s much of the Lamonts' territory was gone and the centuries-long feud between the Lamonts and the Campbells was underway with a vengeance.

In the 1600s life in the western Highlands was remorselessly brutish and short, justice unsparing. As the diary of John Lamont of Newton makes clear, the region's inhabitants engaged in a litany of felonies and misdemeanors from bestiality and incest to patricide and witchcraft. Assaults and battery occurred at the drop of an insult. Amidst the everyday shootings, drownings, and stabbings came a drumbeat of public executions — well-attended hangings, stake burnings, and disembowelment. The gallows at Greyfriars churchyard in Edinburgh was a perpetual motion machine.

All this violence occurred in a land ruled by unforgiving Presbyterians. In the early 1600s there was only one God in Scotland and he was a rigid Calvinist. Not content with the Protestant Reformation, Scotland's churchmen sought to impose on England their own narrow brand of Puritanism with all its thou-shalt-nots. Ignorant of English institutions, convinced that popery was rampant on the streets of London, the Scottish presbytery denounced the Church of England from their pulpits. When Charles I responded to this insolence and sought to saddle Episcopacy and the hated English Prayer Book on his Scottish minions, they rebelled.

The uprising touched off the civil war in England in 1642, Cromwell's Roundheads opposing the Cavaliers who supported Charles and the Established Church.

The fighting moved north and spread across the restive Border districts and West Highlands. The heather was afire with clashing armies, martyrs for the Scottish Covenant littering the moors, zealous ministers of the Kirk (the Church of Scotland) indulging their bloodlust on English yeomen. Among the disunited clans allegiances shifted, some clans conspiring on behalf of the King, others in support of the rebels. The most minor skirmishes — Rullion Green, Drumclog, Bothwell Brig — entered Highland lore along with the most monstrous slaughters like that of the MacDonalds at Glencoe. None of these last surpassed the Campbells' butchery of the Lamonts on a June day in 1646.

The Campbells had for decades acted as a kind of unofficial police force in the West Highlands. Their chief, the Marquis of Argyll, detested Charles I and supported the Presbyterian Covenanters. Argyll's archrival, the Marquis of Montrose, had abandoned the Covenanters' cause in favor of Charles, and the King had put him in charge of Royalist forces in Scotland. Resentful clans like the MacDonalds and Lamonts continually tested the Campbells' dominance.

In 1644 Sir James Lamont and his clan joined a sizable force of MacDonalds to invade the Campbells' territory, aiming to pillage it and link up with Montrose's Royalist armies. It was an act the Campbells were unlikely to forget. A year later, when Montrose was defeated by Scottish government forces, Argyll's Campbells massed in Cowal to descend on Montrose's MacDonald and Lamont allies. The MacDonalds retreated, leaving the Lamonts to face the full brunt of the Campbells' wrath.

Only fifteen years later, at Argyll's trial for treason, did the full details of the carnage emerge. Barricaded in their strongholds at Ascog and Toward, cut off by land and sea, the Lamonts had withstood a fortnight of siege before their provisions gave out. On June 3, 1646, Sir James capitulated, having negotiated a written treaty that permitted his broken clansmen and women safe conduct at the hands of their captors. The ink had scarcely dried on the Campbells' signatures before Argyll's warriors turned their fury on the vanquished, citing no truck with "traitors to God and his covenant."

Ascog Castle fell first; then Toward, bombarded and burnt to the ground. A number of Lamont women and children were slain on the spot, their bodies left as "prey to ravenous beasts and fowls." Sir James and his lieutenants had been herded from Ascog to Toward after their surrender. Guarded behind the blasted walls of the fourteenth-century castle, their hands bound behind their backs, they must have heard in "torment and misery" the cries of their dying kinsmen. The surviving women and children were carried away in boats to an unknown fate.

Just before she was seized and stripped, one Lamont lady, who was somehow spared, managed to conceal in her hair a copy of the surrender document. The Campbells then threw the rest of the prisoners into boats and conveyed them down the coast to Dunoon.

In the kirkyard of Dunoon that June day the Campbells fell on their captives with a frenzy. They slaughtered with pistol, dirk, and shovel, egged on by a wild-eyed priest who stalked the scene as a self-appointed instrument of divine vengeance. There are no artists' renderings, no recordings, of what took place. One can only imagine the murmur of final prayers mingled with the shrieks of victims and, raging above the tumult, the imprecations of the lunatic priest. Perhaps a Campbell piper provided a skirling leitmotiv.

Thirty-six lairds of our Clan were hung from a single ash tree, then cut down, many still breathing, and tossed into the pits they'd been made to dig beforehand. Those who tried to climb out of the pits were pushed back, the earth piled over them till they suffocated. When it was over, there must have been a brief and terrible soughing, a last mass sigh of death, then silence.

All told, the rampage took some three hundred Lamont lives and eviscerated the Clan as a Highland force. The Campbells continued to overrun the Cowal peninsula, sending the Lamonts and other clans fleeing from their retribution. Legend says the ash tree at Dunoon withered and its roots ran blood.

Over the next centuries the Clan faded peaceably into the Highland mists. Among its dispersed remnants was a branch that found its way to Coleraine, a seaport town in the northern reach of Northern Ireland. From the progeny of one John LaMonte of Coleraine came, in the mid-1700s, the first of my line to America.

2

Ned Who'd Chase Earless Dogs and the Man Who Knew Lloyd George

My grandfather Thomas William Lamont entered the world in a nondescript clapboard house just up the road from the cemetery at North Hillsdale, New York, where his Revolutionary forebears lay.

At his birth in 1870, the United States was not yet a century old and just beginning to get on its feet after the trauma of the Civil War. It was a country of less than forty million souls, much of it beyond the Mississippi still "nature red in tooth and claw." Large swatches of the West remained unsettled and stateless; the opening of the transcontinental railroad linking California to the rest of the United States had transpired just the year before.

The decade would see the beginning of America's advance from a largely rural society to the world's preeminent urban industrial power. My grandfather would grow up to become a leader of the business forces that staked that advance.

The New York of 1892 that beckoned him, fresh out of Harvard and headed for his first job on a newspaper, was emerging as the world's second largest city after London.

Its harbor was the world's busiest, its skyline each year peppered with thousands of new buildings that increasingly dwarfed the church steeples that had once dominated it. No subway line existed and streetcars were still horse drawn, which led some locals to worry that all that manure halting traffic on the streets would somehow delay the city's growth.

Tom Lamont plunged into this new world with the gusto of a twenty-two-year-old. An early photograph of him shows a youth of steady gaze, full lips topped by a thin mustache, dark hair neatly parted in the middle; he wears a white wing collar and tie beneath a formal coat and vest. Had he worn that outfit his first day as a general assignment reporter on Horace Greeley's old *New York Tribune*, he might have drawn guffaws from his new colleagues. Except that they, too, working by wavery gaslight in the *Tribune* building on Park Row, then the tallest building in Manhattan, wore dark suits and stiff celluloid collars. Tom, congenial as he was industrious, fitted into the *Trib's* city room just fine. He soon graduated from covering street crimes and sports (he interviewed "Gentleman Jim" Corbett, the newly crowned world boxing champ) to reporting financial stories — a turn that well served him when he left the paper after two years to earn better pay in the business world.

Tom needed the money badly, as he had needed it while a scholarship student at Harvard. For in 1895 he would marry the equally ambitious Florence Corliss and set about with her to raise a burgeoning family.

My Grandmother Lamont was a gilded product of her class and times: brilliant, beautiful, with enough moral uplift to cow a convention of bishops.

She strove to adorn her new husband's world of practical affairs with her own brand of idealism. Her singularity came wrapped in the patronymic of an ancient family of Belgian nobles, de Corlies, who had joined the Second Crusade, eventually found their way to America where they'd renamed themselves, and finally fetched up in Englewood, New Jersey, where Florence was born. Her father had been turned down for service in the Civil War because of acute asthma, a condition he passed down through several generations of family lungs until it reached mine.

For Tom Lamont, he of equable demeanor and the finessing gesture, Florence provided a no-frills counterpoint. She was fierce in her convictions, scornful of diplomatic niceties, intolerant of the conventional. She lustily booed President Roosevelt at the news-reel theatre; went flying in a two-seater with Charles Lindbergh; and took to smoking pipes while on a visit to Japan with Grandpa. She was a spiritual gladiator who radiated what one writer called "a bluestocking intensity."

Florence took a thin-lipped view of the modern world and technology, deploring mechanical appliances if only because they seldom worked for her. In the private elevator of her New York townhouse she regularly pushed the wrong button and got stuck between floors. She was happiest pondering a classical ruin in Tuscany or discussing Spinoza with the British prime minister. Heaven was home in a paneled salon filled with tweedy philosophers and poets. Since these were in short supply in America, she invited the company of English ones. John Masefield, the salt-water bard, became her close friend.

Toward people of a different shade or race Grandma was not overtly biased, simply unaware. As befit her station, she had no innate knowledge of blacks, little rapport with Jews, and a familiarity with Catholics that extended to giving orders to her largely Irish household staff. She expended her most serious passions trying to tame the untamable lives of her four children. She was a one-woman Protection Society against the evils of bathtub gin, tobacco, and racy books. Later she tried her best to discern the patterns and personalities of her sixteen grandchildren. She did not, I'm sure, really know me except by name, and I have no yellowing letters to confirm even that. Still, she loved us all with an endearing imperiousness.

I rather prized being part of her court when the "grands," summoned, would crowd into her sitting room of a Sunday morning in Palisades, the family's weekend estate above the Hudson. I didn't mind a whit being one of her little acolytes, having to answer her persistent questions about what I had done that week to enhance the course of mankind. Who could begrudge a sovereign queen like Florence? Especially one who dispensed homemade vanilla ice cream smothered in chocolate sauce every Sunday lunch? I'd have slain dragons for her.

Even after he'd reluctantly left the *Tribune* to join a local food products company, Tom Lamont would occasionally moonlight at the *Trib* offices, editing copy at night to make a little extra money. Newspapering stayed in his blood even as he moved seamlessly into the larger world of commerce.

In short order, after he'd successfully revived a number of failing companies, including his own, Lamont caught the eye of city bankers. He was hired by the fledgling Bankers Trust where he quickly impressed his bosses, then in 1911 moved to the House of Morgan where, at the age of forty, he was offered a partnership by Morgan himself in what was then considered America's, if not the world's, headquarters of financial power.

Thomas Lamont's rise to financial heights in the first half of the American Century has been recounted in detail elsewhere. In short, the village parson's son, born poor and forced to pinch pennies as a boy, found himself by his fifth decade earning millions, advising the world's movers and shakers how to manage their nations' affairs. He even advised a worried John D. Rockefeller Jr. how to apportion his children's weekly allowances. For more than two decades, according to one historian, Grandpa Lamont would exercise more power in the Western hemisphere than any other figure.

When Lamont joined the House of Morgan, public regard for bankers was at a low ebb. The robber-baron label had sullied their reputation. In the public's eyes Rockefeller, Vanderbilt, Morgan, and their like all fused into the cartoon version of a single cold-eyed monster atop a mountain of gold, feeding on scraps of flayed workers. It was Lamont's task, with his newspaper experience, to explain to reporters and editors not only elementary finance but the larger aims of his bank and profession. In time my grandfather would help change the image of J.P. Morgan & Co., from a heartless money-making machine with a glowering proprietor to that of a firm of public-minded bankers of acknowledged probity.

Early on Lamont moved from helping his bank provide financial aid to the Allies in World War I to playing a key role in the peace negotiations in Paris. He would skillfully exploit the trend of U.S. presidents, starting with Wilson, to use bankers as instruments of foreign policy, encouraging them to adopt diplomatic roles in helping create a more stable international economic order. If Lamont, as the Morgan empire's de facto secretary of state, had to parley at times with unsavory types like the dictator Mussolini, he also befriended respected statesmen like Clemenceau and Lloyd George.

After Grandpa bought the prestigious New York *Evening Post* in 1918, and later bankrolled the birth of *The Saturday Review of Literature*,* the Lamonts' circle of friends expanded to include literary and journalistic figures like Robert Frost, H. G. Wells, and Walter Lippmann.

In the twenties' Jazz Age, between advising presidents and orchestrating global loans, Grandpa danced the Charleston and practiced perfecting his golf swing. He was, noted one writer, "a small miracle of sophistication." It was said that he could, with smiling, effortless ease, keep a half-dozen balls whirling in the air without letting one drop.He shrugged off the occasional close call: in Mexico, bandits tried unsuccessfully to intercept his train and

---

*In a deal whereby Lamont, a charter subscriber of the newborn *Time* magazine, put up $50,000 and Time Inc. agreed to publish Lamont's literary magazine, the first issue appearing in 1924.

kidnap him for ransom. By decade's end, he was acting not only as the public voice of his bank ("Morgan speaks to Lamont and Lamont speaks to the people") but as the man Wall Street turned to in its direst emergencies.

Grandpa misread the severity of the oncoming Crash of 1929, but once it struck he led the rescue party. The group of banking leaders he assembled met daily in the Morgan offices at 23 Wall Street. Behind this group, wrote *Time* magazine in its cover story on Grandpa, "there glittered the world's single greatest pool of liquid wealth" — about ten billion dollars — and "over such a mighty sea raged the winds of panic." The Biblical flourish continued. "The man who steered the ship of U.S. prosperity through the storm, who at length felt the helm respond," concluded the article, was Thomas W. Lamont.

By the time the helm responded, however, the Crash had plunged Wall Street and the nation into the Great Depression.

Not that it was all gloom. The day of my birth astronomers at the Lowell Observatory in Arizona announced the discovery of the ninth planet, Pluto, an icy ball smaller than our moon. Night baseball debuted in Indianapolis.

That year Sinclair Lewis won the Nobel Prize for Literature and the Gershwin brothers lit up Broadway with their new musical *Girl Crazy*. Up in Harlem, Duke Ellington and his orchestra were jamming the Cotton Club nightly with excited patrons. The club was owned by gangsters, a breed that, thanks to Al Capone and screen star Edward G. Robinson, had become a national preoccupation. In midtown Manhattan the Chrysler Building, chrome gargoyles and all, went up smartly to become the ultimate in art deco skyscrapers. And around the corner at Madison and 76th Street the Carlyle Hotel opened. It had been designed in the last moments of the carefree twenties, Brendan Gill wrote, and had made its opulent debut "as the grit of the Depression began to sift down grimly upon the land."

Cooing and gurgling in my parents' Upper East Side apartment, I was oblivious to it all. I was sprouting a head of platinum-colored curls and rattling my crib for attention. I was pathetically small, about six hundred feet shorter than the 602-foot Great Lakes ore carrier that was launched that year by the U.S. Steel Corporation, bearing the name of one of the company's directors, my Grandfather Lamont.

Now in his sixties, gray hair thinning above a sweetly expressive face, Grandpa eschewed the brusqueness of power; warmth seemed the core of his being. He charmed Midwestern bank presidents and newspaper editors, making them feel, as Frederick Lewis Allen wrote, "they saw eye to eye with him and that the power of the House of Morgan must be beneficent." Nor was the locus of Grandpa's power some aseptic corporate throne room high above the tumult of the Street. It was a second-floor office with book-lined walls and an antique Jacobean refectory table serving as Grandpa's desk. On chilly days a wood fire merrily blazed.

It must have been a welcome retreat for a man burdened with constant travel to every world capital from Berlin to Washington. It was said that Lamont and a colleague shuttled in and out of the White House with the regularity of confirmed tipplers visiting their favorite bar. No president, from Wilson to Franklin Roosevelt, could be left unconsulted by the Morgan princes.

The lawyer Grenville Clark, a contemporary of Lamont's, told of how President-elect Roosevelt, the main speaker at the New York Harvard Club's annual dinner in January 1933, had invited Clark to sit next to him at the head table, only to be advised that Grandpa had already been granted that honor. At the dinner Clark observed Grandpa giving Roosevelt "a terrible earache." Presently FDR sent word to Clark to join him for a talk. Clark asked if FDR didn't want to continue his chat with Lamont. "No, no," Roosevelt laughed, "I've had all I can take. He's been telling me how to run the country, and I think I know as much about it as he does."

On the other hand, I would have loved to have consulted Tom

Lamont, to have had him advise me on how to run my affairs in the sandbox, collect the right cereal box tops, and hide those wicked comic books from my mother. I'd have hung for dear life on a word or two from him on how to master long division or wear snappy vests the way he did while sailing up the Hudson on his yacht. I'd have happily invaded his dreams and purloined his game plan on how to become el supremo in any one of his roles as banker, diplomat, journalist, press lord, philanthropist, trustee, and advisor to the gods.

But Grandpa was busy and I was way down the food chain. I had to settle for his melting laugh at Sunday lunches, his melodious descants from the pew behind me when we sang "Jerusalem the Golden" in church, his cheery puzzlement at family functions as to just who I was.

Despite the distance between us, I loved him greatly, not least because in the last year of the nineteenth century he and Florence had delivered my father, Thomas Stilwell Lamont.

Father would live out his days as the distinguished and dutiful first son of a protean figure whose fame he never seriously aspired to.

The Morgan bank in time claimed him as a partner too, though unlike Grandpa he never bent a president's ear. Father traveled minimally and seldom far afield. He sought little more than a passing acquaintance with high culture, acquired no fine art. He avoided the opera whenever possible and nodded off at concerts. Averse to chilly drafts, he once sat through an entire Philharmonic recital with his hat on and was delighted not to be asked back. What my father had in spades was a profound commitment to the cause of education, a lifelong savor for good books, and an unshakable integrity. He was the most honorable man I ever knew.

My mother's people, the Miners, were ancestrally linked to an enduring legend of early-colonial history: how John Alden, speaking on behalf of Miles Standish, had won the hand of the fair Priscilla Mullins.

The Miners traced back to before the Norman conquest, and drew their name from those who worked the dark iron-ore fields of southwest England in the thirteenth century. Generations of Minors, as the name was then spelled, clustered in the Norman English village of Chew Magna in Somerset County. The first of them to reach America, Lt. Thomas Minor sailed aboard the *Arbella,* which docked in Salem Harbor in 1630, nine years after John Alden and Priscilla had tied the knot.

Some two hundred years later, Edward Griffith Miner, progenitor of my mother's line, left his birthplace in Vermont and struck out for the remote new state of Illinois. He settled in Winchester, Illinois, where he met and married a school teacher from Massachusetts named Sophronia Alden, the great-great-great-great granddaughter of John and Priscilla. They were married in the same parlor where eight years later Abraham Lincoln and Mary Todd would be married. Miner's and Lincoln's paths crossed frequently thereafter.

At Edward Griffith Miner's death in 1900, the local editor saluted him as "among the last of those great spirits of our heroic age." Sophronia had borne him six children, one of whom sired my maternal grandfather Edward G. Miner Jr., known throughout his life as Ned.

Ned Miner, born in 1863 in Waverly, Illinois, never attended college. He left home to work as a telegrapher for the old Chicago, Burlington & Quincy Railroad — and never looked back.

By the age of twenty he'd quit the Midwest, bound for Rochester, New York, and a job with a fledgling company, Pfaudler, that one day would become an internationally known producer of glass-lined tanks for dairies and breweries.

Rochester was then a boomtown, a lumber-producing, wheat-processing hub. The city was home to Western Union; to the inventor George Eastman whose Kodak box camera would shortly open up the world of photography to anyone with two hands and a good eye; and to the entrepreneurial Jerome brothers, one of whom was married to a future grandmother of Winston Churchill. The Jeromes, proprietors of Rochester's leading newspaper, built themselves a pair of grand houses, linked by a bridge, in the best section of town.

That last must have been the stuff of dreams for Ned Miner, busy working his way up at Pfaudler, unable yet to afford fancy housing, much less a bridge, for himself and his young wife, Helen Branscombe Ranlet of Holyoke, Massachusetts. By 1911, though, at age forty-eight, Miner had become Pfaudler's president, the same year that another aspiring executive, Thomas Lamont, was made a Morgan partner. By the 1930s Miner, having served as a director of the Buffalo, New York branch of the state's Federal Reserve Bank, was thought to be one of the men outside Wall Street with real financial influence.

Ned was a prolific letter writer — his correspondents included the writer Owen Wister and the artist Frederic Remington — as well as a compulsive joiner.

His records, Jeffersonian in their breadth and detail, show that, not content with conventional clubs, he joined variously the Compania de Café Esperanza, the Societé Anonyme de Dentin et D'Anzin, the Northern Nut Growers Association, and the American Ice Flotilla Committee. He bankrolled or belonged to more than fifty local organizations whose titles began with the word Rochester. He also kept close count of his personal property losses: pearl studs, eyeglasses, umbrellas, etc. This was a man obviously engaged to the point of absentmindedness.

His curiosity was insatiable. "If Ned was on his way to an important meeting and saw an earless dog," a friend observed, "he'd probably forget the meeting until he'd chased the dog up an alley to find out what had become of its ears."

On a business trip to South America, Miner got interested in yellow fever, read up on it, then wrote a paper for the city's Pundit Club, which Rochester's medical fraternity pronounced soundly authoritative. He assembled a collection of old railroad timetables that was so complete the New York Central offered to buy it from him. He composed articles and gave speeches on topics ranging from poison-gas warfare to "The Shipwreck and Wanderings of Alvar Nuñez Cabeza de Vaca." He would have made a fine journalist.

As it was, Ned became Rochester's foremost citizen, winner of its Civic Medal in 1940. A keen observer of the human comedy, he owned the richest chuckle in town. He was perservering in his old-fashionedness. From his home abutting the city's grandest avenue, Ned would sally forth to his downtown office in an electric automobile, a two-seater black-and-glassed artifact that he and a business friend kept in mint condition. I remember riding in it with him and thinking I was the luckiest boy ever to be pottering around in this quaint contraption with my eccentric grandfather.

Those outings happened every other Christmas when we visited Grandpa and Grandma Miner. We'd board the overnight train from Grand Central Station, the first leg of the trip after midnight taking us along the banks of the Hudson. In my lower berth on the Pullman sleeper I could raise the window shade and peer out at the river shimmering under a full moon. For a city boy en route to the provinces it was a wondrous sight.

The three-story house on Rochester's Argyle Street and East Avenue appeared portentous, but inside it had a welcoming feel, faintly redolent of cigar smoke. My grandfather liked to puff away, seated in his favorite green upholstered chair in a corner of the downstairs living room or, when solitude called, in a book-lined den midway between the first and second floors. Somewhere among his various tomes on brewery equipment and the geological rock formations of the Genessee Valley lurked a thin volume containing verses of doggerel written in Abe Lincoln's hand and an inscribed edition of Brigham Young's personal Bible.

At Christmas dinner an ornamented musical tree on a table stand revolved magically while playing old German carols. There were usually one or two well-lubricated great uncles or aunts on hand, in black tie or party dresses with lace collars, plus a covey of boisterous Ranlet cousins with names like "Buddy," "Peachy," or "Butts." Peachy, I remembered, wore a soigné black velvet dress and breathed an indefinable allure. They were all older and a trifle intimidating.

Grandma, with her Yankee thriftiness, habitually toned down our expectations. One Christmas Eve the dessert centerpiece on the dining room table appeared to be an elegant pastry filigreed with red, white, and green icing. On close inspection it turned out to be a decorative wooden cover that, when Grandma lifted it with a flourish, revealed a plain sponge cake underneath. As for Grandma's presents, an exquisite Tiffany box might contain a new toothbrush, or a set of pearls might come wrapped in Kleenex inside a Squibb toothpaste carton.

Grandpa was more constant in his largesse. We had to recite before we got a present. Grandpa would reach into his leather purse and hand us each a silver dollar no matter if we'd mangled the Gettysburg Address or done violence to "The Night Before Christmas." In this home-away-from-home filled with strange relations, my grandfather was a reassuring presence with his warm tenor voice issuing melodiously from under a canopy of snow-white hair. I was mesmerized by his porcelain hands, the beautifully manicured nails, by the flair with which he carved the turkey, and the minimalist way he extinguished the candles after dinner (others blew, he pursed his lips and blipped).

I never doubted he was an original or that when he died at ninety-one and was, or certainly should have been, laid out in his preferred dark-blue double-breasted suit, there was any cause to doubt a friend's assessment that out of the plains of Illinois, in another age, Ned Miner had brought with him to the world a little of Lincoln, much of Mark Twain, and just a suspicion of Paul Bunyan.

It was my sainted Grandmother Miner who tucked me in at night, after the festivities, on the darkened top floor of the Rochester house. She was Ranlet by birth, of distant Southern ties and biases, no taller than five feet, with a crown of upswept silvery hair.

Her father, Charles Ranlet, owned one of the most celebrated rose gardens in New England and ran the Holyoke bank, which had financed the building of the town dam spanning the Connecticut River. When the dam broke one fateful day, Ranlet wired his investors in nearby towns: "The dam's gone to hell by way of Willimansett!"

He had only slightly better luck controlling the flow of his capricious wife and daughters. In June 1887, Frances Ranlet, Grandma's mother, had sailed off to London for a party, Queen Victoria's Golden Jubilee. Great-grandmother Ranlet took in the whole shebang from the Jubilee procession to Westminster Abbey to the party afterward at Buckingham Palace. She watched the Queen's carriage, drawn by eight cream-colored ponies, rattle past the throngs along Pall Mall, the crowned heads of Europe marching behind. Later, as the guest of a Lord, she'd sipped champagne in the palace drawing room with members of the royal family. She must have dined out on the experience for the rest of her days in Holyoke.

Grandma's sister Leighton, or Leight as she was called, settled for partying in the home of the president. Her boarding school classmate Fanny Hayes was the daughter of Rutherford Hayes. A few years before Hayes's death in 1893, Fanny invited Leight to the Hayes homestead in Fremont, Ohio. In the family dining room, now a museum, there's a faded tintype of a luncheon party held there more than a century ago. It shows Hayes sitting at the table in the company of Fanny and her houseguest, a lovely young thing of about nineteen, my great-aunt Leight.

Grandma Miner was a devout Episcopalian with a provincial's distrust of those she considered of lesser faiths or refinement. The story went that Grandma's rakish younger brother, known as Uncle Beau, had married a Catholic lady, an actress named Kitty. Beau, whose line of work was never clear, would periodically show up at our apartment to pester my father for a loan. In his last days Beau was placed by Kitty in a Catholic nursing home where she could look after him. Upon his death Kitty prepared to have him buried in a Catholic cemetery outside New York City. Grandma had other ideas. She arranged to have a private railroad car from the New York Central dispatched to the funeral home to retrieve Uncle Beau and transport him to a Protestant cemetery in Holyoke, Massachusetts, the Ranlet family birthplace. He reputedly rests there today under a proper Protestant headstone.

Well into my college days, Grandma would caution me about the perils of dating Catholics, Jews, or Holy Rollers. I remember listening to her in some bewilderment, for I'd never heard my parents talk of others that way. I chalked it up to a generational lapse or possibly a siege mentality. Grandma saw herself perhaps as a decent, pious woman surrounded by relatives of dubious character — on one side, those of partial Virginia stock fond of their juleps; on the other, those of citified Northern stirps partial to their martinis. Several Ranlet contemporaries, be it noted, turned out to be men of exceptional achievement in business and diplomacy. That they were a spirited, partying lot I always thought a nice counterbalance to the more soberly virtuous Lamonts.

To the last, when frailty of age finally overtook her, Grandma Miner remained a faithful correspondent, curious about all facets of my family and career, signing her handwritten letters with a spidery and increasingly faint "your devoted Granny M."

Granny's only daughter, my mother, was a more complex woman. Born the first year of the new century, she grew up amid the accepted conventions of her small-town class, only to marry into and make her way thereafter in the more progressive social sphere of New York City. She suffused my life from day one.

Elinor Miner Lamont was a woman determined to do right by her cosmopolitan in-laws. She was spurred by a lack of formal education beyond finishing school, in her case Miss Porter's School for girls of the right sort.

She learned to play the mandolin, dance in a white dress around the Maypole each spring, and exchange lavender-colored missives with smitten young Harvardians, some of whom sounded like P. G. Wodehouse characters. One of them showered Ellie with gossipy letters about college life, the war in Europe ("The Germans are so unsportsmanlike"), and his admiration for her selling Liberty Loan bonds to support the U.S. war effort. In his last letter to her before joining the Army in 1918, he bade farewell, declaring, "Well, I must pop off. Toodle-oo!" He signed it "Jimbo."

Mother gradually distanced herself from the world of the Jimbos, although she continued to pay it affectionate regard throughout life. Even as she ascended the heights of cultural and religious philanthropy in New York and London, she kept a warm spot in her heart for her old MPS chums. She was as fiercely loyal as she was unashamedly romantic — half Mary Queen of Scots, the historical figure she most adored; half John Knox.

She had boundless moxie and could sass back an impudent cab driver with the chutzpa of a Mae West. She thought nothing of chewing out street bums or accosting litterers who dared foul the sidewalk in front of our building on 72nd Street. At first, as a small boy in her tow, I cringed at these encounters, then began secretly to cheer her on. I relished her defiance of the proprieties that bound most New Yorkers of her class. She spoke out loud and

21

early for birth control. At a time when women mostly left foreign policy discussions to men, she started a ladies' group that met in our apartment.

My mother seemed forever on the run, rushing to appointments and meetings. I wondered if she ever sat down. She was always bending to remove a dustball from the carpet, a leaf from the terrace, a weed from the garden. Summers she raced small sailboats across the waters in fair or foul weather. She bustled through life, entering and departing spaces with suitable stir. Observing her, I wanted to lie down and rest.

She had perfect pitch. In what passed for her flapper days Mother had sung on the radio in a one-shot appearance. From her would come my crush on popular music and eventually a battleship of a Steinway that had been built for her parents in 1911. From her would come my love of birdwatching. She taught me, as she had my oldest brother, the thrill of tracking an osprey's flight, how to tell a wood thrush from a thrasher, how to spot the telltale markings of migrating warblers. Birding more than anything would hone my powers of observation.

Mother wore her passions on her sleeve, a reckless trait in the bland, emerging world of political correctness. Always the best of company, she was at times maddeningly opinionated, too scathing in her assessment of lesser mortals, too crushing to those who incurred her displeasure. She was never stoic about the swings and fortunes of life; she cared deeply. Like Scarlett O'Hara she moved with grace through her narrowly ordered social world, embracing the company of those who sparked her curiosity, who conversed amusingly, who passed muster. She could be unfair, unbending, but always there was that redeeming warmth and courage. She was never uninteresting.

That must have been the chemical mix that attracted my father to her and led to their wedding in Rochester on an April day in 1923.

3

Officer, He's Only Eight

If my parents thought my arrival a blessed event, it must have been one of the few that first winter of the Depression.

While I slept in a pillowed echo chamber, hearing the sing-song voice of my mother and the yelps of my feuding older brothers, whole families slept in their cars. Right through my teething days things stayed rough on the outside.

In 1931, bread lines and Hoovervilles. Al Capone went up for income tax evasion and the Mob orchestrated a mass house-cleaning: forty Mafia bosses dispatched one evening across the country in what became known as the Night of the Sicilian Vespers, right up there with the Dunoon Massacre. The cruelest year may have been 1932, with seven million folks out of work. That March, a week before my second birthday, the Lindbergh baby was kidnapped.

My grandparents had known the baby's mother, Anne Morrow Lindbergh, as well as Anne's famed husband, Charles. They rushed to the Lindbergh home in New Jersey. The kidnapper had entered an upstairs window and snatched the child from his crib; the baby's body was found two months later in the woods nearby. The senior Lamonts were badly shaken. (TWL's yacht *Reynard* was searched for clues; one of the crew had phoned his girlfriend, the Lindbergh baby's nurse, the night of the kidnapping.) Within weeks they had protective steel bars installed on the grandchildren's bedroom windows at their country home on the Hudson. They hired an armed guard to keep an eye on all of us when we came visiting on weekends.

Later that year the clouds parted a bit. Franklin D. Roosevelt was elected president, promising to restore prosperity. J. P. Morgan Jr. had his picture taken chatting up a woman midget on his lap, which caused people to reassess the image of bankers as a mirthless lot. It was reported that a United States senator in London had startled guests at Claridge's by running down the hotel corridors stark naked and brandishing a bowie knife — testament to the rejuvenation of our national legislature. People crowded the movie houses. Prohibition was lifted.

Through it all I slept and ate and regurgitated my pap.

In our eleventh-floor apartment, in a neo-Renaissance-style building that stretched an entire block along Park Avenue, I became vaguely aware of my two roughhousing older brothers named for their grandfathers. Thomas William Lamont II ("Tommy") had been born in 1924, the year of the Teapot Dome scandal, and, approaching ten, showed a precociousness bordering on genius. Edward Miner Lamont ("Teddy") had arrived in 1926, the year of Garbo's debut, and early on developed an affinity for the sports pages.

At the age of five I was sent for my sins to the renowned St. Bernard's School, a mile north off Fifth Avenue. It was modeled after an English public school with around-the-clock Latin instruction and cold food; everyone was called by his last name. The headmaster, an Englishman named Jenkins, disciplined laggard students by having them jump up and down to "shake their brains into place." The faculty was studded with men bearing names like Musgrove Strange and Captain Fry. Soccer was mandatory, though the masters grudgingly tolerated baseball in the spring.

I didn't mind St. Bernard's, even with the masters hurling erasers at me, except for the daily drive there. Our black Packard pulled up at the school each morning to disgorge me with my satchel of books and homework. After a while I asked Nagle, the chauffeur, to drop me off a block from the school to spare me my classmates' snickers. Nagle participated in the Chauffeurs Race at the school's annual Sports Day. Alumnus George Plimpton recalled that the chauffeurs removed their shoes at the starting line, then raced down the field in their black silk socks. The winner received a tiny silver cup "into which it was possible to squeeze about three cashew nuts."

On one of my first report cards Mr. Jenkins awarded me the lowly mark of 40 for Conduct. My mother circled the offending item and scribbled beneath it, "Do you suppose he bites and kicks, or only bites?" I did little better on the General Knowledge exam, which required us, among other things, to identify Rudy Vallee and Lou Gehrig. My mother huffily told the school that questions like that did not indicate deficiency, adding she was delighted I didn't spend my time listening to radio crooners or dissecting the *Times* sports section. Little did she know.

A few more years of this and we called it quits with St. Bernard's. Nagle and the Packard were retired, and I was allowed to walk each day the two blocks to Buckley School where my brothers matriculated and I could play real football.

Life in the city seemed a perpetual struggle with the elements. Winter snowstorms were bigger, longer, and left colossal traffic-clogging drifts. Summer heat waves were draining and could lead to ferocious storms the likes of which they don't make anymore. There were no TV weather warnings, no air conditioners or electric ice makers. Still, we had organ grinders on the sidewalks and doctors who made house calls. In my bedroom Dr. Van Ingen placed an ether swab over my nose before operating on an infected ear. I figured that was the way things would always be done.

My days were circumscribed within a three-block radius that included Buckley, our apartment, my grandparents' house, and St. James' Episcopal Church. The last was presided over by a plummy-voiced rector named Horace Donegan who sounded like God himself. Donegan was a showman who liked to dazzle the young in his congregation with paeans to heroic role models. One Sunday he replicated Lindbergh's transatlantic flight by rigging a wire across the church's nave and attaching it to a small toy plane that wobbled its way above our heads while the organ pealed triumphantly.

Grandpa, when he wasn't at the White House, held court with Grandma in their baronial townhouse on East 70th Street. The street was lined with showy Beaux Arts chateaus and Italianate brownstones. By contrast my grandparents' four-storied Tudor-Jacobean massif had been hailed for its modesty when it was completed in 1921. In time it became a sort of international inn for the talented and famous on both sides of the Atlantic. You might bump into squeaky-voiced H. G. Wells in the hallway or a besotted Edna St. Vincent Millay weaving down the staircase. In the upstairs library, where guests were served tea and toast glazed with melted brown sugar, I once met Charlie Chaplin and Wendell Willkie.

For a six-year-old my grandparents' house was a forbidding spectre. To be summoned there with my brothers for a holiday dinner was a daunting experience. We'd arrive properly attired at the imposing street entrance and navigate the massive front steps while high above us, beneath a stone balustrade, a row of bossed grotesques observed our progress.

Inside the great oaken front door we were greeted by Metcalfe, the English head butler. Bald headed, in black cutaway and wing collar, he bore an eerie resemblance to the actor Erich von Stroheim. Metcalfe ran the place with a military efficiency doubtless acquired through his service in the Boer War. Encountering an improperly clad guest, he would lead the offender to a closet filled with men's clothing of all sizes, and outfit him on the spot with whatever was required.

Metcalfe would escort us into the main hallway with its somber tapestries, then up the staircase with its gloomy statuary on each landing, and into the living room to be presented to Themselves: Grandpa, master of the universe, and Grandma, wreathed in pearls of wisdom. We would be blessed with a perfunctory kiss on the cheek, a stray pat on the head, then released to the company of our infant cousins. There would be merriment amid the tinkle of silver Christmas bells, the aroma of roast beef and popovers as we pushed around the dinner table. Toasts would follow, much glass clinking, conversational burble, and I would drift off in a haze of content-ment, happy to be in the bosom of my family, yearning subcon-sciously to escape this mausoleum.

There were other family homesteads, and not all of them had scary halls and shadowy recesses to stir my childish fears. North Haven, for example.

On that island afloat in the mystic blue of Maine's Penobscot Bay, my Grandfather Lamont had built a rambling clapboard summer home whose warmth and cheer the dampest fogs couldn't dissipate.

The house, a series of units connected by cooling breezeways, was bathed in muted yellow and stood on a bluff overlooking the bay. It had been a farm once, and the vast firmament above it had moved my grandparents to christen the place Sky Farm. The mead-ows around it teemed with hawkweed, lupine, purple vetch, and buttercups. Finches flashed gold among the birches; birdsong filled the air. On a still southwesterly day, as the clouds drifted languidly overhead, the bay, as a poet wrote, wore "a milky skin." It was a spot for daydreaming by small boys.

From the porch at Sky Farm, I first viewed the church spires of Camden across the bay and the cobalt blue hills nestling the town. From Sky Farm I saw my first aurora borealis, my first three-masted windjammer bowling through the waves. In its fields I first heard the whitethroat's pleading song. On the bay beneath the farm I learned to sail and caught my first mackerel. On North Haven I saw my first drunk, plucked my first chicken, chased my first sheep. On that island I first encountered death and adultery: a drowned fisherman; a wayward uncle. On North Haven I discovered girls.

My brother Tommy called the island his Mandalay, his Tivoli. It was my Elysium, too.

Indians had fished along its shores for three millennia before Europeans reached the area in the 1500s. An Englishman, Martin Pring, had discovered North Haven and its sister Vinal Haven in 1603, naming them the Fox Islands for the silver gray foxes abounding there. The first settlers built permanent homes there in the 1760s. In the northern corner of Penobscot Bay, at Castine, America suffered its first naval defeat of the Revolution. In the War of 1812, settlers near Oak Hill on the island's eastern end could watch the British fleet maneuver up the bay, its frigates pounding the islands along the Camden shore with cannon shell.

North Haveners joined the Union Army during the Civil War. Later, President Grant spent a night at the village inn and left his cigar stub as a memento. Then one summer day in the 1880s a party of Bostonians sailed into the Fox Island Thoroughfare, bought up shorefront property and erected the first of their palatial "cottages." The Haven's summer colony blossomed over the years with a succession of Cabots, Saltonstalls, and other Brahmin clans. They built the first of their twelve-foot, gaff-rigged sailing dinghies that would become the oldest one-design class in America. They consumed quantities of S.S. Pierce gin and erected their own party house, The Paralyzo.

New Yorkers and Philadelphians reached the island about three decades later. They built around Pulpit Harbor on the island's north shore, and they built big. When my grandparents hired the firm of Frederick Law Olmsted to landscape Sky Farm in 1919, and workers began dynamiting the rocky ledges to accommodate the grand new house with its sunken English garden, the Cabots in their rustic cabins across the harbor looked askance.

The island's year-round residents were a breed apart: steadfast, shrewd, demonstrably friendly; drivers on the road habitually waved to one another. They were also flinty, stubborn, and outspoken. At the funeral of one roundly disliked fellow, the minister asked if anyone wished to say a word or two about the deceased. A man in the back stood up and shouted, "His brother was worse!" Insular in code and conduct, the natives proudly brandished their independence. Many boasted pedigrees stretching farther back than the summering Brahmins. Their relationship with the latter was one of mutual respect. Summer folk might complain in vain about the natives' work habits, their indifference to deadlines, but then the clock was seldom the natives' taskmaster; the sea and its weather controlled their timetable.

Sky Farm on the other hand was a disciplined exercise in family recreation: picnics, competitive sports, parlor games, reading-aloud sessions, all planned and carried out with an eye to time unwasted.

When the Lamonts set out across the bay in the *Reynard*, Grandpa's motor yacht with mahogany-paneled cabins and a five-man crew, it was always an excursion with a specific destination and purpose, executed briskly by the captain in charge. Lunch was spartan-light, dessert usually a bland Jell-o, which the Norwegian steward called "yellow." No liquor or wine was served. It was, as the writer Elizabeth Hardwick observed, the Ruling Class at play along the Maine coast, "asserting even in the most costly boats and in their great houses on inhospitable islands, a sort of puritanism remaining at the center of the pleasure principle."

Everyone paid court to the island's summer traditions. I was wheeled up in my wicker baby carriage to the Big House at Sky Farm to be shown off to guests at my grandparents' end-of-season tea for the summer clans and dinghy racers. At these affairs women with cold-cod complexions would lift me out of the carriage for inspection. The men spoke a strange patois full of broad As and wore sweaters with large red Hs on them.

Within a few years I became aware that the island was knee-deep in characters. Every Saturday afternoon on schedule the village drunk raged up Main Street, yelling the most bloodcurdling oaths and emptying the street of women and children. On Sundays two men, togged out in their Sabbath best, trudged down the road from the island church, the same man always in the lead, the other trailing fifty yards back. "There go the Pike brothers," my mother would remark. "They haven't spoken to each other in thirty years."

Enoch Piper was the island recluse. His hermitage was a gabled cottage on a bend of the North Road, the favored port of call for Rose, my Scottish nurse with cheeks the color of heather. Rose was partial to the ballads of Harry Lauder and other songs from the old country. So the two of us would go roamin' in the gloamin' across the fields to Eenie's house and rap on his door. A wrinkled apparition in clamming boots and a wool cap would open the door, beckoning us in. Eenie's speck of a living room was piled high with old newspapers and smelled of cat food and the droppings of a pet canary. But when he picked up his banjo and began singing "The Isle of Capri" in his cracked falsetto, I knew why Rose brought me to this place each summer. A touch of magic amid the grime.

Palisades was the clan's weekend retreat the rest of the year.

I'd have happily stayed in town, watching Tom Mix serials or ogling the dinosaurs at the Natural History Museum. But off we'd roll in our limousine, its over-stuffed seats emitting a sickly sweet odor, across the George Washington Bridge, up Route 9W past the Rustic Cabin saloon where Sinatra first sang, and on to Palisades and the Sneden's Landing road that forked off onto the Lamonts' private driveway.

Atop the rocky palisades that stand like guardians of the Hudson some fifteen miles north of the Bridge, my grandparents had built a Dutch Colonial-style manor house on 135 acres of lawn and woodland. Once again they'd hired the Olmsted firm to do the landscaping. When it was done, more than 27,000 bulbs of crocus, narcissus, and scilla had been planted scattershot in the grass around the myriad apple trees, while the formal garden overflowed with English boxwoods, Virginia bluebells, winter jasmine, and trailing wisteria. Tom and Florence had kept the place's ancestral name, Torrey Cliff, after a nineteenth-century botanist who'd summered there.

The name conjured up visions of dark doings on fog-shrouded heaths. The grandchildren were shunted to the manse's top floor where the doors creaked and shadows menaced. One cousin regularly checked under her bed for spooks before turning out the light. I thought her a sissy, and then started doing the same.

The rest of the house exuded an old-world ambiance with its sculpted marble fireplaces, red damask window curtains, and Hepplewhite furniture. There were lavender bathtubs with lavender soap balls, and a pine-paneled living room made for high tea, backgammon, charades, and other parlor games to amuse the constant stream of family and houseguests. In the living room small fry could play Hide the Thimble or peer through an old-fashioned stereoscope at fin de siècle views of London and Paris. On a corner table sat a china bowl filled with dried rose petals that I fancied would lay there in perpetuity before turning to dust. In her upstairs morning room, Grandma read Mother Goose rhymes to us and poems by William Blake.

Sunday lunches were occasions for verbal food fights around the dining room table. I was too young to grasp the complexities of FDR's assault on the Wall Street banks, the whys of the Spanish Civil War, and other current topics that set my relatives aboil. But I knew enough to duck when the words Stalin or Roosevelt came up. Grandma would start tearing into Uncle Corliss over Stalin's abuse of the kulaks, and Corliss would fire back; Grandpa and Father would start in on FDR, while Aunt Margaret, Corliss's wife, would chew the glassware defending something called the

Kremlin's Five-Year Plan. I was always happy when dessert ended and I could flee outside.

That was where the real action was. In a fairyland of rolling lawns, lily ponds, and grape arbors we cousins chased each other tirelessly at Cops and Robbers and Capture the Flag. Croquet games were intense to the point of violence; Uncle Corliss would hurl his mallet at no one in particular when he missed a shot. On a swing tethered to a hilltop willow tree I floated above it all, stretching my legs, arcing high into the sky. In the dark woods that seemed to stretch forever along the palisades, we skipped down trails, carved our initials on gnarled oak trunks, and dodged copperheads.

Family photo sessions were a trial. Like Kenyan tribesmen ignoring the tourists and their lenses, we seemed intent on shunning the photographer. Old photos taken at Palisades or Sky Farm show members of the family resolutely focusing elsewhere — Grandma offering the camera her profile, Grandpa squinting into the distance, some aunt admonishing a fidgety child, various small cousins staring at their shoes, sulking over a parental rebuke, talking to the dog, picking their nose, or sleeping.

We seemed more at ease performing than posing. At Christmas in the grand entry hall, beside a tinseled tree that seemed as towering as the one at Rockefeller Center, I recited the Boy Scout oath to wild acclaim; Grandma and Grandpa sang "My Bonnie Lies Over the Ocean" in duet; and Aunt Margaret performed the word Internationale as a charade.

One day near the end of the decade my parents asserted their independence and gave up Palisades for a new weekend home of their own on the north shore of Long Island.

The house near Oyster Bay on the Great Gatsby's Gold Coast was a huge yellow-brick thing worthy of the neighborhood's affluent bankers and bluebloods. Across our field on one side lived members of an old-line Wall Street investment clan; on the other side, the faintly declassé heirs of a toiletry empire. The old Tiffany estate was down the road. Country and yacht clubs seemed to sprout at every bend. It all reeked of settled money and St. Grottlesex lockjaw.

Nature seduced me here. In the fields that bordered the sunlit lanes running down our hill to the Cove road, I collected birds' nests, insects, and small animal bones. I hammered rocks, looking for quartz crystals, and dreamed of finding geodes, stray arrowheads and fool's gold. I netted monarchs, red admirals, and tiger swallowtails, scooped up the shedded wing feathers of blue jays, crows, and the occasional pheasant. Through a pair of Woolworth binoculars I started observing the birds more closely, their habits and bearing. I grew attached to the patrician cardinal and the congenial little junco looking, as E. B. White described him, like a dapper nob dressed in gray suit and white waistcoat for an afternoon tea dance.

My growing hoard of collectibles necessitated the erection of a tar-papered shack behind the garage, which became the Fieldside Museum with myself as chief curator. My Grandfather Miner, through his sundry connections, became principal donor for the collection that rapidly grew to include everything from Argentine teapots to vanadinite crystals. Grandpa donated a stream of oddities — a watch chain made of coins from the 1893 Chicago World's Fair; a wooden gavel made from the stair railing of a Rochester arcade circa 1820s — and accompanied each with an explanatory note.

"I am sending you," he wrote, "some stones which my agent said were used by David when he fought Goliath." The agent, Grandpa added, was a distant relative of Goliath. More exotica arrived. Grandpa took to addressing me as "Chief" and invented a name and title for his agent, "William Wigglewhistle, Field Scout." Wigglewhistle, he notified me, "is soon to leave Hong Kong for Manila, and I expect he may get an Igorrote* for the museum. I

---

*A tribesman from the mountainous region of northern Luzon in the Philippines.

told him to get a fresh one, as Grandmother does not like the canned variety."

A box of arrowheads from a Stone Age mound in Ohio arrived. The arrowheads had been secured, Grandpa informed me, by "that eminent field worker, Mr. Billy Butts Macomber." (William B. Macomber, a Ranlet cousin, would one day become deputy under secretary of state in the Nixon administration.) Another time a letter came from Winchester, Illinois, addressed to me as Keeper of the Wampum. It was from Grandpa's brother Earl applying for membership in the museum and enclosing a spearhead as payment ("I'm out of wampum").

Grandpa was full of ideas concerning the Fieldside Museum's management. He praised my handling of its finances while expressing disappointment that I had not increased his salary as first assistant curator. When I balked at his suggestion we procure a typewriter to facilitate business, citing the cost, he said not to worry. "I neglected to inform you that when we dug up the petrified Chinaman we found $2.98 in small change in his pockets." I also had to sidestep him on a tricky personnel matter. He'd proposed making our butler an assistant curator. ("He could give official welcomes to distinguished visitors in your absence.")

I hated to turn Grandpa down. The butler, William Mork, whom I adored, was an imposing fellow, but I didn't think him suitable for a curatorial position. For one thing, he drank and told off-color stories. For another, he didn't know arrowheads from sharks' teeth. Willie was Danish, six feet five inches in his stocking feet, weighed more than two hundred pounds, and had short-cropped blond hair. Decked out in his swallow-tailed black formals for a dinner party, he made an earnest stab at looking dignified despite his unruly girth. He and his wife, Violet, the cook, acted on occasional weekends as surrogate parents when my own were not around.

Off-hours, in his cups, Willie was prone to collapse at his own jokes, most of them scatological verses in Danish. I was enthralled, and committed each verse to memory. Violet, a Scots Calvinist with dark hair, portable teeth, and a violent temper, was appalled by Willie's antics and regularly showered him with unprintable curses, which I also committed to memory.

My weekends in their care were sublime. I could stay up past midnight, guzzle chocolate malteds, and read my comic books in peace. They took me on outings to Jones Beach where I first romped in surf. They took me to the movies in Huntington, movies my mother would have forbidden. Humphrey Bogart in *The Maltese Falcon*. Joel Cairo and the Fat Man, Wilmer the gunsel, sexy Mary Astor. Sheer Nirvana.

I was still immature, not yet ready for those dippy little girls in braces and Mary Janes who would soon be tripping their way through Lester Laninland. But I was shedding childhood in a hurry.

My father realized soon enough that either of my two older brothers would be better suited to follow him one day into the bank. He regarded me with puzzled resignation, a wearied lion try-ing gamely to instruct a wayward cub.

He was a formal man. Cautious, judicious, not one to jump fully clothed into a pool on wild impulse. There were early signs I would be none of these. I wore my little food-stained ties askew and refused to attend dancing class, preferring to stay home and hear the fights on radio.

A discriminating eater, I tossed my tapioca and calf's liver out the window, cheering all the way as they spun down eleven stories onto Park Avenue. After one too many of these flights, the police came knocking, but Rose saved me from the cuffs.

I was hopeless with figures — algebraic, geometric, Arabic, Roman — a cross-off for any future employment requiring preci-sion with profit and loss statements. It didn't help that my mother was arithmetically challenged and that money was never discussed at home. I was still tagged a backslider.

My first attempts at English composition gave Father scant hope. He'd edited his school and college newspapers and was convinced my teachers were giving me a free ride when they returned my compositions with an occasional A. He was a literalist — not one for metaphor or flowery prose; split infinitives were treasonous. As much as anyone, he grounded me in the basics of disciplined writing, of thinking through a sentence structure, a paragraph's course. What I didn't absorb through his strictures, I took from the model of his long, thoughtful letters invariably composed on embossed J. P. Morgan & Co. stationery and assiduously typed by the formidable Miss Keyes, his secretary. Pharaonic tablets had nothing on these missives.

My early education was thus a spotty thing as far as my father was concerned. He tried his best to fill in the lacunae. His one and only sex talk took approximately thirty seconds and was the oral equivalent of one of those Dordonne cave paintings, roughly suggestive rather than explicit. When Buckley finally disgorged me, ready for grazing in the uplands of a New England boarding school, Father remained skeptical of my prospects.

While I was being fitted for long pants, Hitler had come to power. Nazism had begun spreading its toxic weed; the Japanese invaded northern China. Millions of new cars rolled off the Ford assembly lines, and New York's Robert Moses built endless parkways around the city to accommodate them. Fiorello La Guardia, the "Little Flower," became our reformist new mayor. Roosevelt was reelected.

One July day in 1936, FDR steamed into Pulpit Harbor on the presidential yacht *Potomac*. The harbor was bursting with excitement, a cruiser and destroyer circling outside in the bay, airplanes swooping overhead, boatloads of reporters and photographers jostling for position. The American Legion band in full regalia blared away, families and friends crowded the outer point by the harbor entrance.

The Roosevelt sons had joined their father; they'd wended their way up to Sky Farm to borrow a few bottles of milk, some gin, and a tennis racquet. They broke the racquet and to make amends invited my brothers and me aboard the *Potomac*. We rowed out, scampered up the gangway, and were escorted to the fantail to shake hands with the Great Man sitting with Fala, his Scotch terrier, looking relaxed and puffing on a cigarette. I didn't wash my right hand for a month.

For a while good things like that kept coming regular as the milkman. The Depression receded. Mickey Mouse débuted. Our fourth sibling, a brown-eyed charmer of a baby girl, Elinor, arrived.

Abroad, a royal romance captivated the world. Tom and Florence danced the night away in London at a party for King Edward VIII and Mrs. Simpson. Grandpa talked with the king, Noël Coward played the piano, and Grandma nodded in agreement as he sang his latest hit, "Don't Let Your Daughter Go on the Stage."

Then things started to unravel. Gershwin died. The *Hindenburg* blew up. The smitten young king abdicated his throne. The book burnings began, the purges in Russia, the civil war in Spain. Atrocities like Nanking, *Kristalnacht*, and Guernica burned their way into our consciousness. My brother Tommy, who passionately supported the anti-Fascist Loyalists in Spain, attended a private school in Switzerland, where many of the students were Fascist sympathizers. He'd walk into the school yard, giving the Loyalists' clenched-fist salute, and the Fascist kids would lay into him with fury.

We were still trooping up to Rochester on alternate Christmases and I was still the wet-behind-the-ears dupe. One Christmas day after we'd opened our presents, I surrendered West Point, a snazzy F.A.O. Schwarz replica of it complete with a corps of lead cadets, to my older brothers in exchange for a lousy box of wooden Indians.

The next day one of my Rochester cousins, known to me thereafter as Manhole Macomber, deposited me for fun down the innards of Buckingham Street.

About the time I was finally getting acclimated to these Rochester Christmases, our biyearly treks started tailing off. Maybe it was the scent of war in the air. Maybe it was because Father got tired of the interminable waits to use the one bathroom on our floor.

That summer of 1939 — the last perfect summer of the decade, someone wrote — people flocked to see Clark Gable in *Gone With the Wind*. I was taken to the World's Fair in Flushing with its theme, The World of Tomorrow, featuring displays of prototype televisions and all-aluminum kitchens. On North Haven I chased sheep, weeded our vegetable garden, and swam in the frigid bay. One September morning, through the static on our kitchen radio, we heard the news flash that Germany had invaded Poland.

The war had finally come, stealing what was left of our childhoods.

4

"The Germans Wore Gray, You Wore Blue"

— Bogart to Bergman, *Casablanca*

In the war's opening year, the first American to die in combat as an officer was a Lamont. Among the last to die in the war's closing months would be my oldest brother.

The Second World War was the great enterprise of my father's and my oldest brother's generations, the last war that united the nation thoroughly, and was fought to unconditional victory.

It would eventually take my father to London and France with the Army Air Force and brother Tommy to the Pacific on a Navy submarine. Our mother would sign up as a local Red Cross leader. Various uncles would join the U.S. armed forces and go off to fight. One of Father's cousins known as "Skinny" Lamont was refused a commission for being underweight, so he joined the Royal Canadian Flying Corps, which apparently took you if you had a pulse. Even my seventy-two-year-old grandfather would be called to duty to head a civilian committee charged with helping the Army Air Force target enemy manufacturing centers in Europe.

In the war's first desperate years, Churchill's defiant growl offered the one resonant note of hope, although Grandma did her bit. At a luncheon she gave shortly after the hostilities in Europe began, she rose and proposed a toast: "Here's to the victory of the Allies and to hell with neutrality!" One of the lunch guests, the British politician Duff Cooper, recalled how overwhelmed by gratitude he felt.

Rogers Lamont, the forty-year-old son of Grandpa's first cousin and a partner in the New York law firm of Sullivan & Cromwell, had joined up in a hurry. Over the protests of his senior partner, John Foster Dulles, Rogers had rushed to Canada following Britain's declaration of war. In October 1939, he'd reached England, enlisted in the British army, been commissioned a captain in its Field Artillery, and was sent to France. In May 1940, on the eve of the evacuation of British forces at Dunkirk, Lamont was killed when an enemy tank shell struck his armored car.

That September the Blitz began, the first bombs raining down on London, and Britain entered the longest midnight in its history. Incendiary bombs gutted London's business district, reducing it to a mash of flame and ruin. One December night the Germans dropped ten thousand of these silvery projectiles on the city. One of them, a foot-long cylindrically shaped device, failed to explode and was found amid the rubble. Somehow it came into Grandpa Lamont's possession. He had it disarmed and forwarded to the chief curator of the Fieldside Museum.

In the presidential campaign of 1940, Grandpa cast his lot with Wendell Willkie, the Republican aspirant.

Willkie was a transplanted Midwesterner who'd become a leading corporate figure in New York. He shared Grandpa's internationalist views, particularly the urgent need to aid Britain. (For a brief while Grandpa had been convinced that Britain could withstand the German onslaught on its own. At a dinner at the home of *New York Times* publisher Arthur Sulzberger, he'd dismissed the view of a young *Times* reporter just back from London, James Reston, that Britain could not survive without U.S. help.)

Grandpa promoted Willkie with the help of his Midwestern cousins, the Cowles brothers, who ran an influential newspaper-magazine dynasty. He worked behind the scenes as Willkie's key fund-raiser, saw him nominated then crushed at the polls as Roosevelt rolled to an unprecedented third term in the White House. Had Willkie won, Grandpa was reportedly in line for the post of secretary of state.

I didn't see much of Grandpa that year or the next except at the occasional family fête where the meal might be interrupted by Metcalfe announcing that the president was phoning from Washington. But then I was importantly busy, too, running the museum, collecting more bird nests, and trying to dodge the toughs in Central Park.

At Buckley I was flunking math under Mr. Summers with his bristly Prussian haircut; messing up my Latin verbs to the despair of fussy Mr. Gamble; and misplacing my capital cities in Mr. Williams' geography class. Mr. Williams was moved to throw the blackboard chalk at me. A classmate stole my wallet with Charlie Chaplin's autograph; a pair of muggers lifted my wristwatch on 74th Street. It was a rocky year for a ten-year-old in Manhattan.

Things were only marginally better in Maine.

The war had brushed even our little island. A German sub was trapped and sunk off Lincolnville across the bay. A covey of saboteurs landed on a remote beach on North Haven's eastern end; they were flushed out and captured by armed islanders led by a colorful local figure, Goldie MacDonald.

In August 1941, the president paid a return call to Pulpit Harbor following a secret rendezvous with Churchill in Placentia Bay, Newfoundland. The two leaders had blocked out a declaration in principle of the Allies' postwar aims, the Atlantic Charter. This time there was no escort or attendant hoopla when the

Potomac ghosted into our harbor. I wasn't piped aboard with my brothers, but Grandpa was. He listened, enthralled, to FDR's account of his meeting with Churchill, the president's concerns about Japan and the possibility of war in the Far East.

That summer, biking along the island's north road with a pal, I fetched up at Eenie Piper's. The house had that abandoned look, its roof sagging, the trim around the windows peeling paint. The window panes, however, were temptingly intact, all thirty-seven of them. Something in me snapped. I picked up every rock within reach and hurled away. The music of shattering glass, the percussive "pow" of rock and shards clattering on floors, the shouts of my pal egging me on drove me to manic heights of pleasure. I felt released, omnipotent. When I was done, not a pane remained.

The house was not abandoned, it turned out. Eenie returned home enraged. The culprits were shortly identified. My friend was sent packing back to New York. Restitution was made to Eenie. I faced the unshirted wrath of my father and was sentenced to the equivalent of fifty lashes and a month on half rations.

My father didn't need another cross to bear. He was now a Morgan partner, in the public eye, and kidnap threats had been made against him and the family. A night watchman with a revolver encamped in the kitchen of our Long Island house. On top of that, my mother kept dragging him off to the opera.

The strains of Verdi were seldom heard in our home, but I was provided piano lessons from a fellow who had a genius for refining unformed talent and charged five bucks an hour. Pretty soon I was playing old chestnuts like "Marching Through Georgia," which infuriated my Aunt Betty Blue, an unreconstructed southerner. I also dreamed of becoming a Spitfire pilot and thought briefly of entering medicine, so expert had I become on various personal ailments from asthma to whooping cough. Meanwhile I took to twirling my cap pistol like the Lone Ranger and imitating Bogart's snarl.

One night in the fall of 1941, aboard a train headed south to warmer climes and my recovery from a bout of whooping cough, we stopped outside Washington's Union Station. I raised my window shade and glimpsed for the first time the dome of the Capitol, spotlit and gleaming like a great protective beacon. The remembered sight would continue to stir me in the years ahead, long after the shock of December 7th.

We were in the living room of the Long Island house that morning, settling in with the Sunday papers after church. I heard a door slam, followed by brisk footsteps, and my father, looking pale, walked into the room. He'd been alerted by a friend's phone call. He sank to his knees, switching on the big Philco console in the bottom cabinet of the bookcase. It was there a little before noon, listening to a voice crackling over the airways from Pearl Harbor, we heard the news that would change our lives forever.

All at once our daily regimen was filled with unfamiliar urgencies. Air raid drills and the extinguishing of telltale lights after dark. Collection drives for aluminum salvage and waste paper that could be recycled for war use. Gas rationing, sugar rationing, tire rationing.

People placed crossed strips of thick adhesive tape on their windows to reduce the glass-shattering impact of bombs. We bought war stamps for a quarter each and pasted them into booklets that could eventually be exchanged for a war bond. On our classroom walls we studied maps of the European and Pacific theatres of war.

The first newspaper stories speculating on the impact of an air raid over our city appeared: an attack of forty German Stukas carrying incendiary bombs could ignite up to four thousand fires and reduce to ashes most of Manhattan's Upper East Side. That got my attention.

I was coping at school with my own small firestorms, trying to escape the wrath of my teachers, ducking erasers and chalk. Joey Roth stuck a lead pencil in my leg and I cocked my fist at him, cocked it right through a glass window, which sliced off part of my right pinkie.

My father, to cool my temper, took me for rides in his Ford coupe, which had red hubcaps and a rumble seat. Evenings he read to me from *The Home Book of Verse*, poems like "The High-wayman" by Alfred Noyes. I fell in love with poor doomed Bess, the innkeeper's daughter, and her perfumed tresses. She held my fevered imagination until Ingrid Bergman came along a year later in *Casablanca*.

My classmate Allen Dulles Jr. invited me to his family's fishing lodge on Lake Ontario. Allen's father was already building his reputation overseas as a spymaster nonpareil. Young Allen, reserved and brittle, was our class brain. He had dark curly hair, a precious accent, and was even more unathletic than me. We bonded over the campfire, broiling the lake bass we'd just caught. He would become a casualty of two wars: this one which estranged him from his absent father; and a later one which left him with an irreparable battle wound.

In June 1942 my brother Tommy struck a premonitory note in his Exeter senior class oration. His generation would fight not only pro patria, but for the larger principles of peace and freedom, he proclaimed. It was "a rotten thing to die in vain." That fall he entered Harvard.

Impatient to see action, he left Harvard in the middle of his freshman year to join the Navy as a pilot. The following year he washed out of Navy flight school. He'd been found wanting as a flier; he'd also bent a rule or two. Mechanics at the school noticed that each time Tommy's plane returned from a solo training flight the gas tank was mysteriously near full. An officer trailed his plane after takeoff one day and found it some forty miles away parked near a dude ranch filled with girls. Within days of his washout, Tommy had signed up with the most dangerous of the Navy's arms, its submarine service.

My parents, who'd objected to Tommy's leaving Harvard, were

even more dubious about this move, given his shaky displays of sea-manship. On one of the last summer days of 1942 he'd been helm-ing our seventeen-foot Knockabout across Penobscot Bay in a stiff nor'wester, with me and a friend as crew. We took in so much sea the boat swamped and sank in high waves more than a hundred yards off the Haven shore. We'd swum for our lives, my brother clinging to my life preserver. For a few hours, till we finally showed up safe at the farm, the family thought we'd gone down with the Knockabout and perished.

My father had enlisted and flown to London that summer, assigned at the age of forty-three to the Eighth Air Force as a procurement officer with the rank of major. His colleagues would come to admire him as the wizard of scrounge, his ability to acquire by hook or crook a steady supply of scarce parts for the Air Force's over-worked and flak-damaged bombers.

Early one morning near the end of the year, beneath the stands of the University of Chicago's football stadium, a team of physicists headed by Enrico Fermi concluded a secret experiment: the first controlled chain reaction of fissionable material. Fermi's success signalled the coming of the atomic age and America's potential to build the world's most destructive bomb.

That December, Sinatra debuted at the Paramount Theatre in Times Square amid the squeals of bobby-soxers. Grandpa Lamont sold the *Reynard* to the Navy for one dollar, making his initial con-tribution to the war effort and a tidy tax deduction at the same time.

The war filled our lives with remembered images and sounds.

In London the air raids' percussion reminded my father of an approaching summer storm. The mournful wail of sirens like a rushing wind announced the enemy bombers. Then came a stac-cato whisper that intensified, the chok-chok-chok of antiaircraft batteries like the first distant claps of thunder. The crescendo at the storm's eye was earsplitting, the thunder of ack-ack and rocket barrages, the sirens now screaming, the crump of exploding bombs. The air was filled with jagged shards, the night sky crisscrossed by probing searchlights, shell flashes, and flares. The storm passed, the skies cleared, and Londoners emerged exhausted from their subway shelters.

My father went down into the subways only once during a raid, long enough to absorb the sight of whole families huddled together in the tunnels, seeking to revive their spirits with communal singing, sleeping fitfully in corridors or on escalators. The tunnels were dangerously unsanitary, infested with rats, fleas, and lice; people had to use them as bathrooms, creating a continuous stench. After a raid, while they were still digging for survivors, my father wrote, the shopkeepers would clear the debris from their window displays, nail up beaverboard strips to replace the shattered windows, and tack up signs declaring "Business as Usual."

Most air raids Father could be found in the basement of his building, surrounded by children, reading aloud to them from Robert Louis Stevenson. The children seemed enraptured, oblivious to the explosions and clamor above.

At home we marked Armed Forces Day with parades down Fifth Avenue. Mother in her gray blues stepped out smartly ahead of a contingent of Red Cross ladies. *Oklahoma* opened on Broadway two months after the Battle of Stalingrad. Amid the carnage of war the show was a lyrical bouquet of cheer. It sparked my lifetime romance with the musical theatre.

Grandpa's Committee of Operations Analysts, evaluating the growing impact of Allied bombing on Germany's industrial machine, reported in 1943 that the destruction of sixty key targets would seriously impair, perhaps paralyze, the Axis war effort in the West, enough to enable the Allies' invasion of Europe within a year.

At some point, too, that year a secret scientific laboratory was built in New Mexico, high up on a remote mesa. The site was called Los Alamos, and the experiments conducted there would one day shatter the world, altering forever our view of it.

By early 1944, the course of the war had shifted in favor of the Allies. U.S. divisions were storming up the boot of Italy. The Russians were forcing German retreats on the Eastern front. MacArthur's forces were advancing in the Pacific. R.A.F. and Eighth Air Force bombers were pounding Berlin; one barrage obliterated three key aircraft assembly plants, ones that quite possibly had been targeted by Grandpa's committee.

When D-Day came that June, the immensity of the invasion force staggered us. A million more Allied troops followed that first assault, my father among them. By then he had transferred to the Ninth Air Force, which was responsible for direct tactical support of the Allied armies. Father pitched his tent in a pasture near the Normandy beachhead. After the infantry had secured the area, he set up shop in an abandoned château.

The war reduced to mere blips the milestones in our lives at home. I graduated from Buckley with a prize in English composition, which must have dumbfounded my father, though it barely mitigated his view of my uncertain progress. That October, now a lieutenant colonel, he headed home after two years of active service just in time to see FDR reelected to a fourth term. My brother Ted turned eighteen and was drafted for naval training.

Halfway across the world my other brother, now a Seaman 1st Class, saw the tedium of shipboard life change in a flash with his baptism in combat. His submarine, the USS *Snook*, on its seventh patrol, had attacked a Japanese convoy, sinking three freighters and crippling a fourth. The sub had followed up a few days later by torpedoing another enemy ship off Formosa and rescuing a downed American pilot in the seas off Luzon. Altogether the *Snook* had destroyed some 37,000 tons of Japanese shipping on the patrol.

The exhilaration of combat had come after months of Tommy and his mates enduring freezing gales along with a couple of close calls. On an early test dive something had gone terribly wrong and the *Snook* had plunged steeply toward the ocean bottom before righting itself at the last minute. Off Japan's Kurile Islands the ship had struck an iceberg, damaging its superstructure. The incidents may have steeled Tommy for the combat ahead; they'd have also reminded him of the variable dangers of his work.

Many subs carried torpedoes that sometimes failed to explode or turned off course and circled back to sink the ship that fired them. Submariners, along with pilots, were targeted for especially rough treatment by the Japanese; if captured, they'd be assigned to the vilest prison camps. Twenty-two percent of them would die in action before the war's end.

In a letter home, Tommy wrote in his best censor-baffling Latin: *Dulce et decorum est pro patria mori.* To die for one's country is sweet and seemly.

By the end of March 1945, Germany was all but beaten, her military collapse expected at any hour.

On April 1st Parisians floodlit the Arc de Triomphe for the first time since the start of the war. Eleven days later FDR died of a massive stroke at the winter White House in Georgia. Grandpa sent a letter of condolence to Eleanor Roosevelt who responded, noting her special sadness that FDR "could not have lived to see the day of victory."

One night that month I dreamed that an avalanche of water had burst the innards of Tommy's sub, sending it careening down through the ocean's depths. I heard my brother crying aloud in distress.

In May Germany surrendered, and at dawn one morning that July, scientists from Los Alamos test-fired the world's first atomic bomb.

The bomb hastened the war's end, forcing Japan's capitulation in August. On V-J day Americans uncorked champagne and danced in the streets. But in our household the celebrating was tinged with unbearable sorrow.

48

That March the *Snook* had begun its ninth patrol, heading for Guam. By now it had sunk or damaged more than 136,000 tons of Japanese naval and merchant shipping.

The ship was ordered to join a wolf pack of attack subs headed for the South China Sea toward the vicinity of Hainan Island by the Tonkin Gulf. The *Snook* had radioed her position just east of Hainan Island on April 8, her last contact. Subsequent orders to the *Snook* to proceed northeast toward Formosa and the Luzon Straits were not acknowledged. Other attempts to raise her by radio in the days ahead proved futile. She was never heard from again.

The telegram reached our Manhattan apartment on a balmy morning the first week of May. My mother guessed the contents the moment she saw the envelope; there'd been no word from Tommy for so long. "The Navy Department deeply regrets . . ." it began. He was missing in action. My father wrote to say there was no hope of his returning. Tommy and his mates were on eternal patrol somewhere at the bottom of the Pacific.

Only years later would I fully comprehend how grievous a void Tommy's death had left in my parents' lives. He'd been a challenge all along to their best efforts to mold him into the exceptional young man he'd finally become. In a letter to my mother, written while Tommy was at sea, my father had tried to reassure her "that all will be well with the boy over whom we together have worked and fought and suffered and wept so many times for so many years."

They wept for him again at his memorial service in the island church that August, a few days before the guns fell silent everywhere. Here on North Haven, his Tivoli, the friends who mattered most to Tommy gathered to sing the familiar lines of the Navy Hymn and wish him a last good-bye.

John Crocker Jr., marveling at the turnout for his old friend, would write, "Death does teach us how much we care for one another and how much that caring matters."

5

A.O., *Sally Rand, and*
the Athenian Effect

At some point in all this, I'd been shipped off to boarding school.

My mother was convinced I needed stricter supervision at a more genteel correctional facility than the one my father and brothers had attended. So to Father's dismay I was air mailed not to Exeter but to Milton Academy, an ivied cloister of Yankee rectitude situated just south of Boston.

Milton was a brief trolley ride from downtown Boston. The school authorities spent as much time protecting us from the sins of Scollay Square's burlesque and movie houses as they did promoting the virtues of Horace and Cicero. Mostly our sinning was confined to the occasional hike to the village ice-cream parlor.

Life as a lowly boarder was predictably monastic: bone-chilling New England nights, cramped dormitory cubicles, bullying upper classmen, an endless diet of chipped beef on toast. Chapel and Sunday church were mandatory; we dosed out on God. Our housemaster, a genial former pro baseball player, urged us to persevere and "keep rounding the bases." His deputy, a dead ringer for Sidney

Greenstreet, took to calling me "fer-de-lance" (a pit viper) which, in my ignorance I took to be a compliment.

The academy's headmaster, a dapper chap with a clipped mustache, was adept at cajoling checks from the Brookline and Back Bay mothers whose young charges he supervised. The academy also harbored a separate girls school down the road, a very good one, which was run by a formidable dreadnaught named Miss Faulkner; Milton wasn't yet coed, a term that vaguely offended Brahmin sensibilities. The boys school principal was a tweedy beanpole named Arthur Perry who came from a distinguished line of educators and whose eyes perpetually twinkled behind a pair of rimless glasses. Mr. Perry's annual reading at assembly of Dickens's *Christmas Carol* was as eagerly anticipated as the Great Tree Frog Dissection conducted each spring in Mr. LeSourd's science class.

If Mr. Perry had no vaulting ambitions for his school, it mattered little in the scheme of things. Milton was where the first families of Boston sent their sons, the bright as well as the real cream ("rich and thick"). It was expected that, barring expulsion for a serious felony, they would proceed on schedule to Harvard across the Charles.

Milton's motto was "Dare to be true," proclaimed in plain English with none of the fancy Latin varnish favored by other schools. The teachers were a sturdy lot, disciplined, demanding, occasionally fired with passion. If they were more sage than inspired, it may have been because most were seriously aging, their younger colleagues still off finishing the war. All that changed for me with the arrival in 1946 of Albert O. Smith, our new English teacher.

A.O. was lately discharged from the Air Force and eager to get on with his career. He was unmarried and unconforming, a lanky character with smoke-stained teeth and a quizzical smile. Most days he wore a frayed button-down shirt and a tired sportscoat that drooped to his knees. He was rumored to knock down a bourbon or two and some mornings appeared in class a little the worse for wear.

His classroom style was Socratic-casual, something we were unused to. Shortly he became the most subversive, liberating influence in our academic life.

A.O. prodded us to avoid the banal, to think critically and argue succinctly. He pumped us up with the intellectual oxygen we needed, and did so with infectious humor. He seemed free of pedantry, a blithe spirit thumbing his nose at church-school formalities. He became my friend and mentor.

A classmate and I put out a mimeographed four-page newspaper for the lower classmen, my initial foray into journalism. But the writer in me wouldn't crystallize for a while. My first short-story effort was returned with the comment that it lacked a plot. I began polishing my letters home, describing the terrors of boarding life. That would prove a more useful run-up to the trade I eventually chose.

I'd put away the songs of childhood, the Stephen Foster melodies my mother sang, and begun to dig hipper stuff like "Stompin' at the Savoy." I became a swing addict.

Holidays in New York meant camping out in Times Square. Within an eight-block radius stood the Capitol, the Roxy, Loews, Paramount, and Strand movie theaters, kitschy temples to the high priests of swing. The papers would run full-page ads announcing a blockbuster double bill with Bogart or Alan Ladd headlining a movie, followed by the Harry James or the Count Basie or Benny Goodman orchestras live. Ticket lines would stretch for blocks. If you were lucky and made it inside for the early matinee, you might never leave, it was that magical.

When the film ended and the last chords of the intermission organ had faded, there was a pregnant pause while we waited in the darkness. The ushers moved to the edge of the orchestra pit to repel the jitterbuggers. Then we heard the first glorious sounds from deep within the pit. The stage lights burst aglow and suddenly this hydraulic ark filled with men in satiny blue tuxedos, their horns blasting, rose from the depths to envelop us in aural splendor. We sat bolt upright, pounding our feet to the rhythm, digging the saxes' seamless wail, the brass behind them setting our ears afire.

Everything was gale driven, a kinetic blend of harmony and beat punctuated by the sizzle of cymbals. The ark seemed to explode with gyrating bandsmen popping up for solo riffs. We sat there yelling, bathed in the delirium. Near the end, when Goodman's clarinet might interlace the haunting rills of "Goodbye," his signature sign-off, we knew our fix was over. At least till the next holiday.

I wrote for the lit magazine and took up smoking. The ads and movies suggested cigarettes lent spice to life, Bacall languidly blowing smoke in Bogart's eyes, Bogie singlehandedly turning the cigarette into his personal swagger stick. Cigarette-wise, my father was the essence of cool. At the breakfast table he inhaled the nicotine through a silver-and-black cigarette holder he'd bought under the illusion it was a filter. He'd blow a ring or two, then rest the holder in the ashtray, letting tendrils of blue smoke from it curl alluringly across the table's mahogany surface. So I went out and bought my first pack of Camels.

Nice girls didn't smoke, at least not the ones in cashmere sweaters who strolled down Milton's Centre Street. But then we weren't interested in nice girls, we told ourselves. We figured that with the right date, a smooth line, and a few suave Camel exhalings, we could turn nice to bad. It didn't work out that way, but I fantasized about it along with the rest of my hormonally active little pals, especially when the spring prom rolled around.

There in the gymnasium, strung with crepe paper decorations, dimmed colored lights and a revolving sphere that sprayed flecks of blue and tangerine gleam across the dance floor, we lost ourselves in a bower of gardenias and romance. All those girls in red velveteen dresses or off-the-shoulder tulle gowns, me and my panting pals in our scruffy black shoes and crooked bow ties — shuffling cheek-to-cheek through the perfumed air. For a couple of hours we fox-trotted through a darkened world full of ridiculously imagined promise.

My father was making it big as a banker, civic leader and Harvard overseer. A friend commented on his pin-striped virtuousness:

> A stranger, scanning Tommy's solemn face
> And slightly mournful gaze and deadpan look
> Might think he was preparing to say grace
> Or to read verses from the Holy Book.

I figured otherwise. It was all a pose for Father's true role as boulevardier and man-about-town. Strolling jauntily down the avenue on a fall day, he was a profile in dapperness from his brown felt hat to his Oxford loafers. He was customarily sheathed in a natty twilled topcoat and, beneath that, a dark suit from off the rack at Macy's (he was a pal of the owner), enfolding a crisp white shirt and silk tie of impeccable restraint. The tie was clasped to the shirt by a thin gold clip set at a rakish angle. Thus outfitted, Father commanded the sidewalk, greeting friends with a brisk salutation that resembled a greyhound's bark.

In his occasional attempts at the risqué, Father had mastered a sort of Bojangles clog, which he performed in ski boots or black pumps. The peak of his clogging career came at a champagne dinner given by his friend Lewis Douglas, a former ambassador to Great Britain. The guest of honor was the Queen Mother. Father balanced himself atop a piano stool, belting out "We're Having a Heat Wave, a Tropical Heat Wave," while wiggling his backside. The guests roared their applause, the Queen Mother smiled wanly.

Next morning my father awoke to a phone message from one of the guests:

> It really isn't etiquette
> To ask a Queen to applaud

> Songs that appeal to a lush coquette
> Or are commonly sung to a bawd.

He penned his apologies to the Q.M. and hung up his clogging shoes for a while.

These larky bits, though, were rarer than UFO sightings. Father was a man weighed down by worries. Most of them, I was convinced, focused on me. Each time I was summoned to his dressing room, I knew, from the warning rattle as he cleared his throat, I was in for a heavy reprimand.

At such times I turned to my Uncle Ranny for relief. Ranny was my mother's irrepressible younger brother. He had a shock of red hair turning silver and seemed liberated from the Protestant conscience that burdened my father. He laughed easily and made me laugh. At family dinners his repartee would breeze along on wafts of gin until an almost imperceptible slurring of words occurred, at which point my mother would deftly engage him in some distraction while signalling the maid to remove his glass. Ranny was my pal, my blood brother in rebellion against the established order.

On Christmas Eve 1947, in the 70th Street house, Grandpa collapsed at dinner. Various aunts fluttered about the grandchildren's table, trying to block our view of him in distress. Two months later he was dead.

There were ripples of mourning and remembrances from everywhere. They remembered him in Boston where he'd donated the first modern undergraduate library at Harvard. They remembered him in England where he'd made a signal bequest toward the restoration of war-torn Canterbury Cathedral. They remembered him in Greece for his generosity to the American School of Classical Studies in Athens.

Wall Street, one newspaper observed, had had more flamboyant figures than Grandpa but "none of greater ability, of deeper understanding." In *The Saturday Review of Literature* his friend

Henry Seidel Canby noted that character accounted for at least 80 percent of Grandpa's success. It was generally conceded that my grandfather had played some part in practically everything big that happened during his decades-long watch at the Morgan bank.

My Rochester grandparents bequeathed me ten dollars on my eighteenth birthday, obviously relieved I would make it to graduation in June.

I'd made good friends at Milton, some with stars in their futures. One would become a Harvard dean, another a classical dancer; one or two would become spies. Flender would become my banker; Richardson would marry my first cousin. Stevenson, son of a soon-to-be presidential nominee, would become a U.S. Senator. One classmate would confide years later how thoroughly he abominated his years at Milton. Another would commit suicide.

The boys in the class above us would go off to Korea to die and win posthumous medals for gallantry. We clung to our own little zeitgeist. Our senior class voted "Li'l Abner" its favorite comic strip and, wonder of wonders, Harvard decided I was an acceptable risk.

My father figured a taste of the Continent might be salutary for a prospective freshman as culturally impaired as I was.

Everyone seemed to be heading for Europe that summer. Father was particularly happy to be leaving town — some crank with a hate for the Morgan bank had threatened to shoot him. When the *Queen Mary* eased out of her berth in lower Manhattan one July morning, my parents, my sister and I had joined a shipboard contingent that included Clark Gable and a raven-haired post-debutante I knew slightly, Jacqueline Bouvier.

In London, we lunched with the historian Arnold Toynbee, shared high tea with John Masefield, and drinks with the U.S. ambassador. The Olympic Games were in town. The hotel lobbies were aswarm with people like Jack Benny and Alfred Hitchcock.

When you took a cab to the games at Wembley Stadium you might find yourself being trailed by a silver Rolls bearing Tracy and Hepburn.

Life on the road beyond London was more testing. At Loch Lomond, where we dined at the home of the resident baron, Father drove our car into the host's front gate, demolishing it on the spot. After that we hired a chauffeur who rocketed our limo through the countryside at Mach 1. In Geneva, the hotel refused to honor our reservations and Mother got into a fight with the concierge.

The worst was eating out in Paris. The French doted on their pets and dogfights were apt to erupt during meals. The restaurant would turn into a bedlam of yapping poodles, the noise amplified by foreigners demanding service at the top of their lungs. The waiters liked to spill soup on the Americans. At dinner's end, Father would try and decipher the bill, then summon the waiter to remonstrate with him in his fractured French. The waiter would roll his eyes; we'd pay the bill.

The back end of the trip was a drive through Normandy, retracing my father's post-invasion days. In the villages en route to the beaches little had been spared the war's fury. Machine guns and mortars had torn large chunks out of every structure. The countryside was a tableau of desolation: skeletons of trees stripped bare by exploding shells; broken fields filled with twisted metal where armies had blasted through, ripping apart the hedgerows and churning up ugly berms of charred earth; here and there lay abandoned German Tiger tanks in the last stages of corrosion.

Beyond St. Lô, a shattered ghost town that had borne the brunt of Allied shelling, we fetched up at Fuegères and the old chateau that had served as Father's post-D-Day headquarters. On Omaha Beach burned-out hulks of landing craft still littered the sands; above them were the pillbox entrenchments from which the Wehrmacht had rained down a hell of fire. We spared my mother a visit to the American cemetery above the beaches.

But at Bayeux, our last stop before Cherbourg and the voyage home, my father and I walked at dusk to the British war cemetery on the city's outskirts. I remember a woman there, standing with bowed head among the sea of white crosses, sobbing at the grave of her son.

The fall I moved into Harvard Yard, Truman upset Dewey and James Michael Curley was running for mayor of Boston from a jail cell across the Charles.

Long-playing records debuted, consigning to the scrap heap my old shellacked seventy-eights with their Commodore labels. The Kinsey Report had landed in America's lap with a blast. In between the *Iliad* and the *Odyssey* we read that our elders were sexual Olympians. When they weren't jumping into bed with one another, they were putting the pedal to the metal of their new Chevys or erecting suburban split-levels. Everyone was accentuating the positive and finding his or her own groove. I found mine under the stately elms of Harvard Yard.

The place was astir with the ghosts of Eliot, Henry James, "Copey," and Santayana. As a freshman, my grandfather had once seen William Cullen Bryant striding through the Yard near the old college pump. Now there were reported sightings of James Bryant Conant, the eminently elusive current Harvard president. Robert Frost dropped by to read from his works; Aaron Copeland taught a class in contemporary music. Howard Mumford Jones, one of my professors, declared the Yard the natural home of intellectual freedom. I took up housekeeping on the third story of Stoughton Hall, a red-brick colonial pile with sagging floors.

Our entering class, thirteen hundred strong, represented the college's biggest peacetime influx, and was the last to include large numbers of World War II veterans. The vets, making up for lost time, brought a seriousness of purpose to our ranks, though not enough to diminish the usual undergraduate deviltry: beer-fueled rallies in the Yard; football riots in Harvard Square; Saturday night benders in Cronin's where Jim Cronin, in his bartender's apron, tossed the most obstreperous of us bodily out the door.

On weekends there was Boston's peerless symphony orchestra and Sally Rand, the fan dancer. At Storyville off Kenmore Square you could chat up Max Kaminsky, Pops Foster, and other jazzmen between sets. Or you could drop by Lowell House to hear the Crimson Stompers and a singer from Wellesley whose pipes were angelic. I played piano at a settlement house for poor kids and performed Handel's *Messiah* at Symphony Hall with the glee club under the baton of Koussevitsky.

I decided to major in English. Robert Frost said we went to college to be given one more chance to learn to read. The danger, he added, was that we'd overshoot the mark and learn to study what was only meant to be read "and so be spoiled forever for enjoying Keats's *Ode to Autumn*."

It almost came to that. The Shakespearian scholar Harry Levine, with his fussy line-by-line dissections of *Hamlet* or *Macbeth*, came close to ruining the Bard for me. John Ciardi, conversely, was a model tutor in the art of short story writing, a man of incorruptible standards in an age when teachers had not yet caved to student demands for inflated grades.

Other professors dazzled us with their showmanship. Owlish David Owen, whose course in nineteenth-century British history was a sine qua non, regaled us with his bawdy asides. Samuel Eliot Morrison did everything but launch a brigantine in his class on naval history. For sheer unbridled theatrics, though, nothing equaled John Finley, professor of Greek. When Finley was in full Homeric flight, his patrician face in studied profile as he declaimed on dark-prowed ships and rosy-fingered dawns, his classes became stage performances rivaling those of classical Greece.

But then the whole scene was like some idealization of the Hellenic age: helmeted gladiators clashing in the stadium each fall; muscled Adonises sculling on the Charles; and, in the distance, the golden dome of Boston's Statehouse shimmering in an Attic light.

One of the Cabot grandees had publicly proclaimed his family's preference for the Athenian style. So straightaway I presented myself to the dean as a son of Athens — devotee of the musical arts, parlor sportsman, Olympic-style bon vivant — and got to room with a Cabot. We added a third roommate, a Canadian named Lawson, who idolized Hemingway and had a penchant for gambling on the horses. A triad of Athenians. My father choked on the notion.

Charlie Cabot had been head prefect at Milton. He was everything my father despairingly hoped I'd become: studious, athletic, a natural leader of men, a veritable young Sun King. I did the best I could to stay close to his light. He was also a bit of a square. Our unspoken bargain as we bonded was that I'd imbue him with a little big-city slick, introduce him to Manhattan's bright lights, and he would work on my character. I was less than successful in my task, but Charlie held up his end of the bargain.

The Cabots at one time or another pretty much ran everything in Boston — the symphony orchestra, the editorial page of the *Globe*, the local transit authority, and Harvard's gold-plated endowment. For all that, they seemed quite approachable despite rumors they talked only to God (as long as He was from Boston). At worst, they were equal-opportunity snobs. After John D. Rockefeller III bought a summer home on Pulpit Harbor across from the Cabots, I asked one of the Cabot ladies how she liked her new neighbors, the Rockefellers, and she responded sweetly, "Who?"

Altogether, I thought the Cabots an enviable lot. They dressed like hobos, swore like truckers, and thought nothing of rowing across Penobscot Bay in a storm for fun. Cabotville by the Pulpit was a warren of drab little cottages inhabited by an assortment of overachieving judges, business tycoons, lawyers, editors, and scientific wunderkinds.

As part of my self-improvement campaign, I gave up reading purloined Henry Miller paperbacks. I turned my summertime energies to more serious pursuits than chasing debs across the parqueted dance floors of Gatsbyland.

There were still end-of-summer cruises downeast on Cabot's yawl *Echo* — weeklong vagabondages in pea-soupers and tearing winds where our crew of Harvard-Dartmouth brothers would contrive to lose charts and winches overboard, shinny up the mast to grapple with ripped mainsails, set tenders adrift, and hit every submerged rock between Pulpit Harbor and Petit Manan. The world kept intruding, though, on even these diversions.

Nine million refugees had fled eastern Europe since the war's end, many of them to West Germany, which now faced a severe housing shortage. The summer of '51 I signed on for pick-and-shovel work under the sponsorship of the American Friends Service, helping construct new homes for the refugees. I flew to Hamburg, then Berlin, en route to the AFS camp in Bavaria. Hamburg was a city still lacerated by the war, the wind whistling through the blasted entrails of entire city blocks, families living hand-to-mouth in the three-sided skeletons of what had once been homes.

In Berlin, I bicycled into the Soviet-controlled sector.* My guide was a thirty-year-old former Wehrmacht sergeant who'd lost his leg to a Russian mine. We headed past the burned-out Reichstag, through the Brandenburg Gate, and into East Berlin. The avenues were vacant and quiet. On the walls of gutted buildings chalked messages read, AMERICANS, GO HOME. I had visions of being stopped by KGB agents and spending the rest of my days in a gulag. A half-hour later we emerged, to my relief, at Potsdammer Platz and crossed back into Free Berlin.

---

*My Harvard classmate George J. W. Goodman, on his way to becoming a best-selling author, had slipped into East Berlin a few weeks earlier, posing as a U.S. delegate to a Communist youth festival. An official there had lectured him on the evils of capitalism, a subject she had learned years before at a monetary conference in Switzerland while working as an assistant to an "imperialist Western banker" named Thomas W. Lamont.

The rest of that summer I dug holes and hauled cement. The AFS camp at Geretsreid housed fourteen German boys in lederhosen, a half-dozen Americans, two French Moroccans, and a pair of useless Italians. Everyone worked long hours except the Italians. The Italians hated the camp and its rules. They'd heard of a dream camp farther east that had no rules and a nice river to splash in. When our work at Geretsreid was done, they persuaded me to go with them.

The dream camp turned out to be smack on the Czech border. The Czech border guards had killed a West German policeman in a firefight there the month before. The camp was encircled by barbed wire; we could splash in the river only under the wary eyes of German cops and a U.S. tank crew. A woman picking flowers on the wrong side of the river had been snatched by the Czech police a few days earlier. On my first swim I dog-paddled to the Czech side, stretched out on the rocks to catch some rays and dozed off. I was roused by shouts from the opposite bank and plunged back across the stream moments before a Czech patrol spotted me.

We lived in tents that were drenched by frequent rainstorms and smelled of mold. At night the Czechs harassed us by firing their rifles in the air. I felt the Italians had pulled a swindle on me and requested, and got, reassignment to another AFS camp near Ingolstadt.

The den mother there was a young Prussian whose father had known Rommel. She'd spent the war in air raid shelters, swearing eternal vengeance on American pilots. She hated the Russians worse: they'd beaten and raped one of her cousins.

Mr. Noel was the camp's senior advisor, another war veteran. One day he accidentally stepped on my foot. "I didn't realize," he apologized, "I have no feeling in that leg." I watched him limp away as I had watched so many of his compatriots that summer, limping, jockeying their wheelchairs, or squatting on their pitiful stumps.

I came of age my last year at Harvard. Baptism in sex. Confirmation in the church. Midnight reflections on opportunities missed, doubts about self-worth. The first wrenching truths about life's fragility.

The freshly minted Marine lieutenants I knew became cannon fodder in the fighting that raged across the mountainsides of the Korean peninsula. Their forward outposts were overrun, mortar shells shredded their bodies. Rod Skinner, a wrestling star at Milton the year ahead of me, threw himself on an enemy grenade to save the men around him and was posthumously awarded the Medal of Honor. Allen Dulles Jr. was directing fire on an enemy gun emplacement when a shell fragment ripped into his brain, ending his brilliant future. "Whatever you do, don't join the Marine Corps," 2nd Lieutenant Adlai Stevenson III wrote from Quantico, Virginia, later that year.

Stevenson's father was being touted as the Democratic nominee in the upcoming presidential campaign. Robert Taft, the Ohio conservative, would challenge General Eisenhower, a moderate, for the Republican nomination. Election politics suffused the Harvard campus. I schemed to somehow crash the GOP convention that July.

That last spring in Cambridge one remembers with a sweet ache. The lovely windblown Cliffies dashing between classes. Chestnuts blooming on Linden Street. The Charles meandering beneath the bridges, past sunlit greenswards. A hint of sexual longing hung in the breeze — reveries of Laura, the housemaster's wife in *Tea and Sympathy*, unbuttoning her blouse and whispering endearments to the young initiate, Tom, who would be played in the movie version by our classmate John Kerr.

We reveled in our last undergraduate surges of exuberance and outrage. We condemned with fury the louts who burned a cross near the campus quarters of some black students. We ignited a brawling rally in Harvard Square for Pogo, a cartoon character running for president. On our little patch of ivied turf we thumbed our noses at the stereotype of us as the Silent Generation. We bowed out with high-decibel zest.

Commencement week, Cabot slammed a two-run homer against Yale and, under the elms in the Yard, I joined that company of Harvard graduates described by Emerson as "the long winding train reaching back into eternity."

A month later I was sitting in the rafters at the GOP convention hall near the Chicago stockyards, helping plot a balloon drop the moment Eisenhower's name was offered in nomination. That fall, Ike was elected in a landslide.

6

The Blonde on the Beach, the King of KP

My larval years behind me, the fifties were just beginning.

It was the decade of electric dishwashers and Liberace. We fell in love with tailfins, barbecue pits, Lawrence Welk, and anything Formica. I had matured into an unbeat generation of dull conformists anxious to start marrying, raise families, and get on with life.

The Eisenhower years offered little excitement beyond peace and prosperity. The DNA's structure was unveiled; polio vaccine made available. The Korean War ended in 1953. Some historians even concluded the fifties were America's last idyllic time.

Except for McCarthyism. As Cold War tensions spread the Red-scare virus across America, the Republican senator from Wisconsin became its most notorious carrier. Few people cared to antagonize Joseph McCarthy, master of the reckless smear. Uncle Corliss relished the challenge.

My oldest uncle had been a rebel since his Harvard days, forever cutting against the grain. He delighted in tweaking Grandpa's and Father's capitalist noses, deriding the financial system of which he was a prime beneficiary. He exasperated enough people to have earned, it was said, the most impressive collection of epithets hurled on any man in America. "Silk-shirt Communist" and "barefoot proletarian millionaire" were among the milder ones. Corliss rarely went barefoot, never wore silk shirts, and professed to his dying day never to have been a Communist.

If he was more naif than realist, an incurable romantic, he was also an unabashed extrovert, a man who loved to sing and dance as well as aggravate. In his youth, Corliss had amorously pursued the Morrow sisters, Elisabeth and Anne, eventually falling, wrote Charles Lindbergh's biographer, "deeply in love with Anne's lambent beauty and smoldering nature." Anne regularly shrugged off his proposals, but for the rest of his life Corliss privately carried the torch for her.

His public torch bearing he reserved for the Soviet Union. From its socialist vision to its role as wartime ally, Russia, in Corliss's eyes, was a paragon among nations. He dismissed all doubts about its multiple oppressions, its cruel economic failures, its purges, its gulags, its grasping foreign policy. My father had written Corliss, to no avail, urging him to use his influence "to open the gates of Russia to truth and the free exchange of information." Corliss's busy pamphleteering, which condemned the "imperialistic" West while lauding the "peace-loving" Soviets, moved a New York Times book critic to cite his views as "so fantastic they are not even wrong; they enter a science-fiction universe of meta-wrongness." Nonetheless, Corliss pressed on. Bye and bye he caught McCarthy's eye.

In his campaign to root out Communists — real or imagined — from government, McCarthy had run roughshod over constitutional principles, bullying much of the liberal establishment while cowing the mainstream press.

Henry Luce, editor-in-chief of Time, had initially been ambivalent about McCarthy. Luce expressed his views privately one evening at a dinner in Rome with the Paul Cabots and my parents. Luce and Cabot, a pioneering investment banker and member of the Harvard Corporation, got into a hell of an argument, according to Luce. Cabot defended Dean Acheson, an early McCarthy target, and roundly excoriated McCarthy for trampling on Americans' rights. Luce later told a colleague, referring to the Cabots and Lamonts, that what annoyed him most "was not Commies but these Park Avenue and Cambridge muddleheads."*

In September 1953, McCarthy summoned Corliss to appear before the Senator's Permanent Subcommittee on Investigations. Corliss stood his ground, citing the First Amendment and challenging the subcommittee's jurisdiction. McCarthy had him indicted for contempt of Congress, a charge that was promptly dismissed by the courts. Corliss went on to successfully sue the federal government and the U.S. Post Office for censoring his mail. McCarthy's star faded as the country wearied of his antics. Condemned at last by his senate colleagues, he retreated into alcoholism, a sick and broken man.

In late 1956, Stuart Symington, one of McCarthy's severest senate critics, send an aide to McCarthy's Washington home to convey a personal message of concern for his health. The aide rang the bell, and when the door opened he beheld an unforgettable sight: McCarthy standing in the doorway in his skivvies, unshaven, disheveled, a half-empty snifter of brandy in one hand, and a Colt .45 revolver in the other. Within three months McCarthy was dead.

Corliss, on the other hand, was exhilarated.

My brief tenure at the Harvard Business School was a mistake. I would not be the next Carnegie or Mellon, I soon realized, and shed no tears when I wasn't asked back the second year.

I made a last hurrah, however, before cashing in my chips at

---

*In fact, Paul Cabot and Father were anything but muddleheads, although Cabot could turn combative in argument, especially after a few drinks. Adlai Stevenson, veteran of many a bruising political campaign, once recalled that after a long, wet dinner with Cabot he felt "more bottle-scarred than battle-scarred."

HBS. I forewent a spring vacation spent cramming for finals in factory management and took off for the beaches of Florida. The very first day, on the sands of a Fort Lauderdale beach, I met the love of my life.

She was swimming in on a lazy roller, gracefully stroking through the water, the sun catching her blonde bangs and tanned limbs. I posted myself in front of her, caught an outgoing wave, and smacked into her with more force than planned. "I think you've broken my nose," she said. I mumbled apologies, convinced this would be the shortest romance ever, that I'd lose the girl before I'd even gotten her name.

It turned out to be Ada (compact, Biblical) Jung (German-American, fourth generation). She was a business major at Northwestern, outdoorsy, reserved, from a large merchant clan in Wisconsin. All I kept thinking was she owned the most winning smile east or west of the Hudson.

I was dazzled by her; she was curious about me. An encounter of the third kind. She had never met an Easterner, let alone a Harvard man; I'd never heard of her Greek sorority. She'd been raised in a small town, Sheboygan, with middle-American values; I came from a city run by the Mob. Her people spoke a folksy burr; my people avoided r's and called their hometown New Yawk. All I knew about Wisconsin was McCarthy, cheese, and that my Grandfather Miner had once drunk champagne with the governor in the Milwaukee Club; all Ada knew about New York came from the Warner Brothers back lot. It was a perfect match.

We kissed on our first date and neither of us would ever regret it.

Grandma Lamont stayed a contrary spirit to the end. She despised hospitals. I saw her for the last time at home, lying on her canopied bed, under an oxygen tent, impatiently awaiting death.

She had deeded Torrey Cliff to Columbia, which would transform it into the Lamont Geological Observatory. The staff, known as "Lamonters," would make their observatory the world's foremost research center of its kind. At the time, though, I was appalled at the prospect of the old place being converted into an office complex, a great earthquake-detection space crammed with seismometers and sediment cores.

We would lose Grandpa Miner next. He left some money for me and my siblings, but his lasting bequest was the kindness and laughter remembered. That and the swellest collection of arrowheads a boy could ask for. The city of Rochester, which he'd served so well, mourned him as it had honored him over the years.

Early one October morning in 1953 I reported for duty at the Battery Park induction center in lower Manhattan. My locks were shorn, my civies stripped, and I faced with bleak anticipation the start of a new life in the United States Army.

Within a short time I'd been processed out of Fort Dix, New Jersey, to a scrubland waste in Alabama called Camp Rucker. Rucker was home to the Third Army's 47th Infantry Division, known as the Viking Division. (My father briefly thought the Army was trying to make a sailor out of me.) The nearest town, Ozark, was twenty miles away. I was assigned for basic training to the 164th Infantry Regiment, Fox Company, 2nd Platoon, 4th squad.

At Fort Dix we'd had a psychopathic first sergeant who kept a pet rabbit in the barracks and reportedly fed it carrots laced with a mind-altering substance. At Rucker the sergeants tried to derange the recruits instead. This was carried out over eighteen-hour days that began at 4:00 A.M.

Under an onyx sky we stood braced at attention. The dawn chill penetrated our fatigues, forcing the last bit of sleep from our systems. Orders for the day were barked. The cadremen moved us out for a three-mile run before breakfast. We swept down our barracks and cleaned the latrine for inspection. I was assigned to polish the small brass drain on the main urinal. I gave it the finest lustre I could before surrendering it to the kidneys of the 2nd Platoon.

Afterward there was Police Call, a clean-up exercise in which we moved en masse across the parade ground, eyes peeled for cig-arette butts and gum wrappers. If you inclined your head toward the camp's main gate and kept walking slowly with your eyes on the ground, you could go AWOL with no trouble.

The field marches separated the men from the boys. We'd double-time through the swamp and sand, chanting dirty rhymes in cadence, feeling the dead weight of our M-1 rifles and bulging packs. A truck followed to pick up stragglers and the comatose. One day we were double timing out to the firing range and the CO ordered that no one was to fall out of formation. The last two miles I half-carried, half-dragged a Hispanic kid who'd collapsed.

Retreat sounded at five, but the work clanked on. After supper we cleaned our rifles, spit shined our boots, and burnished our can-teens till they iridesced. When we thought we were done at last, the sergeants ordered us on our knees to scour the barracks until "lights out." In this fashion I came to feel a long overdue bolt of steel being welded onto my backbone.

On pain of death I avoided the camp infirmary. Only once did I go on sick call with a 101° fever. The infirmary was jammed, no place to sit. It smacked of a Turkish jail; if you fell asleep on the floor, the orderlies kicked you on the soles of your feet to wake you. They fed me aspirins till my tongue turned white. There was a trainee in the next cot with a dose of the clap. At night he emitted a death-rattle snore; every time he inhaled it was like a hundred whistling teapots. I thought of smothering him with his pillow, a mercy killing.

The NCOs tried their best to shape us into a fearsome fighting machine. Our platoon sergeant, one Romulus Ambrosino, was a figure of such Neanderthal force I quake at his memory. He had a voice that could crush cement. Ask a stupid question or display two left feet, he'd have you on KP faster than a coon-hound. My first week with him I reckoned I rinsed, dried, and stacked over a thou-sand trays, and assorted cutlery. Afterward, in the grease pits we'd scrub down the garbage cans while the cooks yelled at us.

Diary Extract: Nov. 20. One of the cooks got court-martialed for cussing an officer. They ought to court-martial all the cooks.

In time, under Ambrosino, we morphed into the semblance of a disciplined infantry unit.

After basic, I became an assistant machine gunner. The rest of the guys I'd originally shipped out with from Dix were either transferred or stuck around in new guises. Ramos, the company boxer who did a disappearing act whenever his bout was announced, transferred to the Quartermaster Corps. Cohen got a section eight for hurling a pair of footlockers through the barracks window.

I missed my old buddies and tired of lugging a machine gun over half of Texas, where we'd gone on maneuvers. I yearned for the purifying life of an officer. When the regiment was reassigned to Ft. Benning, Georgia, I applied to Officer Candidate School.

In six months I was retooled from a shabby private first class to a gold-barred leader of men. All I had to do was manage on four hours' sleep a night and execute enough push-ups to break a horse.

That September Ada and I were married in the Lutheran Church of Sheboygan. Several of the Eastern guests ended up in Cheboygan, Michigan, by mistake. Otherwise the affair was a smash. My father stood around at the wedding dinner in his pinstripes and gamely joined in the cornballery of his new Midwestern in-laws. They kept slapping him on the back, shouting, "Drink up, Tom!" We had a forty-eight-hour honeymoon before I had to report back to Benning.

My new commission as a second lieutenant in the infantry elicited mixed emotions in the family. I'd graduated eighty-fourth out of an OCS class of eighty-six, a ranking that would have exhilarated my anti-militarist grandmother but disappointed others. On the other hand, my father, who was always grateful for the smallest favor when it came to my progress, assessed my new status and recognized that a miracle on the scale of Lourdes had occurred.

My orders were to proceed to the Lesser Antilles, which I assumed were somewhere near the Canary Islands off Africa. When our ship steamed into Puerto Rico's San Juan Harbor two weeks later, I jumped for joy.

It was short lived. We were trucked across the mountains to an army post on the island's back side far from the fleshpots of San Juan. Camp Losey, home to the 65th Infantry Regiment, might as well have been in Botswana. It was surrounded by sugar cane fields and squalid native shacks. Goats roamed untethered along a coastal road littered with the skeletons of abandoned cars. Naked children urinated under the acacia trees. The nearest town, Ponce, had a quaint firehouse and square, but not much else.

The regiment was commanded by a paunchy bird colonel who took one look at my records and probably smelled a fellow loser. I was sent to the field to train a platoon of cutthroats from the barrios of San Juan and Spanish Harlem. Most of them had trouble with English; my Spanish was nonexistent. At noon in the bush the temperatures reached one hundred degrees and the sun blistered your face into a patchwork of sores. Every blade of grass or leaf we touched seemed a variety of poisonous nightshade. Afternoon rain showers left our gear drenched, the dirt floors of our tents muddy deltas.

At the end of a month, with the help of a tough top sergeant named Mendez, I'd drilled the socks off this crew and managed to turn a few into halfway decent soldiers. One of them threatened to slice my ears off when we got stateside. The CO was impressed enough to transfer me to a job editing the regimental newspaper. At some point, in a priggish moment, he spotted a cheesecake photo I'd inserted as a morale booster. I was terminated as editor and reassigned to legal duty defending troops who'd gone AWOL. They'd have done better hiring a chimpanzee.

The AWOLs were mostly noncoms who pined for the pleasures

found in the ramshackle brothels that flourished among the cane-brakes. After dark the AWOLs would slip out of camp and run to the fields. A jeepload of MPs would take off after them, careening down the paths that crisscrossed the fields. The MPs would catch the AWOLs in flagrante delicto, haul them back to camp, and I'd be summoned to plead their cases at the courts-martial. My record was consistent and perfectly congenial to the Army: all my clients ended up in the stockade.

When the regiment was disbanded on higher orders from state-side, I gave up defense lawyering and was transferred with my family — which now included our firstborn son, Douglas — back to Fort Dix where my tour had begun. I closed things out as a public information officer.

On a gray November day in 1956, the first Hungarian refugees landed at McGuire Air Force base near Dix. They'd fled during the revolt against Hungary's Communist regime and had found their way, bedraggled and exhausted, to U.S. soil. An interpreter and I quickly debriefed those families with the most compelling stories, coaxing from them tales of oppression in their occupied homeland, their harrowing escape from the border guards. Then we directed them to the waiting newsmen. I kept for years the image of the mothers and children, shy smiles of relief finally emerging through listless eyes.

My promotion to first lieutenant came through about the same time Ada delivered our first daughter, Lisa. A few days short of my twenty-seventh birthday the Army discharged me. Samuel Johnson had said, "Every man thinks meanly of himself for not having been a soldier." All I knew was I'd begun to think better of myself after three and a half years in khaki.

Following the advice of a corporal in our public information office, I applied to and was accepted at the Columbia Graduate School of Journalism.

My grandfather's stint at the old *New York Tribune* had left its mark on him. Forever after, he was proud of having once been a newspaperman. Not that everyone shared his perspective. My mother believed I was joining a lesser breed of humanity.

Columbia's journalism school was the best in the country even with its share of faculty burnouts and cranks. It had the incomparable John Hohenberg, a former Hearst foreign correspondent, who advised us novitiates to "listen, listen, listen like a good bartender," to check everything out, "even your mother's stated age." Columbia taught us the ABCs of journalism, but it was the out-of-school work that earned us the career entry tickets we sought.

I made extra points as Columbia's Teachers College stringer for the *Times* and as a night grunt on the Associated Press radio news desk at the AP's headquarters in Rockefeller Center. That's where I heard one night that my boyhood idol, Bogart, had died.

Now I had other idols. "Scotty" Reston of the *New York Times*, Vermont Royster of the *Wall Street Journal*, Edward R. Murrow of CBS News. The city was our laboratory, its streets our virtual classroom. A half-century earlier, my grandfather had found himself covering fires, murders, and gang shoot-outs in Manhattan's grimier districts. In his footsteps I took my first street assignment covering the aftermath of an underworld killing.

Albert Anastasia was chief executioner for Murder Inc., the enforcement arm of organized crime in the New York area. With every Mob hit the tabloids plastered his photo across their front pages. On a fall day, while strolling along Central Park South, I came face-to-face with Anastasia as he emerged from a restaurant. A squat, bulky man, he was wearing a camel's hair overcoat and a pearl gray fedora that shaded the cruelest pair of eyes I'd ever seen. A week later he was dead.

He'd dropped by for a shave in the ground-floor barbershop of the Park Sheraton Hotel on Sixth Avenue. The barber had wrapped his face in hot towels and prepared the lather; the bodyguard had gone to the men's room. Two gunmen rushed in, shoved the barber aside, and emptied their revolvers into Anastasia's head. The force of the bullets sent him hurtling out of the chair. He crashed against a mirror, upsetting a bottle of bay rum, then toppled back between the chairs. One of the gunmen popped a last bullet behind his ear, the coup de grâce. The killers had calmly dropped their guns, walked out onto the avenue, and vanished into the crowds.

The papers were still blaring the story when I visited the barbershop a day or two later. I asked Mr. Bocchino, the barber, for a haircut. I didn't want to risk a shave; Mr. Bocchino was still shaking. No one attended the fourth chair where Anastasia had sat. The place was empty except for a worker replacing the linoleum flooring where the bullets had torn it up.

Mr. Bocchino was not a good interview, too terrified from the experience. I filed a mood piece, ending it with a flourish that must have made John Hohenberg wince: "The mirror facing chair No. 4 still reflected the potful of purple iris that Anastasia would have glimpsed in his dying seconds." Tabloids, ahoy.

The summer I graduated from Columbia I made another educational investment. Ada and I packed our bags, parked the children with my parents, and set out to see the world in a three-month odyssey.

We'd laid out an itinerary that would take us some thirty thousand miles to more than twenty countries and had put ten thousand dollars down with American Express to cover all travel costs. For that we got the splendors of Angkor, the slums of Bombay, firefights in Beirut, riots in Paris, Alpine dawns, Carpathian nights, and much more. Along the way I posted articles to the Quincy, Mass. *Patriot-Ledger*, which paid me pittance but gave me a byline.

Much of the world was in armed conflict. Civil war raged in Lebanon; the Marines had been dispatched there. Cyprus and the Holy Land were seething. Mau Mau terrorists had left a trail of bloodshed in Kenya.

Our first night in Beirut machine gun and mortar fire erupted in the rebel Muslim quarter; I crouched on the hotel balcony with binoculars, trying to spot the flashes. Outside Nairobi we spent a restless night on the edge of the Aberdare Forest where the last of the Mau-Mau were holed up; at Tree Tops, the wildlife observation post that perches above a natural salt lick, the Mau-Mau had decapitated one of the cooks. In Jerusalem, Palestinians and Israelis were violently disputing claims to the holiest of the shrines we visited.

We figured Paris would be mellower. But the country was immersed in civil strife over the Arab insurgency in French-occupied Algiers. De Gaulle had been returned to office following the fall of the Fourth French Republic, and had been given near dictatorial power to quell the growing unrest of France's left.

On a September afternoon, I found myself squeezed into the Place de la République, bobbing in a sea of Parisians. A hundred thousand people had packed the square to hear De Gaulle proclaim the new powers of his government. Student radicals, Marxist workers, and other anti-Gaullists had infiltrated the crowd, spoiling for a fight.

The jeering intensified, firecrackers exploded, steel-helmeted gendarmes rushed the protesters. The barricade I was standing on collapsed. A woman next to me went down screaming beneath the stampede. The gendarmes swung their lead-weighted capes with abandon. I climbed the nearest lamppost for a better view. Ambulances and stretcher crews were tending the wounded. In the side streets, bleeding rioters tore up paving blocks to hurl. One block narrowly missed me and smashed into a police van. Tear gas filled the air; the police kept charging. The rioters finally scattered. A photographer asked me, "Your first Paris revolution?"

We dined out on our odyssey for years. No dry readings of world history would have sufficed.

7

Hello, Sweetheart, Get Me Rewrite

That fall of 1959 I arrived in the Capital, armed with a letter of introduction from Columbia to the editor of Washington's preeminent evening newspaper.

Grandpa Lamont had renounced the conventional wisdom that young men should start their journalistic careers in smaller cities where lightly staffed newspapers offered grounding in all aspects of the trade. Success, he wrote near the turn of the century, was "to be found surest on the newspapers in the large cities, where the opportunities for development and advancement crowd thick upon you."

Grandpa would likely have applauded, then, my apprenticeship at the old Washington *Evening Star*, the hoary Tory grand dame of Washington journalism. The *Star* was owned and run by two families for whom the paper was a cash cow. It was known for its accuracy, sobriety, and reliably prosaic reportage. It was the local Establishment's paper, its proprietors doyens of the city's clubby, inbred society.

The paper paid its employees rock-bottom wages and had more than its share of debilitated old-timers who'd filed one too many fairy tales, missed one too many deadlines, rung up one too many hangovers. I spent my first Christmas in Washington picketing the paper with colleagues from the Newspaper Guild who were striking for a few dollars more a week. Still, I was thrilled to be a starting reporter at a great metropolitan daily in the world's most powerful capital.

The city editor was an ex-Marine with a gravelly voice named Sid Epstein. When he assigned reporters to the police siege of a gunman holding a hostage in a suburban department store, he deployed us tactically like the battlefield sergeant he'd once been. One night on the late shift I got to cover my first homicide. It was a cop-shooting in a dark alley and the story made page one with my byline. I thought I merited a Pulitzer nomination. "Nice job, kid," said Epstein. I took that as a papal blessing and forgot about the Pulitzer.

Ten months into my stint at the *Star* I was assigned to cover Municipal Court hard by the U.S. Capitol. On lunch breaks I sneaked off to the Capitol to mingle with the veteran reporters who covered the House of Representatives and the Senate. One of them told me about an opening available with one of the regional news bureaus that serviced groups of client newspapers.

After a year with the *Star* I left to take my chances with a smaller outfit on a bigger pond. My father thought I was unwise to leave, but Sid Epstein saw that I was in a hurry to make up for lost time, and wished me well. Ten years later the *Star*'s owners, weary of losing readers and advertising to the ascendant *Washington Post*, would put the paper on the block.

In the fall of 1959, I became one of two reporters in a news bureau covering Congress for sixteen New England dailies. It was a half-step into the big leagues. I had a higher paying job as well as a colleague and mentor, Don Larrabee, who seemed to know

everyone of importance in the New England Congressional delegation. I could observe firsthand the workings of the elected political class. I got to share occasional cold lunches with Senator
Leverett Saltonstall, a man so kind and courtly he was known to his
colleagues as "Old Oil on Troubled Waters."

Our downtown office, which I generally avoided, was a small
warren on the twelfth floor of the National Press Building. There
the bureau's owner, a tall septuagenarian of dignified bearing,
shambled around with a distant look in his eyes. Everyone called
him "Buck" and treated him with deference, including Jim
Hagerty, the president's press secretary, who issued me my first
White House pass.

Journalism, I was finding, resembled a wonderful sort of vacuum
cleaner. It sucked up all the stray dustballs like me — inquisitive
but unfocused chaps — thus clearing the stage for those budding
masters of the universe in other supposedly weightier professions.
In turn, we journalists would spend our careers examining *them*. It
seemed a fair trade-off.

In our game they taught you to ask the right questions. What
other profession did that? What other profession would pay me to
be informed about the great dramas and players of our time? What
other profession, come to think of it, would have had me?

Washington was my escape from the New York of my parents'
circle, nice people who congenitally distrusted the notion of big
government and whose conversations revolved around the stock
market and the shortage of good help. Washington was terra incog-
nita to them. Or, as my grandfather once averred, "I make it a settled principle so far as possible never to go there except under
subpoena." My father felt pretty much the same.

Washington was still a culturally challenged southern town,
belittled as a place that kept gaining in importance without ever
acquiring a style. What style it had lay in its discourse. It was, as
Henry James observed when he first visited it in 1905, "the city of

conversation." Whether on the floors of Congress or in the salons of Georgetown, that conversation was seldom less than pulsing, argumentative, or freighted with political consequence.

It was also a capital that, with the exception of Beijing, another observer had noted, was unequalled "for the relentless brilliancy with which the spotlight of public attention is fixed upon the comings and goings . . . and the amours" of those running the city's official life — a clique that in New York might have comfortably squeezed into a corner of the Plaza Tea Court. The most private whisperings might enter the public domain in the twinkling of a tipster's phone call to a reporter.

Washington was already shedding many of the orthodoxies and icons of its past by the time Ada and I settled our family into a home in the northwest section of the city.

There were fewer great oaks left. Men like Acheson, Marshall, and Kennan — luminaries from that memorable generation of public servants who'd served the postwar presidency with such panache — were mostly gone from the Washington scene. Some things, though, seemed impervious to change: Congressional customs, racial and sexual taboos, the cellar-dwelling Washington Senators ball team.

Southern grandees ran congress for the most part and their prejudices permeated the far reaches of Washington. There were real estate covenants binding home owners from selling their property to people of color. The only blacks admitted to private clubs were the ones who worked in them. Sweltering summers by the Potomac were another constant. They contributed to the city's reassuring sense of languor.

It was all about to end.

America was girding up to confront new Cold War threats across the globe. In Southeast Asia. In Africa aboil with Soviet- and U.S.-hatched conspiracies. (A CIA man I knew was ordered to assassinate a Communist-leaning strongman in the Congo.) On the heels of Sputnik the nuclear arms race was accelerating. The

Soviets had test fired the first intercontinental ballistic missile. Friends of ours were building well-stocked bomb shelters in their Virginia backyards.

One by one the last connectors to an older world were dying off. The last Confederate veteran died in 1959. Alice Roosevelt Longworth, surviving daughter of Theodore Rex, had finally surrendered her throne as queen of Washington's old-guard society. I glimpsed her that year among the spectators at a Senate hearing, peppery and regal in a resplendent, out-sized blue chapeau. Ike was yielding the Oval Office.

The Kennedys were coming, riding the winds of the Cold War buildup, heralding America's determination to rise to the challenges of the new age. The landscape was rearranging itself amid the tectonic shudders of massive social change. The divisive sixties were underway. Professionally, I was moving up again.

Washington in the first days of 1961 seemed on its face unruffled by the coming transformation. The Capital was still under the holiday spell, the season's first snow framing the familiar tourist scenes. Icy gusts whistled across the White House ellipse where the nation's Christmas tree, a seventy-foot Oregon fir, bowed under its heavily festooned limbs. Skaters cut merry figure eights on the reflecting pool by the Lincoln Memorial.

The Capital's heart, though, was fluttering in anticipation of the inaugural of the nation's thirty-fifth president.

Not that John F. Kennedy had overwhelmed the electorate during the campaign. Many Americans had complained that neither Kennedy nor his opponent, Richard Nixon, seemed qualified for the job — a perspective that led me, foolishly, to vote for neither man — and the almost dead-heat returns in November had seemed to confirm it. Still, growing numbers of people saw in the young president-elect a promise of something excitingly different, something daring and idealistic that bespoke a newly empowered generation. He had wit, good looks, great hair. He'd married a pedigreed younger socialite of rare beauty and charm. Washington couldn't wait for the Kennedys' arrival.

You could feel the excitement building on Capitol Hill where reporters buzzed with speculation about Kennedy's "New Frontier" plans and carpenters' hammers beat a quickening tattoo as they nailed the inaugural platform into place. You could sense it in the thrum of conversations swirling through the Democratic Party clubhouses and patronage offices, in the noisy chatter that dominated cocktail parties.

Hotels were jammed, ticket offices swamped, everything sold out from inaugural ball tickets to bleacher seats along the parade route. On Pennsylvania Avenue the VIP viewing stands were already in place across from the historic Willard Hotel, and sixty thousand people were expected to fill them. Never before, said veteran observers, had an inaugural stirred such world attention, such ravenous press curiosity. I would be among the throngs as the newest correspondent in *Time* magazine's Washington bureau.

Hours before the preinaugural gala the snow had started, not a lazily spiralling snowfall, but a wet blinding onslaught that paralyzed traffic throughout the city. VIPs in their stalled limousines cursed the outgoing Republicans for the storm; they commandeered milk trucks, police cars, and other conveyances to reach the gala in a downtown armory. While she was trying to connect with me, Ada's car broke down in the storm; she spent the evening drying out in the *Time* bureau. I went on alone by cab to report the gala. Every star in the show-business firmament was there. Frank Sinatra and Ethel Merman sang, Gene Kelly in a green topper danced. Jimmy Durante complained he was staying at a hotel, the Pierre L'Enfant, he couldn't even pronounce.

The inaugural parade next day was held under cloudless blue skies. Ada joined me in the stands for one of the longest, coldest such processions on record: skirling pipers, strutting buglers, drummers, twirlers, Shriners, Mummers, and Apache dancers; rockets, missiles, mule trains, dog sleds, Army tanks, a model of JFK's World

War II Navy PT boat; endless floats and marching bands, plus enough horses and their excreta to have fertilized the Great Plains.

Across from us, on the presidential reviewing stand, the afternoon sun lit up a tableau of chilled and famous faces: the Kennedys; Harry Truman, jaunty as ever under a gray fedora; Justice Felix Frankfurter deep in conversation with the new president; Adlai Stevenson, lips pursed in discomfort; Dean Rusk, the poker-faced new secretary of state — a panoramic sweep that personified the succession of power from one Democratic generation to the next.

That evening I donned a tux and escorted Ada to the main inaugural ball. Everyone there seemed giddy on champagne plus large draughts of triumphalism. The Basie band played on a revolving stage. Kennedys were everywhere. *Time* had rented a box by the dance floor and everybody of note dropped by. I waved to a fellow who looked vaguely familiar. It was Jim Cronin of Cronin's Bar & Grill in Cambridge. Kennedy had asked him down for the occasion. "I used to throw him outta my place," said Jim.

Later I delivered the first "take" of my first *Time* cover file.

Time, with its eye on the trendy and glamorous, had fastened on Jackie Kennedy for its inaugural week cover. She was the new fairy godmother dispensing silver dust with her wand, about to orchestrate the social transformation of the Capital from Midwest dowdy to Newport chic. Long after her passing it would become clear how importantly, if only in a fleeting Camelot moment, Jackie had influenced Washington's, and the nation's, growing cultural sense of itself.

The cover story, by tradition a team reportorial-editing effort, was the first of more than fifteen I was to report for *Time* in as many years with the magazine. The issue was a sellout on the newsstands.

John Kennedy, our first commander-in-chief born in the twentieth century and the youngest elected to office, would oversee a transforming presidency. The press, with its fledgling cousin televi-

sion, sensed what lay ahead and had geared up to cover this presidency as never before. The Washington news bureaus were expanding, *Time* included. I had been hired at a profoundly right moment.

It was not as though *Time* and I were strangers. My godfather, Harry
Davison, had been *Time*'s first investor, my Grandfather Lamont an
original subscriber. My first image of war was an early *March of
Time* newsreel that showed Japanese soldiers in Nanking forcing
Chinese prisoners to dig their own graves, then bayoneting them
into the graves. *Time*, with more than four million subscribers and
probably triple that number of readers, had become the world's
preeminent news magazine, an influential opinion shaper without
equal.

I began my political education as a member of the Washington
press corps in a city where print journalism still drove things. The
trade had not yet been subverted by the unbearable lightness of
television. Our oracles, men like Walter Lippmann or the *New York
Times*'s Arthur Krock, resonated a not-to-be-slighted gravity. So, too,
did the owners of their publications — figures like Henry Luce, the
Sulzbergers of the *Times*, and Eugene Meyer of the *Washington
Post*. Such men thought seriously about their influence for good on
public opinion. Bottom lines and shareholder benefits were not
their guiding obsession. Luce used *Time* adeptly, if often unfairly,
to skewer those in public life whom he felt had violated his philosophical or moral code.

The congressional landscape had its tall markers as well, men
like William Fulbright, Richard Russell, Hubert Humphrey, and
Leverett Saltonstall, senators who believed they were engaged in a
calling whose potential for bipartisan achievement could benefit
all Americans. The Senate, wrote the historian, Robert Caro, was a
place of "courtesy, of courtliness, of dignity, of restraint, of refinement, and of uncompromising austerity and rigidity."

I thought myself especially fortunate to have landed in a news
bureau filled with so many engaged, tough-minded men and

women. Our bureau chief, John Steele, was a savvy, cigar-chewing veteran of United Press; the chief congressional correspondent was a chain-smoking redhead who liked to brag of his Scots ancestry and knew more about Congress than most congressmen. Every week he transmitted what he'd learned to the New York editors who just as regularly printed less than a tenth of one percent of it. This was the unremitting frustration of all *Time* correspondents.

Time was famous for its church-state wall separating the editorial and business divisions. Less noted was the implicit barrier between its editors and correspondents.

Under *Time*'s managing editor, Otto Fuerbringer, whose sharp professional instincts were often subverted by his iron-fisted conservatism, the editors tended to dismiss the correspondents' output as marginal to their needs. Space in the magazine was at a premium. In their warren of cubicles in Manhattan's Time-Life Building the editors read, conferred, and struggled to compress their stories for publication. Small wonder they resented the freewheeling work style, the celebrity shoulder-rubbing, the exotic travels of the correspondents, a raffish and self-regarding lot.

As ultimate arbiters of what appeared in the weekly newsmagazine, the editors enjoyed the power; we had the fun. If at first that was limited in my case to covering the Post Office department and a few key regulatory agencies, it gave me time to poke around and sniff the flavor of the larger Capital scene.

Politics then was not held in contempt. At its best it was inspiring; at its worst, pure carny. Most of the time it reflected America's continuously argumentative conversation with itself. Its practitioners could be bloviating bores; most of them I found to be decent, hardworking professionals. More than a few were borderline insolvent, scraping by on modest paychecks. Many were regularly conflicted between personal principles and the pressures of their constituencies. They could be gracious in public, churlish in private, always durable troupers in the theatre of democracy.

The political parties were still vital organisms unimpaired by ideological excess. Pragmatic centrists controlled them, dispensed the monies and patronage, applied the organizational clout, and planned the strategies that made the system work. The conservatives I came to know were unshowy plainspoken types who regarded politics as duty. The liberals I got to know were spirited, idiosyncratic types who enjoyed politics as blood sport. The conservatives you had to respect; the liberals you preferred to drink with. What with all the partisan yin and yang, I leaned toward the centrists.

I tried to accustom myself to the protocols of Capitol Hill. I never quite fathomed the House of Representatives. It was without doubt a mirror of America's clashing interests, a forge of democracy to its champions. It was also a monkey house, a piece of designed chaos. Debate in the House was always, as one commentator wrote, "a shambles of low humor, violent partisanship, clamor, confusion, and burlesque." It had its learned barons as well as its clowns. But just as you were prepared to give your last measure of respect to, say, the formidably gnostic House Ways and Means Committee chairman, the poor man would succumb to drink and go off cavorting with a local fan dancer on his way to permanently forced retirement.

The Senate took itself more seriously. Like the House, it was ruled by a gerontocracy and a rigid seniority system. It lived, wrote William S. White, "in an unending yesterday where the past is never gone." It was an institution above all designed to withstand the passions of the day, especially those proposals approved by the lower house in the heat of anger or exhilaration. The Senate prided itself on thoughtful deliberation and, when that didn't work, the filibuster. Over time it had settled into a body of competent legislators amiably tolerant of the gadflies, demagogues, and scene stealers in its midst.

Everett Dirksen, the lion-maned Republican leader with the pouchiest eyes since Fred Allen, mesmerized the Senate chamber whenever he rose to speak. Dirksen's "floratory," a mix of honeyed persuasion and plain hooey, had the mystical power to sway colleagues to his side; he was known as "Senator Ooze." Lyndon Johnson, the pre-Kennedy Democratic majority leader, was a Texan tornado whirling about the Senate floor in search of deals and votes. Watching Johnson cajole, confide, bend arms, and bellow orders was to witness a primal force at work.

Louisiana's Russell Long, the irrepressible chairman of the influential Finance Committee and the Senate's fiscal guru, was a prodigious drinker and versifier ("Don't tax him / Don't tax me / Tax that fellow behind the tree"). Late one evening in the press gallery I watched, incredulous, as Long, awash in bourbon from a long dinner hour, tore down the aisle, shirttails flying and tie askew, hollering at the top of his lungs to be recognized by the presiding officer.

No mention of Long's performance appeared in the press the next day. We viewed the peccadillos of the pols we covered more tolerantly then. We turned deaf ears to the rumors of wenching congressmen and sexual dalliances in the White House. It was not in us to pull down the reputations of useful public servants as long as they didn't scare the children. We lived and worked on more agreeable terms.

It all led to too many late work nights and missed dinners at home. After a while the kids got used to seeing me only at the breakfast table or on weekends.

Our second daughter, Virginia Alden, had arrived on a muggy June day in 1959. She was platinum-curled and coquettish, already determined to go her own way before she was barely out of the cradle. Our second son arrived in November 1961 and was named Thomas Stilwell after my father. The litter was complete, four towheads of surpassing charm.

In vain their great-grandmother in Rochester wrote them to "keep your daddy at home for a while." For most of the tumultuous sixties it was Ada who nurtured our children. Which, of course, was a blessing. Their patience, good sense, and moral grounding was solely their mother's doing.

The Kennedys shook the starch out of Washington.

Jackie redid the White House, restocked its cellars with fine Bordeaux, and gleefully indulged her home-decorating tastes for anything Louis Quinze. Out went the heavy drapes and the rest of the Waldorf decor. Pablo Casals performed in the East Room.

In her shimmering Oleg Cassini gowns, Jackie presided at glittery state dinners, captivating her dinner partners with her breathy whisper. To converse with her, said one guest, was like talking to fog. Haute couture became the rage. Women aped the "Jackie Look"; the men adopted Continental airs. Lyndon Johnson, Kennedy's new vice president, ordered five suits from a Savile Row clothier, confiding to his tailor that he wanted to look like a British diplomat.

When the youngest Kennedy brother, Edward, came to town as the freshman senator from Massachusetts, Ada and I hosted a small dinner for him and Joan in our Spring Valley home. The Kennedys reciprocated, inviting us to a candlelit party in their Georgetown garden for Ethel and Robert Kennedy, the new attorney general. The whole clan showed up along with an astronaut or two, a supreme court justice, a clutch of flamenco dancers, and the Kingston Trio. Everyone frugged and fox trotted into the wee hours.

At the annual White House Correspondents dinner, usually a dull black-tie affair, I observed the dais where the president sat with his guest, the British prime minister. Harold Macmillan, a worldly old Oxonian from a society that still treated reporters and entertainers as backdoor tradesmen, seemed bemused at the spectacle of the world's most powerful man hugely enjoying himself in the company of newsmen, standup comics, and a young chanteuse making her Washington debut, Barbra Streisand.

The Kennedys' highly charged competitive streak extended to sports. They fancied themselves invincible as touch football players. Sailing was another matter. One summer weekend they appeared on North Haven at the invitation of an island family.

On a chartered fishing schooner Bobby, Ted, their wives, and several friends had made their way up from Cape Cod in a thick fog, aided by a malfunctioning compass and an Esso road map. They'd consumed quantities of vodka and shredded every lobster pot in their way. At North Haven the brothers decided to enter a dinghy race, intent on besting the resident Episcocrats at their own game. North Haven dinghies require a certain touch unfamiliar to outsiders. First across the finish line that day was Leverett Saltonstall. Bobby finished eighteenth, Teddy twenty-seventh.

Back to touch football.

At the Georgetown home of the director of the Central Intelligence Agency I met up again with my boyhood friend Allen Dulles Jr. He'd been in and out of sanitariums ever since the shrapnel wound in Korea had cut short his brilliant future. My first sight of him was of a figure slipping unannounced into the dining room, hugging the wall in crab-like fashion as he made his way toward us. He spoke in a lifeless monotone. It was a long, sad lunch.

Most of the CIA men and their wives we knew, unbowed by personal tragedy like the Dulleses, were a jaunty part of the social mix. They toiled away in Langley, Virginia, bright Ivy Leaguers fitting pieces of intel together till they formed a mosaic of the bad guys' intentions. Affably opaque about their work, they seemed almost eager to be regarded with a certain mystery: one fellow gave me the number of a Georgetown drugstore as his phone contact. Another, a top hand at the agency, grew tentatively illuminating after his second martini. He never revealed details, but knew how to suggest obliquely a strategic op in the making.

The CIA took the fall for the 1961 Bay of Pigs debacle. Afterward Kennedy took care not to scapegoat the agency, and went a questionable step further.

I learned the White House was quietly planning a ceremony in the Rose Garden to honor the CIA's Richard Bissell, who'd been fired for his role as ringmaster in the affair. I phoned the White House for confirmation and promptly got a call back from McGeorge Bundy, the president's national security advisor. I was to come over right away to the White House operations room. There Bundy advised me in no uncertain terms to forego publishing anything about the ceremony "in the interest of national security." Naively, I assented.

A year later an item on the Bissell ceremony appeared in a book on the CIA by my friend David Wise. I was learning the ways of duplicity in Washington officialdom.

One reporter who nailed the Bay of Pigs story in such authoritative detail that it caused an uproar in administration circles was my bureau colleague, Charles J. V. Murphy, the Washington editor of *Fortune*.

Charlie Murphy was a silver-haired veteran of Time Inc.'s earlier days and latterly one of the reigning savants on national security affairs. One of Luce's favorites, Murphy boasted a Richard Harding Davis-like career full of scoops and colorful capers. His creative expense accounts (he once charged the company for a $700 fur coat he'd bought for an assignment to the Antarctic) were the despair of Time Inc. accountants.

Murphy had a roguish charm, complete with theatrically raised eyebrow, that fit well with his patent Anglophilia. He was an expert on the Royal Family, the author of a biography on Edward VIII whom he'd come to know. His sources were legend, impeccable as his bespoke double-breasted suits. A White House aide confided that Murphy had so many highly placed sources "we treat him as a separate State Department."

When you ate with Charlie it was always four-star. Late in the week when our heaviest filing was done, if fortune smiled, my phone would ring and Murphy's melodious voice would issue a luncheon invitation. We would decamp to a favorite hangout of his off Connecticut Avenue. There Murphy would ensconce himself on a banquette, light up a filtered Parliament, and order a dry martini straight up. When the entrée arrived, Murphy would seamlessly switch gears from dishing out the latest Capital gossip to dispensing his wisdom on weightier matters. I'd ask a leading question. Murphy would blow a lazy smoke ring, lean back expansively, and begin the tutorial. For the next hour I'd be instructed on everything from the intricacies of breaching the Berlin Wall to the inanities of television reporting. All on the company's chit.

If I had doubts about Murphy's sumptuous expense accounting, I was soon set right on such matters by my boss, the chief of correspondents, Richard Clurman. Clurman called me in one day to complain that my expense accounts were subpar for a *Time* correspondent. I obviously wasn't taking enough sources to lunch. Henceforth, I began taking my sources' culinary needs more seriously.

Dick Clurman was a bundle of enthusiasms, his professional and social ambitions writ large. He was a cheerleader fiercely loyal to his correspondents, especially those with the requisite panache. He was addicted to stories with lots of flash and gunpowder. A perennially youthful blond in his natty button-down blue shirts and knit ties, Clurman was the apotheosis of the Dick Daring school of reportage, always eager to be on the next Hong Kong- or Moscow-bound jet on which invariably he'd reserved two first-class seats — one for himself and one for his typewriter.

On his occasional forays to Washington, Clurman would relay breathless accounts of the latest infighting in the upper precincts of the Time-Life Building. We may have been preoccupied with larger national happenings, but we sensed what Clurman was up against in New York: waging an often lonely battle on our behalf against the editors' niggardly use of our reportage or their indifference to our judgments about the stories we covered — Vietnam the most glaring example. We may have been bemused by Clurman's name-dropping and all those safari-jacketed dashabouts to the front lines, but the man took care of us.

Thanks to his perseverance, the editorial regime that succeeded Fuerbringer's accorded *Time's* correspondents the respect they'd been too long denied. In time, they were even granted bylines.

The great dislocations of the sixties hadn't yet begun: the surging rates of crime, premarital sex, and family breakdown. Vietnam had not yet metastasized into the draining ordeal that would ultimately take fifty-eight thousand American lives and become our first lost war. The napalm and carpet bombing were still a ways off. The civil rights struggle had yet to command our full attention: Birmingham, the Freedom Riders, the tear gas, and attack dogs. We were, for the short time still left, a people in an upbeat mood, blithely diverted by the groin-thrusting excesses of rock 'n' roll, and the easy riders drifting across a landscape scented with pot and mescal buttons.

Hollywood came to Washington to film *Advise and Consent,* the best-selling novel of political intrigue in the nation's capital. The film company brimmed with stars like Gene Tierney, Henry Fonda, Walter Pidgeon, Charles Laughton, and Peter Lawford, the president's brother-in-law; Otto Preminger was the director. It was just the tonic the Capital needed after a summer coping with crises in Berlin and the Belgian Congo.

Preminger decided to stage and film a lavish black-tie party given by the fictional Washington hostess played by Tierney. Three hundred of the city's elite were invited to come and dance as extras under an enormous marquee at Tregaron, the Rock Creek mansion owned by a former U.S. ambassador to Moscow, Joseph Davies. The bureau sent me out to report the scene.

Otto Preminger had gained fame playing hissable Nazi villains in war movies. His native Austrian accent, applied thickly at top decibel, assured his reputation as one of Hollywood's *enfants terribles*, a director who brooked no errant behavior on his set. When I arrived at Tregaron that evening, Otto was in an elevated chair atop a camera boom, trying to assert command. The scene was pandemonium — carpenters hammering together makeshift catwalks, production assistants tripping over coils of electric cable as they raced about with their walkie-talkies, harried waiters with trays of canapes and drinks, threading their way through the jumble.

Just as the music began and the cameras started rolling, I heard a loud crash. A waiter had dropped his tray. He was promptly shown the exit. "Und keep valking!" yelled Otto. A photographer popped out of the bushes and started clicking away. Otto leveled on him. "But I'm from *Look*," the lensman explained. "*You* look! Get oudt!" Otto bellowed. A local gossip columnist found herself obstructing Otto's line of vision. "Vy are you in ze way?!" he roared. She protested in vain. "I dun't care eef you *are* from a noospaper, you are veesible!" She quickly made herself inveesible. "Action!" ordered Otto.

Preminger had called for "shadows," extras to stand inside the mansion by its front windows and pantomime partygoers while the scene was filmed from the outside. I volunteered along with a production aide and one of Ambassador Davies' granddaughters. We were told to tread a specially constructed catwalk behind the upstairs windows and look animated. "Action!" We started treading the catwalk, but kept bumping into each other. "Cut!" yelled Otto. "Tell zose idiots in ze left window zey look like zey're on a skating rink!"

Otto kept shooting the dance scene over and over. (The "shadows" bit ended up eventually on the cutting room floor.) After the fifteenth take he called a wrap. By then everyone was catatonic. Crash! Another waiter with a tray full of glasses went sprawling. "Granddaddy's house was never like this," the Davies granddaughter chirped.

The America's Cup races summoned me on assignment to Newport one summer. Yachting's greatest trophy match, an exercise landlubbers liken to watching paint dry, had a history forged in national pride and stupefying extravagance.

The prize was an ugly three-foot-high silver pitcher that had once been in sole possession of the British, but had been wrested from them in 1851 by a U.S. challenger. Renamed the America's Cup, it had been toted back across the Atlantic to the baroque quarters of the New York Yacht Club. There, through countless vain attempts by the British to win it back, it had stayed securely bolted to a pedestal above the club's main staircase.

In the first America's Cup race of the sixties the Brits had yielded challenge honors to the Australians. The Aussies fielded a sleek twelve-meter sloop, *Gretel,* owned by a rough-edged Sydney press lord named Frank Packer. Packer had sunk three-quarters of a million bucks into *Gretel* and was hell-bent on recapturing the Cup from the snooty New York Yacht Clubbers. *Time* had scheduled a cover on him.

My most recent sailing trophy dated from the North Haven Midget dinghy series of 1940. I didn't know a clew from a "coffee grinder." But I got to know Packer well enough so that he invited me aboard *Gretel* for a trial race. The day we went only mad dogs and Aussies would have ventured out. It was raining and blowing a twenty-five-mile-an-hour nor'easter, the roughest weather *Gretel* had sailed in. I was ordered to help raise the huge mainsail, winching up four hundred feet of wire on one of the grinders. Once on Block Island Sound we engaged *Vim, Gretel's* sparring partner, manned by fellow Aussies. Our race was over a twelve-mile course.

The winds slammed against *Gretel's* straining blue main, the roiling seas swept her lee rail under as she revved up to speeds of more than twelve knots on the starting six-mile spinnaker run. The crew bent to their task, the foredeck men fighting to control the yawing spinnaker boom and keep the ballooner full. The helmsman, a seasoned warhorse named Jock Sturrock, drove the ship with a vengeance, issuing crisp commands amid the chaos of weather, pitching seas, and snapping canvas.

The six-mile weather beat home was even fiercer. *Gretel* plowed through one monstrous trough after another. The crew flattened themselves against the windward rail as the spume whipped them then raged aft to drench Sturrock and the mainsheet man. Directly behind Sturrock I gripped the stern stanchion and hung on for dear life.

Gretel rode the mountainous seas like a thoroughbred. Gradually we footed past *Vim* and established a lead. A quarter-mile from the finish at Brenton Reef lightship off Newport, Sturrock ordered a fresh genoa jib to be rigged. Suddenly the main clew ripped, leaving the jenny thrashing as the crew tried frantically to haul it in. Sturrock swore as *Vim* bore down from astern. A new headsail was swiftly hoisted and *Gretel* crossed the finish line barely two boat lengths ahead of her partner. There were smiles of relief. I went home to dry out and file an exclusive.

The actual Cup series against the American defender *Weatherly* was anticlimactic. The Aussies narrowly took one race, riding a giant roller across the finish line. It was the first win by a challenger in twenty-eight years and the Aussies celebrated by demolishing one of Newport's finest bars. But the Americans won the series as expected.

The Sicilian mafia, broadly known as the Mob, was a very unpleasant group of men who specialized in narcotics, prostitution, shylocking and, when necessary, murder. They made Bogart and Cagney look like choir boys.

They liked to break the legs of delinquent debtors and kill rival mobsters. They operated largely out of New York, home to the five principal crime families, or *borgatas*. Their victims usually ended up in cement boots at the bottom of Brooklyn's Sheepshead Bay or compressed into the wrecks at selected automobile junkyards. The magazine assumed that I, a New Yorker of the briefest acquaintance with the late Albert Anastasia, was Mob savvy. I was assigned to cover the latest round of Senate hearings on organized crime.

The Justice Department had found a mafioso, Joe Valachi, willing to break the code of omerta and testify about the Mob, its operations, and its governing structure of dons, capos, and "soldiers." In the chandeliered Old Senate Caucus Room, crowds of the curious packed in to watch Valachi illumine the senators on the workings of the Mob, or Cosa Nostra to its members.

The squat old mobster with the peach-tinted crewcut and raspy voice walked the senators through a litany of shootings, ice-pickings and garrotings — many of which he'd participated in as a made "soldier" — from Joe Jelly's demise in an olive oil warehouse to the midnight embalming of "Little Augie" Pisano. He recounted the workmanlike dispatching of characters like "Charlie Blades," and "Kid Blast." By the time he was through, he had exposed in unprecedented detail the extent of the Mob's grasp on lucrative businesses from gambling and pornography to construction and restaurants — at a staggering economic cost to the public.

The Valachi hearings led to new federal laws that substantially weakened organized crime's control while enabling the successful prosecution of its leaders. Cosa Nostra would continue to exert influence in dark corners of the urban economy, but seldom again as brazenly. The freewheeling days of the Mob were over.

In a decade that had threatened to stall with the shame of the TV quiz show scandals and the Bay of Pigs, John Kennedy's ringing declaration that America would outdo itself to beat the Russians to the moon rekindled our spirits. All at once we were engaged in an enterprise the likes of which had not been seen since the Manhattan Project of World War II.

I went from covering the little known National Aeronautics and Space Administration (NASA) to covering one of the imperishable stories of our time. The race to exorcise the ghost of Sputnik focused the nation on a heroic new breed, the Mercury astronauts. Amid their thunderous liftoffs from Cape Canaveral and their adventures in the black silence of outer space, the astronauts would become the icons of the new age. I soon became a regular shuttler between Washington and the Cape in eastern Florida.

In their silver spacesuits, riding their fire-spewing rockets to the edge of the heavens, the astronauts gripped the public's imagination in profound new ways. Less so did the largely anonymous support team behind them. The faceless technicians and administrators driving the multibillion-dollar space venture were themselves a special breed, bright and visionary. They operated in a world of slide rules, humming computers, and gnawing doubts. One of them whom I got to know became the subject of an early *Time* cover story on the space race: Brainerd Holmes, director of NASA's manned space flight program and the closest thing the country had to a moon czar.

A Brooklyn-born electrical engineer, Holmes had been picked to coordinate the effort on which Kennedy had staked his and the nation's prestige. In a series of interviews Holmes patiently abided my attempts to grasp the arcana of space technology. *Time* had assigned the story to an aging science editor in New York and, in the trenches of Washington and Cape Canaveral, a thirty-one-year-old generalist who had flunked freshman science: me. With unerring logic my bosses, also technological illiterates, reasoned I might reduce to readable English the details of fueling, firing, operating, and docking a manned capsule in space. I might also provide several million readers with the human-interest side of the astronauts.

The problem was that the astronauts were machine-tooled products of the space age, consummately professional, superior military officers, but essentially uninteresting men outside their element. Whatever colorful quirks or demons they possessed were airbrushed out of the chivalric image of them fed by NASA to the media. Moreover, interviews with the astronauts were embargoed, *Life* having bought the exclusive rights to their and their families' personal stories. So for a while the public was treated to the myth of the Mercury astronauts as flawless flyboys with Boy Scout virtues and stout-hearted wives, telegenic fellows with chestfuls of service medals, the seven bravest guys around.

Our cover story brought to life one of the key unsung figures of the space race, Holmes, while clarifying the enormous challenges he and his NASA team had taken on. It preceded a string of cover pieces as one after another the Mercury, and later the Apollo, launches set the path to the moon.

My earthbound father thought it all flapdoodle, a waste of time on short-lived heroics and national preening; the monies would be better spent on unmanned space research and more compelling needs at home. I argued with him, appealing to his sense of history and adventure. His view at the time seemed as constricted to me as those who'd scoffed at the dreams of Columbus and Magellan. Their voyages had immeasurably expanded the Old World and given man a new view of himself. So would those of the astronauts. Still, over time my father turned out to have been at least partially right.

In the spring of 1961, excitement built like a gathering hurricane for the first manned space shot at Cape Canaveral. By late April Cocoa Beach, the nearest community to the launch complex, had taken on the flavor of a boomtown. Contractors, short-order cooks, bartenders, reporters, TV crews, groupies, and gawkers poured in. Motels and hamburger joints sprang up along the beachfront. At night the scene around the motel pools resembled a fraternity bash. Everyone made the scene, even the Germans from Werner von Braun's rocket team.

Just before dawn on May 5, Alan Shepard strode across the launching pad and rode an elevator to the top of the gantry where his tiny Mercury capsule perched atop a Redstone rocket eight stories high. Over the next three hours of the countdown, Shepard checked and rechecked the array of buttons and circuit switchers on his instrument panel. He began obsessing on a particular problem, how to relieve his aching bladder. He ended up peeing in his thousand-dollar space suit.

Seconds from liftoff, the giant "cherry picker" crane backed away from the rocket, the umbilical cord of fueling cables fell free, and with a shattering roar the rocket's engines scorched the pad in a sea of flame. For a heart-stopping moment the rocket hung motionless, balanced above its incandescent tail, then slowly rose, thundering skyward.

Three hundred miles downrange, on Grand Bahama Island, I waited with a small contingent of newsmen for Shepard to complete his historic flight. I was part of a pool of reporters representing the world's newspapers, radio, television, and periodicals. I would relay the drama of Shepard's splashdown and recovery to the scores of magazine reporters back on the Cape.

We could only imagine the gravitational forces battering Shepard as his capsule reached the outer fringe of the atmosphere; the defining moment of weightlessness when a stray washer floated before his eyes; his descent, with the capsule's orange and white parachute blossoming like a zinnia at ten thousand feet; then the splashdown and rescue.

Once they'd fished Shepard from the drink, choppered him to a waiting aircraft carrier, then flown him to our scraggly island for a medical check and debriefing, my job as pool reporter kicked in. My initial sight of the nation's first man in space came when Shepard emerged from the plane that had borne him from the carrier. In his flight suit and silver jump boots he was pumped up, grinning from ear to ear. Two days later when a group of us flew back with him to Washington for a celebration at the White House, Shepard was still in conquering-hero mode.

In midflight, thirty thousand feet above the Atlantic, our Air Force jet suddenly pitched to the left, yawed to the right, then dipped woozily. Everyone thought the captain had had a seizure, but it was only Shepard who'd elatedly taken over the controls.

🜋

Alan Shepard's triumph kindled an explosion of public enthusiasm
for the manned space flight effort. The nation was now committed
to landing a man on the moon by 1970. Americans were swept up
in moon mania and the new space lingo. Everything was "A-Okay,"
all systems "Go."

A couple of months after Shepard's flight I covered Gus
Grissom's suborbital launch. The flight went well, but moments
after his splashdown Grissom prematurely blew the hatch on his
capsule. Grissom barely escaped as the capsule swamped and
sank like a stone in the three-mile-deep seas. Grissom's luck would
finally run out: he became the first astronaut to perish on the job
when his capsule caught fire and incinerated on the launch pad.
His death cast a brief pall on the space program.

Gordon Cooper's flight was the last of the Mercury mission and
the longest aloft, demonstrating that a trip to the moon was feasi-
ble. It, too, was a close call and underscored the essentialness of
having skilled humans at the capsule controls in these early flights.
I was at the Cape with Ada tracking Cooper's craft as it approached
reentry into the earth's atmosphere at seventeen thousand miles an
hour. Suddenly there was a glitch that knocked out the autopilot
system. For a seeming eternity Cooper had to pilot his crippled capsule manually before it made a safe landing on target.

The feat earned him a rapturous reception in Washington. At
the White House the Kennedys fell over Cooper like delighted
schoolchildren. Along the motorcade route to the Capitol grown
men whooped like adolescents; giggling girls dashed from the curb
to touch Cooper's convertible as though it bore a rock star. When
Cooper entered the chamber of the House of Representatives to a
deafening ovation, the congressmen forgot all protocol and rushed
to paw or shake some part of him.

So it was then. Everyone wanted a part of the astronauts, to
share in the bedlam of their triumph. The exhilaration reached its
peak with John Glenn's history-making orbital flight. The nation

simply went bonkers. We wanted to cheer like hell and keep cheering forever.

Even as the hugely popular manned space flight program had seized the country's imagination, the long-range, man-to-the-moon effort was lagging for lack of aggressive funding.

NASA's overall boss, James Webb, I learned, didn't share Brainerd Holmes's sense of urgency and single-minded commitment to the lunar program. Webb had denied the program the extra funds Holmes requested; the manned lunar schedule had slipped as a result. I went to the White House for confirmation from the president's science advisor, Jerome Wiesner. Wiesner offered what he thought was a plausible explanation. But, as he later told the president in a memo, "I don't think I changed his (Lamont's) views much." *Time*'s story that November concluded that the nation's lunar program was in danger of bogging down.

For all the space launches I witnessed, I never lost that sense of awe watching man break the surly bonds of earth.

The moments before liftoff, the tension and beauty of the scene, always brought goose bumps: the dawn thunderheads on the eastern horizon heralding a spectacularly vivid sunrise; the silvery Redstone rocket on its launch pad, ghostly under the glare of arc lamps, liquid oxygen swirling like dry ice around its base; the announcer's voice metronomically counting off the last seconds; then the gigantic explosion of flame sending rocket and its human payload streaking across the skies. It invariably brought a gasp and sigh of relief to those of us on the ground. I never got over the moment.

Time wanted to illuminate the personalities of the men who were making nuclear and space history.

The Soviet-U.S. arms race had escalated alarmingly ever since the Soviets had tested a nuclear bomb in 1949. In the early 1960s the U.S. Arms Control and Disarmament Agency along with the Atomic Energy Commission, two of my prime beats, led the way in persuading Congress and the country of the enormity of the nuclear threat and the urgent need to curb weapons testing across the board. For weeks I haunted the Senate chamber where the issue was being hotly debated. Senate doves urged an immediate pact with the Soviets; conservative hawks, wary of entering any agreements with Moscow, opposed the idea. What resulted was a series of testing moratoriums, which the Soviets violated with impunity.

In 1961 the USSR set off more than thirty nuclear blasts over a two-month span, rupturing a three-year moratorium. The largest, a fifty-eight-megaton blast, was the most monstrous manmade explosion in history. The U.S. promptly readied its response: a series of tests in the South Pacific that would ratchet up the arms race to ever more dangerous levels.

Time scheduled two cover stories — one on Glenn Seaborg, chairman of the Atomic Energy Commission and codiscoverer of the element that had led to the development of the plutonium bomb; the second on William Ogle, the man in charge of the next round of U.S. tests in the Pacific. I was to be the lead reporter on both stories.

Seaborg, a gangling six-footer with Mephistophelian eyebrows and guileless eyes, knew that unless the momentous scientific discoveries he'd helped unveil were handled wisely, mankind might in one nuclear winter vanish from the face of the earth. A devoted family man, Seaborg particularly feared the effects of radioactive fallout from the latest Soviet tests, the killer doses of strontium 90 that would multiply the risk of genetic defects in the children of future generations. He had also just informed the president that the results of the Soviet tests had in all likelihood diminished America's lead in the nuclear arms race. Yet with all that on his shoulders, what seemed to preoccupy Dr. Seaborg the day I interviewed him was the imminent birthday party for his baby daughter.

The following spring, the U.S. detonated its own series of tests in the skies above a scrubby South Pacific atoll called Christmas Island. The operation was code-named Dominic. *Time*'s cover subject was Dominic's scientific director, Bill Ogle, a pipe-chewing Nevadan who favored aloha shirts and who, more than anyone in America, had played an integral part in the nation's nuclear testing program every step of the way. I was dispatched to Hawaii to cover Ogle and his preparations for Dominic.

I booked a seat on the same flight out of Washington that Ogle was on and arranged to sit next to him. As we waited for takeoff, I noticed that Ogle was holding tightly in his lap a briefcase stuffed with classified documents, pipe cleaners, and hair tonic. He seemed unusually edgy. He was about to take charge of a fearsome exercise involving twelve thousand scientists, soldiers and sailors, one hundred planes and forty ships — and what had seized his fear buds at the moment was our takeoff. He held out his palms, moist from anxiety. "This flying," he whispered, "it's scary." I spent the next hours aloft interviewing Ogle for what, *Time* later wrote, was a "fascinating look into the mind, analytic and apprehensive" of the nation's foremost nuclear warrior.

We parted company in Hawaii. Barred with the rest of the press corps from traveling to the test site, I spent the next days tracking down military sources and contractors who'd helped prepare the site. I combed the local newspaper morgue for useful tidbits and frequented bars where I might bump into a rummed-up engineer or two who could regale me with tales of life on Christmas Island. Then I filed an advisory to my editors, claiming that despite the security lid I had a full rundown on how Dominic would unfold. I was confident we were ahead of anyone else on the story, and I was right.

Dominic would prove to be a milestone in the superpowers' race for nuclear supremacy. It proved the reliability of America's nuclear weapons. Its megaton blasts obliterated much of the four hundred eighty thousand-square-mile test area and set the Pacific skies aglow for much of that summer of 1962. The cover story bumped up my ratings at *Time*. My office mail increased exponentially — handouts and importuning letters from missile companies and defense officials. An ex-Army officer wrote me about a scheme he had for sending Vice President Johnson on a one-way trip to the moon.

However exotic the life of a Washington correspondent seemed, the work was inordinately demanding and fiercely competitive. Well into the weekend we were refiling with updates and answering lame queries from researchers in New York.

The achievers in our trade, as the columnist Joe Alsop liked to say, were the guys who wore out the most shoe leather. For a journalist Washington was a cornucopia of bright, knowledgeable sources. Many of them — the ones I trusted to tell it to me straight and who trusted me to respect their candor by keeping them anonymous — became fast friends. So too did any number of fellow reporters and diligent young lawyers in the eddies of the Washington tide.

Much as I loved my work and growing family, I feared that our oldest son, Dougie, more into baseball than books, missed the fatherly attention I was able to give him only sporadically. Our oldest daughter, Lisa, in her sixth year, had Pepsodent teeth destined for braces and already the suggestion of a winning femininity. Our younger daughter, Ginny, had long shed infancy and, with her platinum beauty and smarts, was struggling in vixenish ways for her place in the sun. Our youngest, Tommy, had a combustible temper that, sufficiently teased, swelled in seconds to Vesuvian proportions. All four children doted on our dog, a wandering basset hound named Beauregard.

Ada's midwestern style, unadorned like her beauty, played well in a city where success rested on forthrightness and discretion. She had no side to her, no false fronts, no tolerance for cheap gossip. Women trusted her implicitly; quite a few men confided to her

Thomas W. Lamont, the author's paternal grandfather, on the cover of *Time*, 1929.

Grandpa Lamont on the phone to the White House or a J.P. Morgan client.

Author's mother, Elinor Branscombe Miner, at a young age.

Ned Miner, in bowler, Mother, and
Grandmother Miner on the Riviera, 1922.

Four generations of the Lamont family, Palisades, N.Y., ca. 1933. *Back row, left to right:* Corliss and wife Margaret; Austin and wife Nancy; Eleanor Lamont Cunningham and husband Charles; Elinor and Thomas Lamont, my parents. *Middle row:* my grandmother Florence Lamont, my great-grandmother Julia "Mimi" Corliss, my grandfather Thomas W. Lamont. *Bottom row, left to right:* Thomas W. Lamont II (Tommy), my oldest brother; Margot Lamont, Corliss's oldest daughter; Lansing Lamont; Edward Miner Lamont, my second brother.

My father, Thomas S. Lamont, in his thirties.

U.S. Army 1st Lieutenant Lamont in front of the *Columbine*, President Eisenhower's plane, preparing to meet the first Hungarian refugees at McGuire AFB, Fort Dix, New Jersey, November 1956.

With Happy and Nelson Rockefeller, governor of New York, during Rocky's 1968 campaign for the Republican presidential nomination.

Author (*front row*) gauging President Kennedy at a 1963 press conference in Washington, D.C.

With Vice President Hubert Humphrey at his Waverly, Minnesota retreat, reporting for a 1968 *Time* cover story.

With Senator Robert F. Kennedy aboard the campaign train in Oregon, shortly before his May 1968 assassination.

Covering Canadian Prime Minister Pierre Trudeau, during Canada's 1972 elections.

Lyndon Johnson and author
(taking notes) at LBJ's ranch,
Stonewall, Texas.

Jimmy Carter and author,
North Haven, Maine.
(Photo by Thomas J. Watson Jr.)

Author and CBS newscaster Walter Cronkite,
during an interview for *People* magazine.

Author and David Rockefeller, the banker.

Author as foreign correspondent in *Time*'s London bureau, 1971.

Lansing and Ada Lamont family photo, 1975.

things I wouldn't have told my shrink. She was as guarded with her confidences as the Queen's Lady of the Bedchamber. Together we shared the city's rich weekend life: hikes along the old C&O canal; drives to nearby Civil War battlefields; canoe trips down the Shenandoah; picnics in Rock Creek Park; and Sunday tennis in Virginia with friends — the ones building a bomb shelter in their meadow.

Soviet missile rattling had spurred paranoia about the prospect of a nuclear strike against the U.S. Schools held classroom drills on what to do in case of attack and the government announced plans for federally built fallout shelters. The craze to build one's own well-stocked refuge spread following the Cuban missile crisis in October 1962. That would presage a turning point in the arms race.

Having stared into the abyss of nuclear Armageddon, the super-powers soberly reassessed their rivalry and tried for the first time to resolve some of the mutual tensions. The Kremlin-White House hot line was installed. Within a year agreement came on a partial test ban treaty, the first significant arms control agreement between the U.S. and USSR. I had covered its progress through the Senate. The treaty was, in the president's words, "an important first step — a step toward peace — a step toward reason — a step away from war." Some of the tensions abated.

When the first shots rang out in Dallas a little after noon, I was lunching with colleagues in a restaurant in our Washington bureau's building.

It was a Friday in November, a typically slow day, the bulk of our workweek over, the magazine already partially written. We were relaxed, chatting about the week's stories. I'd just started on a cup of soup when the headwaiter approached. He whispered that the radio was reporting the president had been shot. He implored us, as we sprang from our seats, to leave quietly and not disturb the other diners.

Along Connecticut Avenue and elsewhere the news was already

transforming the city. Restaurants quickly emptied. A crowd formed in front of the ABC News studio next to our office building; ABC staffers posted bulletins in the window on Kennedy's condition. Minutes after the president's death was confirmed, sirens wailed across town as ambulances sped to hospitals with heart-attack victims. The bells of St. John's Church in Lafayette Square, the president's church, began tolling.

Everything seemed discombobulated. Distraught taxi drivers lost their way. A woman ran barefoot out of a downtown shoe store. At the Mayflower Hotel across from us, a man in a homburg walked dazedly into a revolving door. People clustered together, peering through the windows of electronics stores where giant TV sets carried images of the presidential motorcade entering Dealey Plaza moments before the shots struck. I saw a congressman I knew slump in tears against a lamppost. A blind black woman on a street corner choked out a bluesy lament on her guitar.

I began interviewing people on the street. The anger and pain overwhelmed. Men shook their heads in despair, blaming the ugly racial climate for Kennedy's death. They spat at the mention of Dallas: the day before Kennedy arrived there, the city's leading newspaper had condemned the president for pushing for more widespread desegregation. Later that afternoon, when a soft rain had begun to dampen Washington's streets, I went to the White House.

The bureau had already swung into action, assigning reporters to various pieces of the breaking story. The magazine was switching to a cover on Lyndon Johnson, the newly sworn-in president. The first man I ran into at the White House was my friend Jay Iselin of *Newsweek*. We joined the throng of reporters jamming the tiny lobby in the West Wing, pouncing on every scrap of news from the beleaguered press office. Everyone focused for the moment on when Air Force One, the president's plane, would arrive with his body.

That evening the new president landed by helicopter on the

south lawn of the executive mansion. The scene more than forty years later is still etched in my mind. On the White House grounds the fountains continued, almost playfully, to jet their streams of water. Southward across the Ellipse, the Washington Monument gleamed in splendor; eastward through the elms the Capitol, too, was bathed in light. The city's familiar symbols shimmered in almost festive denial of the tragedy. The backwash from the rotors of Johnson's chopper scattered the fountains' spray across the lawn as though harbingering a Lone Star gale. From the Rose Garden colonnade we watched the new commander-in-chief emerge and stride toward the Oval Office.

On Saturday they transferred Kennedy's body from the East Room of the White House to the Capitol to lie in state in the Great Rotunda. Thousands came to view the catafalque, the eminent and the anonymous, standing patiently in long lines to say good-bye. The city was consumed by the terrible television images out of Dallas and by an endless gray rain.

The churchmen, led by Bishop Sayre, eulogized the fallen president while declaring we all bore a share of guilt. Our culture had not only accepted violence as a norm, an entertainment even, it had willfully encouraged the violent hatemongers in our midst. We wept for ourselves as well as for our slain president. "Somehow the worst in the nation had prevailed over the best," James Reston wrote.

Sunday evening I drove up to the Capitol. The multitudes were still filing past the flag-draped bier. Weeping mothers and children, old men on crutches or in wheelchairs, the scrapbook historians with their clicking cameras. Many had waited in the cold for up to eight hours. But two, who had not, mingled quietly with the mourners.

Jacqueline and Robert Kennedy had returned to the Rotunda for a final visit. So intent were the crowds on the spotlit bier that few noticed at first the veiled figure stepping softly into the enclosure where her husband lay. She knelt, lifted her veil, and brushed her lips against the coffin. A woman in line reached out to her, a man tried to whisper words of comfort. Bobby, detached, stood by the wall, brooding over the scene.

Arm in arm the widow and the brother walked past the line of mourners that wound down the Capitol's front steps and out into the Plaza. The sky had cleared and a half-moon hung amid the stars. The two moved like specters across the Plaza, Jackie clinging to Bobby in her grief. I felt somehow like a voyeur dogging their steps, transfixed by the scene. At the bottom of the Hill I saw them look back at the Capitol as they climbed into a waiting limousine. The widow turned to Bobby and, for the first time perhaps in two horrific days, managed the trace of a smile.

The odor of incense hung heavy in St. Matthew's Cathedral where the funeral mass was held. Hugh Sidey, our chief White House correspondent and a friend of Kennedy's, had been asked to serve as an usher; I was to cover the service. St. Matthew's is no St. Peter's or St. Paul's, but this day a service took place there rivalling those that had honored other fallen heads of state through the ages.

Long before the muffled drums announced the arrival of the cortege — the caisson bearing JFK's body trailed by a riderless horse and ranks of world leaders — the cathedral had filled with more than twelve hundred mourners. Governors, diplomats, former presidents, and justices of the Supreme Court mingled with the prelates in their lavender chasubles. At the church entrance I stood beside the new president, observing him, he returning my stare with the mournful look of a bloodhound.

The Kennedy clansmen and wives crowded in, accompanied by pewfuls of friends and retainers. There was JFK's boyhood nurse and his valet. There were doorkeepers, drivers, fixers, and court jesters who'd attended the president, with names resonant of a County Cork wake: O'Donnells, O'Briens, Timiltys, Twohigs. The cathedral ran out of seating room.

We heard the slow clip-clop of hooves outside, the martial strains of "Hail to the Chief." The choir began singing softly. Jackie entered with her children, her face a haunting mask. The choir hushed and organ notes sounded. The procession of foreign leaders who'd marched behind Jackie down Connecticut Avenue to the cathedral followed her solemnly down the center aisle. Charles de Gaulle wore a world-weary look, lumbering along like some noble mastodon. He'd have stumbled into the rear of the Kennedy entourage had not Queen Frederika of Greece pulled him up short.

Behind de Gaulle trailed West Germany's Chancellor Erhard; Britain's Prince Philip; Ethiopia's Haile Selassie, the bearded Lion of Judah; the young King Baudoin of Belgium; and Russia's deputy premier, Anastas Mikoyan, looking ill at ease among his sashed and bemedalled peers. Kingly relics of the Old World, they seemed frozen in expressions of official sorrow as though they'd seen it all before. There came a moment near the end of the service when de Gaulle rose to his feet spontaneously to face the altar and Kennedy's casket. The Lion of Judah and Baudoin joined him while the rest of us stayed glued to our seats. The three stood together alone, heads bowed, an indelible tableau.

They carried John Kennedy across the river to Arlington Cemetery where an eternal flame would burn beside his grave. On Thanksgiving Day we took the children out there and stood on a rise overlooking the grave. There was a commotion below. Once again I watched as the widow returned to pray over her husband. The veil was gone and she looked stunning.

The assassination shocked us to the core. We didn't know what had hit us, only that something unspeakable had upended our lives.

The impact was magnified beyond any previous national trauma because of television. People followed with a terrible fascination the images of Kennedy's limo speeding away from Dealey Plaza; the chaos at Parkland Hospital; the transfer of power in the White House; the funeral service and burial. Then, when they must have been nearly surfeited by pain, they witnessed the televised shooting of Kennedy's accused assassin by a deranged Dallas nightclub owner.

In a darkened back room of the Washington Bureau, I watched with several colleagues a strip of uncut film shot in home-movie color by a bystander on the motorcade route. Abraham Zapruder had just sold his film to *Life*. The frames showing the president's head exploding sickened me physically. Years later I would visit the Texas School Book Depository in Dallas, stand in the very spot on the sixth floor where Lee Harvey Oswald had aimed his Mannlicher-Carcano rifle at Kennedy, and recoil at the ease with which the deed had been done. Outside, the cars and people below were shockingly near at hand. Oswald had probably not even needed a telescopic sight, the president in his open car was that vulnerable.

The grieving was visceral and universal. A song from the musical *Camelot* had been a favorite of Kennedy's. In Chicago's packed Opera House where the road show was playing, King Arthur in the last scene reached a line from the song:

> Don't let it be forgot
> that once there was a spot
> for one brief shining moment
> that was known as Camelot

The audience erupted in a sudden rending wail. The play stopped and everyone, actors, stagehands, and audience, wept unashamedly.

I had trouble explaining to my oldest son why so many of us had come to the hill above JFK's grave that Thanksgiving Day, bareheaded and stricken by the new coldness in our lives. Kennedy had been no Lincoln or Roosevelt. At best he'd been a modest profile in political courage; he had achieved few monumental things in his short stewardship. Yet he had offered us, with his personal gifts, something rare: the inspiration of a young leader unfettered by the past, summoning the very best in us. De Gaulle would later write in his memoirs that Kennedy had seemed to him "to be on the point of taking off into the heights, like some great bird that beats its wings as it approaches the mountain tops."

John Kennedy called us to the life of the engaged. He spoke to us in the rhetoric of a shared adventure. His public discourse was informed not by polls or focus groups but by the readings of scholars and historians whose work he'd absorbed. His grace was unfailing, his laughter the kind that lit the dark. It seems mawkish now, but at the time we almost believed we'd been given, in Kennedy's death, the iconic hero we had sought for our generation.

In wrenching ways the Kennedys and their court adjusted to the tragedy. Jackie left the Capital for New York City to begin her sad odyssey in search of a new life. The surviving Kennedy brothers turned guarded, wondering whether they, too, had a rendezvous with the gunman. In restaurants Ted Kennedy warily eyed the approaching waiters, their white serviettes draped over hands that might conceal a revolver. A friend chauffering Ethel Kennedy recalled the moment a passing car backfired and Ethel reaching across the front seat to clutch her in fright.

Like others of my generation I grew up fast in the shadow of that event. We put our shining ideals on hold and faced the world for the first time in all its ugly uncertainties. We learned to temper our hopes and brace for the worst. We lost our youth that November day.

8

A Daisy in the Gun Barrel: The Gathering Storm

Every morning about eight Lyndon Johnson's motorcade sped down our street en route to the White House from his temporary digs in our Spring Valley neighborhood. The roar of the engines jolted us to the realization that a new president had taken charge.

Lyndon Baines Johnson, about to embark on the most ambitious legislative program since the New Deal, was in full rush to set his own visionary stamp on America. He was a Texan hatful of contradictions. Part bully, part saint; wily as a fox, blunt as a blackjack; kind to underdogs and mean as a skunk to nearly everyone else.

He was a rabble-rousing populist, partisan from his boots up, and dirt proud of his Western roots. He came from a state that O. Henry once said had but three laws: don't commit murder before witnesses; don't get caught stealing horses; and don't vote Republican. Johnson, the onetime Senate leader, had been a master at corralling votes, dean of the grab-'em-by-the-balls school of persuasion, which I'd observed at close range. For all that, he was a mass of insecurities. His efforts to overcome them in often compulsive, ill-advised ways would lead him and the country to trouble.

As vice president, Johnson had chafed under the Kennedys and their barbs at his hick vulgarisms. He was hung up on the Kennedys, their New England pedigree, their Harvard polish and sense of entitlement. He'd once complained to me that Harvard, M.I.T., and the University of California got all the scientific talent, leaving "diddly squat" for Texas. He took that as a personal slight and was determined to transform Houston's Rice University into the Harvard of the Southwest.

His large ears soaked up everything. A friend of mine who was squiring one of the Johnson daughters recalled an intimate lunch at the White House, just himself, the Johnsons, their daughter, and a couple who were parents of a young State Department officer on the rise. Johnson turned his charm on the couple, noting their son's good work. Then his smile hardened. "By the way," he said, "if that smart-assed boy of yours doesn't quit his little Ivy League jokes at my expense, mimicking my accent all over Georgetown, he can start looking for another job tomorrow, y'hear?"

On a guided tour of his ranch near Stonewall, Texas, I'd observed LBJ's mastery of the arts of animal husbandry. Following a beer-and-barbeque lunch, Johnson had piled five reporters and an Air Force general into his yellow convertible and taken the wheel. Off we roared down the hot dirt roads of his spread. We stopped at a cemetery where generations of Johnsons reposed in the shadow of a stand of live oaks. Johnson proudly identified each headstone. The next moment he'd spotted several of his prized Hereford bulls dozing on the banks of the Pedernales. Johnson let out a piercing bellow and scrambled from the car to deliver a swift kick to the flank of one of them. "That's where the meatiest tender-loin is," he drawled.

I remembered little of the Johnson ranch house except that

there were Muzak speakers in the trees by the swimming pool and virtually no books in the library except for a dozen or so *Reader's Digest* condensed volumes.

My family thrived in Washington, blossoming like the city's eternally beautiful springs. The pink and white azaleas in our backyard gladdened the heart. The Capital slowly came to terms with the new president.

Where the Kennedys had turned the White House into a salon for the literati and classical cellists, the Johnsons infused it with big-shouldered oilmen and country fiddlers. Lady Bird Johnson exuded a down-home warmth, and Capital insiders concluded over time she was among the very best of modern first ladies. The Johnson loyalists in the West Wing, a few Kennedy holdovers included, gradually acquired a more confident grip on things.

One of them, Harry McPherson, had a daughter, Courtenay, in our five-year-old Virginia's play group. Virginia came home and asked me why I didn't hobnob with the president like Courtenay's father. She refused to believe I'd even met the president. Despite *Time's* less than reverent coverage of LBJ, I called on McPherson for help. In due course a handwritten note arrived from him for my daughter. "Yes, Virginia," the note read, "your daddy *has* talked to Lyndon Johnson. Mr. Johnson says he will never forget your daddy for all the nice things your daddy and the other men from *Time* have said about him. Mr. Johnson is the big daddy of us all."

So I regained the esteem of my youngest daughter and made a fast friend in McPherson, one of the most humane and gifted members of the president's inner circle.

The decade accelerated with alarming speed. The last cultural traces of JFK, like the crisply urbane 007 of the Bond films, were replaced by the Beatles and the Rolling Stones who symbolized the new counterculture. The Beatles and Stones sang to a generation that flaunted long hair, drugs, casual sex, and the needling mantra,

"Don't trust anyone over thirty." The cultural territory of their elders was shoved somewhere south of the antipodes.

The generational clash was abetted by scenes of escalating violence in the U.S. and abroad. Television was aswirl with images of young civil rights workers stirring up homicidal racists in the segregationist South; of youthful rioters in the seething black ghettos of America's cities; of Buddhist monks immolating themselves on the streets of Saigon. It all scared a lot of older, tradition-bound Americans. They watched nervously as the lines hardened across the socio-political spectrum: hawks versus doves; "segs" versus integrationists; the police versus peach-fuzzed antiwar protesters shouting defiance.

In Washington, the old decorum frayed amidst the increasingly heated public debate. Congressional seniors, like their graying countrymen at large, sensed their world was coming unglued, their comfortable assumptions challenged on every front. They blamed the kids and the times.

The sixties were becoming an unforgettably wild ride.

My days reporting in the back tributaries of Washington's big muddy — the regulatory and space agencies, the Kennedys at play, etc. — were ending. I was involved more than ever now in the mainstream reporting of national politics.

In January 1964, I watched from the House press gallery as Lyndon Johnson declared in his first State of the Union address that Congress must at last pass a civil rights bill with teeth as testament to the memory of John Kennedy. The joint session of Congress erupted in cheers that evening, most of them from northern legislators. Six months later the Civil Rights Act became the law of the land, establishing equal rights for *all* citizens — in voting, education, and access to public accommodations. The act finally and firmly put black Americans on a legal par with their white compatriots.

The new president, who'd begun his political life in the Texas hill country with mixed feelings about the rights of blacks, had become a fully committed leader in their struggle for equality. In hammering the final nail in the segregationists' coffin he had also waived his party's long-held control of the South.

The public was shortly embroiled in the raging debate of the 1964 election campaign. Barry Goldwater, the Republican senator from Arizona, had challenged Johnson for the presidency.

Goldwater was leading an insurgency to recast the Republican Party and the country in his right-wing image. He would rid the party at last of its once powerful Eastern internationalist wing. The Goldwaterites' fervor appalled my Republican father who was persuaded his party had been highjacked by reactionary crazies. At the first chance, he joined a bipartisan citizens committee for the president, whose membership read like an honor roll of the nation's top business leaders. *Newsweek* called the group's formation "a circumstance unique in modern presidential politics."

That July most of the Washington Bureau departed for the GOP convention in San Francisco. At thirty-four I was covering my first political convention. Television and primaries hadn't yet turned these events into scripted coronations. There were still battles over the party platform, tense internecine struggles over the party's stance on key issues. But this year the Goldwater forces had a near lock on the outcome of the balloting before it even began.

From day one, the proceedings at San Francisco's Cow Palace were in an uproar. The Goldwater delegates screamed their anger at the hated "liberal" media personified by the CBS News anchor, Walter Cronkite, seated in his broadcasting booth high above the arena. In a crescendo of boos the delegates drowned out Nelson Rockefeller, the moderate New York governor, as he tried to address them. The moderates went down like tenpins before the Goldwater assault. The senator was nominated overwhelmingly on the first ballot.

Instead of healing the breach and reaching out to the defeated moderates for his running mate, Goldwater chose an obscure conservative congressman from upstate New York, William Miller. Miller had a hard-edged style and an ill-concealed disdain for Goldwater's campaigning skills. It fell to me to cover his run for the vice presidency.

Political campaigns have been dignified as the vehicles whereby a great people conduct the peaceful disposition of power and authority. In reality, of course, they are something less exalted. In the weeks I spent with Bill Miller one thought kept recurring: How could this acid-tongued, poker-playing provincial ever become vice president or, God forbid, president?

Yet I came to like him. He was refreshingly plainspoken in a business rife with forked tongues. He had few illusions about the sacredness of the Goldwater cause, his own talents, or the campaign's chances. Still he soldiered on, cocooned in his propjet when he wasn't delivering speeches on airport tarmacs from Erie to Wichita, doomed to fly the friendly skies into oblivion.

After a while I grew as depressed as the candidate. When I was finally able to break away for a week to cover the campaign of Miller's opponent, I was rejuvenated.

Hubert Horatio Humphrey was Miller's polar opposite, a whirling dervish of a campaigner. In his fifteen years as senator from Minnesota, Humphrey had been point man for a host of groundbreaking initiatives from civil rights to the nuclear test-ban treaty and the Peace Corps. In 1948, as mayor of Minneapolis, he'd electrified the Democratic convention with a speech calling on the party's Southern leaders to "get out of the shadow of states' rights and walk forthrightly into the bright sunshine of human rights." Humphrey's brains, his heart and hustle had later earned him the job as floor manager of the historic 1964 civil rights bill.

He was an excitable man with a high, infectious laugh, never at a loss for words. A senate colleague cracked that Hubert approached every problem with an open mouth. For all his partisan passion, he retained the affection of his colleagues. Humphrey was easily the senate's most popular figure because he rarely personalized political differences; he was incapable of hatred. I caught up with him just as his campaign breezed into New England, a traditional Republican redoubt.

Humphrey was in full logorrheic mode on the stump, from the autumnal hills of Vermont to the greeny campuses of Connecticut. Where Miller's speeches clanked along lifelessly, Humphrey's soared, a bubbling mix of civics, history, social relations, and child psychology. In Massachusetts, excited students mobbed him. In Concord, New Hampshire, he shook every hand in sight, even a cripple's crutch. In Newark, New Jersey, on Columbus Day he got carried away, shouting *"Bon giorno, discendenti di Colombo!"* as he waded through crowds of Italian-Americans.

By week's end I'd tracked Humphrey through eighteen cities in as many states. The man was exhausting; still, I thought him someone I'd like to spend more time with.

On election night Ada and I watched the returns with Bill Miller in the basement den of Miller's Chevy Chase home. I felt sorry for him, but he was probably as relieved as I was at the outcome. The Johnson-Humphrey ticket won handily.

The administration was challenged immediately: by the mounting crisis in Vietnam, where the U.S. military buildup had begun in earnest, and at home where racial tensions were boiling over. The president was also forced to confront the demonstrable popularity of the surviving Kennedy brothers.

Adulation greeted their every appearance in the Senate chamber, for example. On any given day the chamber was host to crowds of tourists bent on glimpsing the new Democratic senator from New York, Robert Kennedy, and his sibling, Edward, the junior senator from Massachusetts. At sight of the pair, a rustle would sweep the visitors galleries, a collective gasp and craning of necks. Women lifted their children for a better view, pointed, and whispered excitedly in their ears. Bobby, coiled and abrasive in tone, gave off the aura of a restless man not banking on a life's work as a legislator. Teddy seemed less hurried. The smile came more easily; he was respectful of his elders.

Russell Long observed to me that Bob Kennedy was the more diligent, "but Ted has the makings of a senator's senator." He was right. Long after Chappaquiddick and other lapses had doomed his chances for the presidency, the youngest Kennedy would become arguably the most effective U.S. senator of his generation.

On my earlier rounds of the Atomic Energy Commission I'd discovered that no one had ever published a full lay account of the creation of the first atomic bomb.

The more I dug, the more I realized it would make a dramatic story. I began researching the project, spending weekend hours at the AEC poring over hitherto classified material on the bomb. With enough in hand for a story outline, I approached Simon Michael Bessie of Atheneum who'd had success with other *Time* writers, notably Hugh Sidey and Theodore White. He agreed to publish the book. A friend at the *Washington Star* found a small cottage on the grounds of an estate in Virginia's horse country where I could write in peace. The magazine granted me two months' leave to do the manuscript.

By then I'd flown to New Mexico to interview every physicist at the Los Alamos Scientific Laboratory who'd participated in the final stages of the Manhattan Project. I talked to the Army's wartime boss of the project, Maj. Gen. Leslie Groves. I spoke with dozens of lesser participants and observers from buck privates to the locals who lived near the Alamogordo test site or along the pine-dotted mesa where the bombmakers worked in secret. What struck me most, aside from the magnitude of the project and the single-mindedness of those involved, was the unalloyed beauty of the surroundings in which this ugliest and most devastating of weapons was fashioned.

Near the end of my research I paid a visit to Robert Oppen-

heimer, the scientific leader of the Los Alamos team and now director of the Institute for Advanced Study in Princeton, New Jersey. It
was the mystic Oppenheimer who, conversant with the Holy
Sonnets of John Donne, had chosen the code name for the bomb's
maiden test: Trinity.

Everyone on the mesa had called him Oppie. Much later, after
the war's end that his work had hastened, when the cheering had
stopped, Oppie had become a target of controversy over the moral
issues of the bomb's use, his Communist-tinged past, and his cava-
lier attitude about security matters. The government deemed him a
security risk and, following a farcical show trial, denied him further
access to the nation's nuclear secrets. In 1964 I'd attended a ceremony in the White House where President Johnson hung the Fermi
Medal, the AEC's highest honor, around Oppenheimer's neck —
belated atonement for the government's shabby treatment of him.

The day I drove to Princeton I was half-seized with dread.
Oppenheimer, who possessed a mind as complex as a jeweled
chronometer, was known not to suffer fools and reporters gladly.

He was in a petulant mood when I was ushered into his sunlit
study. There was a plan afoot to dramatize his security hearings for
the theatre, a prospect that not only offended Oppie's taste, but that
would likely revive the anguish he'd suffered from the ordeal a
decade before. As we sat down, Oppenheimer, bent and fragile
beyond his years, abruptly changed moods. He apologized for the
red tape it had taken to arrange our meeting. He began talking softly, poetically, and I felt myself succumbing to the spell of the man.
He talked of the bomb, his bomb, the days leading up to the
moment when it exploded with the force and radiance of a thousand suns on the desert flats of Alamogordo.

He had no remorse, he said, for having made the bomb and
overseen its baptismal test. He regretted only his miscalculating the
immensity of the explosion and the otherworldly light it produced.
A pyrotechnic display over Tokyo Harbor might have convinced the

Japanese to surrender just as quickly, he mused. "We should have acted with more foresight and clarity in telling the world and Japan what the bomb meant." Instead, we had let Hiroshima express that clarity in its annihilating extreme.

I sympathized with Oppenheimer's reservations, but in the end sided with the decision to drop the bomb and save, ultimately, the lives of hundreds of thousands of Americans and Japanese who would likely have perished in a last-ditch defense of the enemy's homeland.

I left him with mixed emotions: exhilarated to have been briefly in the presence of one of the world's great minds; sad at Oppenheimer's worn, tormented state. Once he'd come into the lives of the Los Alamites like some mythical frontier scout of old, wiry and sunburnt under his porkpie hat, riding his horse up the yellow canyons in search of the site for his laboratory. Now he was this scarecrow in tweeds, wizened, hair prematurely white, done in by his critics and his vanity. He was still withal a transcendent figure, I thought as I trudged back across the Princeton meadows that day.

For weeks I holed up in Virginia, typing out the manuscript. Each finished chapter I relayed by prearrangement to the AEC for clearance by its security people. In July 1965, on the twentieth anniversary of the historic test of the atomic bomb, *Day of Trinity* was published to international acclaim. It became an immediate best seller.

The book went into three foreign-language editions and was published separately in Britain. It was selected for the White House library. A year later New American Library publishers issued a paperback edition, the deal involving the largest fee to date paid for paperback rights to a work of nonfiction. Feeling flush, Ada and I bought a half interest in an Aspen condominium and a parcel of land in Virginia for a weekend retreat.

Among the many letters I received, one especially moved me. It was from Oppenheimer, a warm enigmatic critique in which he observed, "It is just possible, I suppose, that the whole episode seems so remote, so vastly overtaken by the times, that no one will care to read about it."

In fact, twenty years later and counting, the explosion of the first atomic bomb would stand, so the *New York Times* declared, "as the central moment in the history of our time, the threshold event of an age."

The Aspen condo was small with flammable, paper-thin walls, but located a three-minute walk from the main mountain lift. Our neighbor a couple of doors down was a German-born former B-movie star who'd played Nazi villains in a string of wartime black-and-whiters, including one or two with Bogart and Peter Lorre. He still had the old menacing hiss.

The land in Virginia was an eighty-four-acre spread in the upper Rappahannock Valley, situated between the Rappahannock River and a tributary stream, the Jordan. The nearest village was a drive-through-in-a-blink called Flint Hill. Our land was stunning.

Gentle hills ran down to bottom pasture fronting the Jordan. The woods teemed with quail and wild turkey. In the spring indigo buntings skimmed across the fields beneath azure skies. There were two ponds filled with tadpoles, and along the river a big rock that we picnicked on with the children. The only dwelling, a small tenant's cottage, was falling apart. From its hilltop perch we could view the Blue Ridge Mountains to the west. They seemed perpetually bathed in a warm Renoirish haze. It was our Arcadian dream. We christened the place Loverly.

We were an hour-and-a-half drive from Washington, but seemingly on another planet. Ours was an isolated patch somewhere off a dirt road that wound along a ridge speckled with a handful of natives and rusticating city folk like ourselves. We hired a local named "Chicken" Welch, with a molasses-like drawl, to check the place when we weren't there. Chicken advised us not to post our property because the deer hunters would consider it an unfriendly gesture. I posted just one sign by the entrance gate to warn off trespassers; it was promptly riddled with shotgun pellets.

It dawned on us that the locals were a bit peculiar. The good ol' boys congregated in Boo Bradford's general store and listened to Boo tell stories through a mechanical box in his throat. They cooly scrutinized outsiders. There wasn't much evidence of the law around, though there was said to be a sheriff in Front Royal some fifteen miles off. There'd been only two or three recorded murders over the years and no one had ever been apprehended.

A year or two after we'd bought Loverly, a fatal shooting happened down the road on Halloween. It was a bushwhacking with the victim, a local doctor named Lynn, gunned down in the driveway of his home. The assailant was reportedly wearing a jack-o'-lantern mask, so the case became known as the Halloween Night Ambush. A thousand-dollar reward was posted for the killer, but no one ever claimed it. Chicken told me it was common knowledge the shooter was a local with a grudge against Lynn. Flint Hill was a tight community and the shooter belonged to a prominent family. The sheriff never pressed charges.

Ada was having second thoughts about Loverly. It was so remote, the cottage beyond repair, and one day she'd found a live snake in the toilet bowl. The idea of a bushwhacker on the loose didn't help her frame of mind; clearly the kids wouldn't go trick-or-treating in Flint Hill.

Then came the Saltonstall-Spellman affair. A woman named Saltonstall, an outsider like us, had bought a farm near Flint Hill and hired a man named Spellman as the manager. The two had a falling-out with the locals over a right-of-way issue. An enraged neighbor shot Spellman, was indicted for murder, and eventually acquitted. Saltonstall had the manager buried on her farm. We could always spot the plot from Loverly because the grass was a distinctively vivid green.

Shortly thereafter, Ada decided she'd be happier visiting Loverly less frequently and only during daylight.

When Hubert Humphrey took over as vice president in January 1965, he inherited a job whose occupant's primary responsibility, as John Marshall had once joked, was to drop by the White House each day and inquire about the president's health.

I watched Humphrey the day he was welcomed back to the Capitol as president of the Senate, his other key responsibility. In his new quarters off the Senate chamber there was a large chandelier that had once hung in Teddy Roosevelt's White House bedroom. The night breezes had kept it tinkling, depriving TR of his sleep. TR had ordered the chandelier removed and sent to the vice president's office "where it can keep *him* awake." Keeping Humphrey awake, though, was never a problem. "Forget sleep," he told me. "You want to die in bed?"

The son of a South Dakota pharmacist, Humphrey was so hyper that, according to one of his colleagues, he must have swallowed all the vitamin tablets in his father's drugstore and washed them down with a missile-fuel chaser. I thought him probably too windy and decent to make it to the highest office. He was an old-fashioned liberal idealist at a time when liberalism was already on the wane.

Moreover, Humphrey was in danger of coming under Lyndon Johnson's thrall. He owed Johnson politically, and Johnson demanded fealty to the point of abasement. If Johnson said, "Dance on your hands," Humphrey danced. The relationship was bound to become strained as the president plunged deeper into the morass of Vietnam. Humphrey, following lockstep in espousing the growingly unpopular war, saw his support from liberals dissipate. Robert Kennedy, who'd soured on the Vietnam venture, was already maneuvering against Johnson's and Humphrey's renomination two years hence.

In 1966, the opening salvos of the coming upheaval in America sounded during the off-year congressional and gubernatorial elections. The vice president hit the campaign trail with gusto as the Democrats' new "happy warrior," and I hit it with him.

Humphrey preached the politics of joy to an increasingly surly electorate that fall. Vietnam had become a millstone. In the South white voters bridled at the headlong pace of civil rights enforcement. Inflation and a volatile job market were frustrating large numbers of Americans. Humphrey's upbeat oratory — "scattering sunshine and optimism among bleak, beleaguered millions," as *Time* wrote — grated on the national mood.

The ugliness showed itself early. The administration's civil rights offensive had hit a wall in the blue-collar neighborhoods and low-income white suburbs of Chicago and other cities. The plight of America's blacks cut little ice with working men and women vehemently opposed to welfare handouts and racially integrated housing. On the road with Humphrey we heard the constant refrain about blacks: *They're pushing too hard.* The backlash grew and violence followed. Humphrey was torn. He applauded the civil rights protesters, but their excesses were endangering the Democrats' election chances. "The violence will hurt us," he confided. As he spoke, two thousand National Guardsmen were being dispatched to quell racial rioting in San Francisco.

Much of the anger was directed at the war. In California's San Fernando Valley, student hecklers drowned out Humphrey's speeches. "Get out of Vietnam!" they howled. "Wipe the blood off your hands, Macbeth!" As he moved northward up the coast, the disruptions intensified. In Portland, Oregon, a protester splashed red dye on herself, crying at Humphrey, "The war dead indict you!" It was the same in town after town. In the middle of one Humphrey speech, protesters pulled the plug on the sound system.

Humphrey, a quintessential man of goodwill, was unprepared for this. He was accustomed to lively but civil discourse; the new politics of protest left him shaken and confused. Confronted by shrieking fury, he responded like an irritated schoolteacher, lecturing the demonstrators on their need for good manners. He got nowhere. His unabashed cheerleading on the war caused voters to question his seriousness. Many felt the urge to flatten all that Minnesota bubbly.

At some point in his roller-coaster tour Humphrey was chosen by *Time* for a cover story and I, a national political correspondent by then, was assigned to profile him.

One day on a flight East with Humphrey, I was interviewing him over lunch, wolfing down a hamburger between questions. An unchewed piece of meat lodged in my esophagus and sent me scrambling to the w.c. behind Humphrey's seat. I gasped and retched trying to clear the blockage. Still choked up, I emerged, discreetly asked the steward for assistance then, feeling better but still not quite right, resumed the interview.

Without my knowing, the steward called ahead for a doctor at the next stop, the Strategic Air Command base outside Omaha. I detected commotion on the tarmac as we touched down, military jeeps and an ambulance raced toward our jet. When we came to a stop the cabin door flew open and an Air Force medic dashed aboard, demanding to know where the veep was and the serious-ness of his heart attack. A visibly upset Humphrey asked who was responsible for the mix-up and fuss. The steward pointed my way.

Humphrey rounded on me. "If you'd told me, I could've helped," he blurted. "Sounds like you've had an esophageal spasm." He scurried to his private quarters and returned with a pill. "Take it," the one-time druggist ordered. An hour later I was back to normal, saved by the vice president of the United States from possibly suffocating on my own saliva.

The elections that fall didn't alter the makeup of Congress immediately. The Democrats remained in control of the House and Senate but the Republicans ended up with a pair of precedent-setting markers: the first black senator ever elected by popular vote, Edward Brooke of Massachusetts; and the first film star to become governor of a big state (California) — a ruggedly handsome, dyed-in-the-wool conservative named Ronald Wilson Reagan.

Nineteen-sixty-seven. The unrest spread. Antiwar demonstrators marched on the Pentagon. Armed students forced their way into administration offices at Cornell. The year's indelible images were of a flower child jamming a daisy down a soldier's gun barrel and a glowering militant in an Afro, bandoliers crisscrossing his chest, confronting university officials.

In April, my father prepared to go under the knife at Columbia Presbyterian: open-heart surgery for the disease that had shut down his arteries after decades of smoking. When the surgeons opened his chest, his lungs, one of them recalled, resembled a tar factory.

Father must have known for quite a while that he was in trouble. Years before, when he'd declined a request to join a presidential advisory committee, the response from a disappointed JFK indicated that Father's reasons had been medical. The president had noted in a letter that he, like Father, "would certainly not want to cross swords" with Dr. Paul Dudley White, then the nation's preeminent heart specialist.

It was another matter, however, that had aggravated my father's condition.

The Securities and Exchange Commission, led by a recklessly zealous chief of enforcement, had charged Father and a dozen officers of the Texas Gulf Sulphur Company with violating insider-trading laws.

The SEC was determined to make it a landmark case, to clarify once and for all the murky insider-trading laws and set new legal precedents to curb the abuse of them. Father, as a Texas Gulf director and ex-vice chairman of the Morgan bank, was the most prominent of the defendants, dragged into the SEC's suit for the publicity value of his name.

Father had known in advance, well before it was announced, of the company's discovery in Timmins, Ontario, of copper and zinc deposits worth up to two billion dollars. But he'd kept the news to himself and done nothing until after the official announcement of the discovery. He was the only one of the defendants not charged with benefiting personally from his insider knowledge. The case against him collapsed to no one's surprise; he was fully exonerated. But the damage had been done, his good name sullied.

The trial had been played out on the front pages of papers like the *New York Times*. The publicity took its toll on Father. The effort to restore his hitherto unassailable reputation wore him down and broke him. Family and friends rallied to his side as his health declined. He maintained a wearied sense of duty: to us, his family; to his bank; to the other institutions he cherished like Exeter and Harvard.

His failing heart led to lapses of temper. In the last summer of his life, he climbed the porch of our wing at Sky Farm one morning out of breath and spluttering with rage. Our pet hound had gotten loose among the sheep.

He tried to sound his jaunty old self preparing for the then unknowns of open-heart surgery. It would be his great adventure, he said, just before entering the hospital. By then I was readying to leave with the vice president on a fortnight's tour of western Europe. "See you when you get back," were Father's parting words.

Hubert Humphrey's dash through the capitals of Europe that spring was the Continental version of a U.S. political campaign.

Ostensibly the trip was to reassure nervous European leaders of America's commitment to NATO and our continued military presence in Europe. It also gave Humphrey the chance to personally plead the case for America's war in Vietnam. More important for him, it was a chance to acquire the statesmanlike bona fides essential to a politician eyeing a future run for the presidency.

On my trusty Olivetti I typed a string of reports on the veep's marathon as he chomped cookies with Queen Juliana in The Hague, glad-handed the West German chancellor in Bonn, knocked down the grand crus with Queen Elizabeth at Windsor Castle, and motorcaded down the old Appian Way to Vatican City to meet the pope. At the Elyseè Palace, he tried unsuccessfully to pierce the sangfroid of General de Gaulle who had just proclaimed the U.S. to be the greatest danger to peace in the world. As usual, the French were being difficult.

For all the ceremony, Humphrey could not escape the Europeans' anger over the war. They tossed everything at him from cabbage heads to cobblestones. He took verbal flak during a private session with two hundred British Parliamentarians. In Berlin there were reported threats on his life; an edgy member of the Secret Service detail crouched in the well of our bus, pistol cocked, ready to repel intruders. When Humphrey attended the opera in Rome, waiting protesters hurled smoke bombs and yellow paint.

Paris was the worst: egg-hurling demonstrators at Orly airfield as we landed; howling picketers at the Arc de Triomphe where Humphrey bowed before the Tomb of the Unknown Soldier. Outside his hotel five thousand demonstrators clashed with gendarmes in a head-clubbing melèe.

When we reached our hotel in Brussels there was a message waiting for me. My father's surgery had gone well, but there were post-operative complications.

I reached his hospital bed forty-eight hours later. He was in intensive care, unconscious, and slipping away. I was too late for an exchange of last good-byes.

I could thank Humphrey for seeing that I'd reached Father in time for a last look and prayer, at least. The veep had arranged for me to fly home from a NATO base in Frankfurt via military air transport. My father would have appreciated the gesture. His own life had been about doing favors for people in need.

It wasn't just running a United Way campaign or some other cause. After Father's death, friends wrote to recall the many instances of his kindness going back decades — the way, for instance, he'd reached out to a Milton classmate of mine whose parents had abandoned him on graduation day or extended a sympathetic hand to some junior bank officer who'd messed up.

His friend Judge Charles Wyzanski wrote, "If I could amend my ways, I would want to imitate his courtesy, his sympathy, his goodness . . . Tommy was the finest gentleman I ever met."

We buried Father under a pink granite headstone near his parents in the crowded family plot in Englewood. He left a generous and beautifully composed will. The SEC prolonged its appeal of the court's decision vindicating him, before finally dropping all charges upon his death. "Too little, too late," one paper commented.

Father's legacy far overshadowed the sorry Texas Gulf tale. His deep commitment to the worlds of finance and education had enriched the best institutions in both. I thought it no small achievement that he had signally helped better the quality of higher and secondary education for future generations or that, like his father before him, had burnished the image of the banker as an engaged humanitarian. He had nothing to apologize for except his leaving us so soon.

God knows, he never flagged in his efforts to upgrade *my* performance. If he was spare with praise at first, he had reason to be. He was unimpressed with my record at college, though I had a grand time unimpressing him. After the Army took me, Father had a glimmer of hope that the discipline of barracks life would correct my downward arc. Just to keep his oar in, he wrote my commanding officer, thanking him for taking on the job of shaping me up. "It was too tough for me," he wrote.

The tide began turning in my favor after I made it through Officer Candidate School and got my commission. He perked up even more when I received my master's degree from Columbia. He congratulated me on entering the newspaper business. He actually beamed when my first book was published. I think he glimpsed a breakthrough, though he made sure to thank my publisher for having taken a flier on me.

The pity was he had only a short while to enjoy my success.

9

"The Whole Damn City's on Fire!"

Say a prayer for 1968.

It was not a year you tipped your hat to. Depending where you were coming from and the number of years you'd racked up, it was either the most exhilarating or the most unhinging year in modern political times.

The embittering war broke one president and trailed its poison into the administration of his successor. America's cities exploded; so did its campuses. The election race attracted some of the worst violence. The shrill new feminist movement moved aggressively to curb sexual inequality, but at the same time abraded people's nerves. The young liberated themselves from old taboos, to the consternation of their elders. The generational gulf widened.

In a span of twelve months the old politics was washed out by the tides of change. Party orthodoxies were tossed aside along with outdated fealties to union, city, ward, and precinct bosses. The pillars of congressional seniority cracked. The practitioners of the new politics moved to retire the stale establishmentarians, yesterday's men; they set about restructuring the whole campaign process. Out went the backroom pols, the cigar-chewing tipsters and get-around guys. In came the cool new breed of professional managers, computer-driven pollsters, and consultants with their focus groups.

The big connector in the mix was television. Mass audiences could now view history in the making within hours of the event, from the anti-Soviet uprising in Czechoslovakia to the student revolts on campus. The impact was incalculable. Once television's cameras focused on the Prague Spring, the Soviets' image was irrevocably tarnished; once they focused on Vietnam and the Tet Offensive, the war was lost. When TV entered America's politics it took over and changed the whole dynamics of campaigning.

Nineteen-sixty-eight served as the ultimate petri dish in which these phenomena were cultured and magnified to a staggering degree. Over many months I logged thousands of miles for *Time* in the quickening presidential race, reporting on most of the political figures who dominated that incredible year. I was there at their triumphs, their defeats and, in one case, their murder. I came home only to shower, pack a fresh set of duds for the road, and blow farewell kisses to my wife and children.

Good-bye, dear; good-bye, Daddy, have fun in Iowa.

The road to the nominating conventions that year led through dozens of county caucuses, state conventions, and primary elections. The untested new presidential hopefuls opted for the primary route; that way, with the help of television, they could skirt the backroom maneuvers of the party bosses. Primaries could make or break a man cruelly. They became the favored preliminary on the presidential fight card.

In February 1968 all roads led to New Hampshire, site of the year's opening primary battle.

New Hampshire had assumed iconic status as a presidential

weather vane. The outcome there would start the winnowing in both parties.

The Republican hopefuls were the veterans Richard Nixon and Nelson Rockefeller; they would duel alone in this opener. The GOP princelings who might enter the lists later were men like California Governor Ronald Reagan, Pennsylvania Governor William Scranton, and the darkest of horses, John Lindsay, the golden-boy mayor of New York. The Democratic field included the not yet officially declared president; the candidate-in-waiting, Robert Kennedy; and the man who'd just announced his decision to contest Lyndon Johnson over the conduct of the war, Senator Eugene McCarthy of Minnesota.

In early February, when McCarthy started ambling through the mill towns of the Granite State, a Gallup poll had the president beating him nationwide by more than fifty percentage points. By the time I arrived in New Hampshire, its rolling hills and town greens shivering amid the last snows of March, the equation had shifted dramatically.

McCarthy's primary race had started as a joke. Nobody appeared to give it serious thought except possibly McCarthy, and he seemed to be campaigning in reverse. His style was low-key and lackadaisical, almost detached. He seemed unbothered by the sparse turnouts or by any notion that his sardonic wit might not play well with blunt-spoken New Englanders. He and his campaign moved above the normal bluster and brio of politicking. If McCarthy couldn't, or wouldn't, utter the epigrammatic sound bite that turned a humdrum speech into quotable front page copy, so be it. He was acting true to himself, a living symbol of this maverick year in U.S. politics.

Slowly the New Hampshire men and women began to sort him out from the others. McCarthy didn't come on like Nixon who sounded like a recorded announcement; or like Johnson who reveled in barnyard rhetoric. McCarthy displayed none of the intensity of Kennedy; he was no glad-hander like Humphrey or

Rockefeller. McCarthy offered rational, commonsense talk in lieu of slogans. What he said about Vietnam connected. For the war had sorely touched the people of New Hampshire's townships and valleys. One had only to watch the communal grieving over a single flag-draped coffin awaiting burial in the town cemetery. McCarthy grasped the pain of it.

He caught, as well, people's growing sense of doubt about a president who wielded his vast authority like a mace. New Hampshire's Democratic leaders, bludgeoned by Johnson operatives into endorsing the president early, must have felt like branded steers on the LBJ Ranch. They were shaken further by the antiwar students who poured into the state to stump for McCarthy, seeing him as the antidote to the culprit-in-chief in the White House.

The out-of-staters for McCarthy included the likes of Paul Newman, the actor, who rode on the press bus with us, guzzling Coors from the can; and a character with shaggy black eyebrows and pockmarked face, named Dick Goodwin. Goodwin was a veteran of the 1960 Kennedy campaign, a gunslinger who gravitated to the political action. He'd come north to offer his speech writing services to McCarthy and had found a campaign so marooned there wasn't even a bottle of whiskey on hand, let alone any typewriters or speechwriters to use them.

By late February, as the primary approached, things had turned around; the marooned campaign had become a juggernaut.

When New Hampshirites went to the polls in subfreezing temperatures on primary day, you could sense something extraordinary about to happen. I was at the McCarthy control center in Manchester where excited volunteers ripped reports of the first promising returns from the wire-service tickers. That evening, while the McCarthy vote continued to mount, the candidate packed a pair of aides, a CBS reporter, and myself into his car for a drive to the nearest television studio. McCarthy seemed eerily composed, still bitter at the White House for having so airily dismissed his challenge.

Only a few weeks before, he had walked the snowy lanes of New

Hampshire alone, unrecognized and ignored. Now, on the cusp of an upset, his televised image was about to circuit the nation.

The next day dawned on a stunningly altered political scene. The president had won in New Hampshire, but with less than half the Democratic vote; McCarthy had polled more than 42 percent, a minor miracle. Now hailed as a serious contender, he was the first candidate in sixteen years to have successfully challenged an incumbent president in the opening round. He'd struck a blow for all those underdogs who dreamed of getting in the ring and decking the Big Buy for an eight count.

The dominos had been rearranged. Nixon trounced Rockefeller in the primary, giving himself a big head start in the Republican race. With McCarthy's impressive vote propelling him into the national spotlight (*Time*'s cover showed him as a heroically declaiming figure, which he was not), Robert Kennedy now reassessed his plans. The president and his men, meanwhile, were in a state of shock. Pretty soon the dominos started falling.

Kennedy declared his candidacy, quashing the McCarthyites' brief euphoria, raising all the old suspicions of Kennedy ruthlessness and a Camelot restoration. He had delayed entering the race while he calculated the force of the antiwar movement in New Hampshire, then ridden in on McCarthy's back. The move infuriated McCarthy's supporters and other Democrats. It also sealed Lyndon Johnson's decision on his own future: he announced his withdrawal from the presidential race.

The president who'd won passage of the civil rights bills, the antipoverty, federal aid to education, Medicare, and other transforming Great Society bills was stepping down to avoid further political humiliation. The decision shocked just about everyone except Dick Goodwin. Weeks earlier he'd bet me even money that Johnson would not be the Democratic nominee. The loser of the bet would buy the winner dinner at New York's pricey Four Seasons restaurant. I avoided New York the rest of the year.

Johnson's decision automatically revived the prospects of Hubert Humphrey who jumped into the race with little urging. Then in mid-April Martin Luther King Jr. was assassinated in Memphis, and America's cities started going up in flames. Chicago, Baltimore, Pittsburgh, Cincinnati, and on. Hours after King's death, Robert Kennedy despairingly quoted Aeschylus to black audiences, urging that they tame "the savageness of man." Humphrey, too, warned blacks not to lash out in retaliation. It was too late.

I was in the cockpit of Humphrey's press plane approaching Washington right after the assassination, when the pilot pointed out the window. "The whole damn city's on fire!" he shouted. The view below was sickening, the Capital blanketed in an ugly yellow pall. Pockets of flame winked across the city's downtown. The control tower at National Airport reported shooting and killing in the city's black districts. The rampage would mount over a week.

Three days later the great and humble jammed into Atlanta's Ebenezer Baptist Church to bid King a last farewell. They recalled his stirring "I have a dream" moment at the Lincoln Memorial. They remembered him at Montgomery and Selma, walking, head high, into the sheriffs' truncheons and police dogs. In the airless red brick church where King and his father had preached, they sang and wept over his walnut casket, undone by the beauty and shame of the occasion.

I'd flown down with the vice president and somehow squeezed into the last piece of unoccupied floor space in the church. I crouched in front of Humphrey a few paces from the casket and King's widow. Coretta King was as regal in her grief as the other anguished widow of five years before, who now sat just behind her. Jackie Kennedy had joined the gathering of those who'd known King as family: the choirgirls in their tears, the desolated colleagues who'd fought alongside him in the long struggle for justice.

When the last "hallelujah" had sounded, they wheeled King down the aisle past the peeling pink walls and out into the crowds waiting in the sun. They hitched his casket behind a pair of mules and set out for the cemetery, a shirt-sleeved procession of close to half a million, singing the "Marseillaise" of their revolution, "We Shall Overcome."

The death toll was rising in Washington when we returned. Whole sectors of the Capital had been turned into smoldering piles of rubble. Much of the business section was gone. As the burning and rioting spread, a curfew was imposed through the city. Helmeted troops and tanks from nearby Fort Meade patrolled the streets.

The first thing I did was jump in my car and race downtown to see the madness for myself. The curfew was still an hour off and I made it without challenge to the epicenter of the conflagration. It was a scene out of a Hieronymus Bosch painting. Entire blocks were aflame, liquor stores the targets of choice. A whole store would explode, the fires illuminating the silhouettes of looters dancing about in a carnival of frenzy. No police or troops were to be seen. One heard no shots or screams, only the ceaseless crackle of flames and the whoosh of disintegrating walls as the inferno roared into the night.

By early May I'd rejoined the primaries fray.

The triumvirate of Democratic candidates — Humphrey, Kennedy, McCarthy — had been joined by the leading Republican contenders: Nixon, Rockefeller, and Reagan. There was a line-up, too, of "favorite sons" and other hopefuls. The air was filled with rumor and projected dream tickets. Nixon-Rockefeller. Rockefeller-Reagan. Reagan-Lindsay. And so on. None of the pairings accorded with reality, the candidates' deep philosophical and personality differences.

Time began plotting various covers as new faces kept popping up in the scrum. I was assigned to look over the budding third-party candidacy of Alabama Governor George Wallace.

George Corley Wallace was a nasty piece of work: a pint-sized demagogue with oily black hair slicked into a pompadour and a defiant dimpled chin. Wallace was the poster boy for southern racism, a cigar-chewing primitive who'd gained national notoriety by standing in a schoolhouse door to block federal authorities from integrating Alabama's schools. He was contemptuous of civil rights laws, "pointy-headed" Washington bureaucrats, and the "pseudo-liberal" reporters who covered them. He played on the parochialism and prejudices of millions of southerners, claiming that the mainstream candidates looked down their noses at them. His was the true politics of resentment. He pursued it artfully.

At an outdoor rally in Fort Worth, Texas, Wallace was in his element, firing up the crowd with his usual invective. He stood on his tiptoes behind the podium, flanked by a couple of big-bellied state troopers, and lobbed his verbal grenades. "I support the police!" he yelled. The snickers began; on cue he responded. "We gonna get rid of you thugs 'n' anarchists!" He turned on a bearded heckler. "You a he or a she?" he sneered. The hecklers were screaming at him now and Wallace was lapping it up, tossing back insults. The protesters finally turned their backs on him and departed. The show was left drained of its venom and edge.

Within four years a would-be assassin's bullet would leave Wallace partially paralyzed and an object of pity. For now, he was an unnerving factor in the political race, a threat in particular to Republicans who worried that Wallace would dilute their party's vote in the South and cost them states they'd won four years earlier. One of those concerned was the leader of the party's true-blue conservative crusade, Ronald Reagan.

Barely a year into his first term as California's governor, Reagan was still viewed as a fringe figure in national politics. But people were taking notice of him, the sunny new face of the GOP's ascending right.

Reagan had been persuaded to enter the race by western Republican leaders who saw him as a bright star and heir to the party's Goldwater wing and who viewed Richard Nixon as worn goods. Reagan more than anyone could help tamp the Wallace boomlet that threatened to lure away conservatives faced with choosing between the liberal Rockefeller and the also-ran Nixon.

Reagan was a former Democrat who'd repackaged Goldwater's scary reactionaryism in a soothing way that addressed the anxieties of America's white middle class. His corporate sermons on behalf of General Electric had championed a more muscular, self-reliant nation; they had touched millions via radio and television. His smooth nonthreatening style masked the revolutionary zeal of his message.

Ada and I met Reagan at a Republican governors conference held aboard a cruise ship in the Virgin Islands. It seemed an appropriately glamorous setting for the newcomer. Reagan may have been only a middling actor (Bob Hope said Reagan wanted to be president, but didn't know where to go read for the part), but he'd learned more than a bit about business and politics as longtime head of the Screen Actors Guild. He'd also learned how to captivate audiences with the homey quip and nod of head. He was a charming libertarian and foreign policy hawk.

For all his allure as the right's new messianic darling, Reagan would have to bide his time. His entry added spice to the race, but he was too untried to corral the party's nomination that year.

Nelson Rockefeller was about to be turned down by his party for other reasons.

The New York governor was out of sync with Republican conservatism, a maverick accused of not playing on the team unless the team captain suited him. And Nixon was not to his taste.

To conservatives Rocky was the embodiment of the arrogant easterner disdainful of the homely values of Middle America. His earlier divorce and remarriage to a younger woman had left a sour taste among the heartlanders. Now he was about to spend six million dollars, most of it his own, securing the nomination. It was a bald effort quite unlike anything that had happened before in our political history.

When I caught up with the Rockefeller campaign, the candidate was demonstrating why a lot of people questioned his seriousness as a contender. He appeared far removed from the lives of ordinary folk. Rockefeller thought pay phone calls still cost a nickel, and on the hustings beyond New York he could get confused between Milwaukee and Minneapolis, things like that. His delegate wooing was amateurish.

Rockefeller hadn't a clue about what impressed delegates in the hinterland, men like Ben Boo, the mayor of Duluth, or Archie Gubbrud, the senate candidate from South Dakota. He thought it was the newspaper, radio, and TV ads he'd spent a mint on; or the cheering rent-a-crowds and Rocky Girls in their red-white-and-blue frocks who pepped up his rallies. He was above the drudge work of courting delegates like a supplicant and too honest to buy them. He could at least have schmoozed with them aboard his roomy campaign jet or invited them to his New York homestead in Pocantico Hills as he did the reporters. He did neither.

Instead he staged enough gimmicky photo-ops to dazzle Barnum. With "Happy," the second Mrs. Rockefeller, he rode a bell-clanging trolley in St. Louis, meandered up the Ohio River on an old-fashioned stern-wheeler, and motored down the canyons of Manhattan's financial district in a convertible showered with confetti. When he worked the crowds, the women moved up to him fast, their eyes glowing and expectant. People reveled in the once-in-a-lifetime moment of touching a Rockefeller. Rocky stood there amid the adulation, winking and grinning, endlessly effusing. "Hiya-wunnaful-to-see-ya, besta-luck-all-the-way, it's-a-pleasure."

His speeches were eminently thoughtful, his position papers well crafted. But it was all subsumed by the clangor. Rockefeller's was a campaign running on pizazz, noble intentions, and little more. So everyone enjoyed themselves.

Henry Kissinger, his foreign policy adviser, joined in the camaraderie when he wasn't locked in his cabin fashioning a Vietnam peace plan. Johnny Apple, the *New York Times* man and Baedeker on the culinary pleasures of small-town America, regaled us over feasts at the great four-stars of Toledo and Dubuque. And who could deny the governor's traveling physician his jollies? One day aboard the plane he appeared in an Indian headdress and war paint, racing up the aisle, emitting war whoops.

Rockefeller's press secretary, a Renaissance character named Les Slote, referred to critics of the governor as "fascist pigs," and expounded wittily on Mahler and Hellenic art, subjects he preferred to the mundane care and feeding of reporters. Hotel reservations were known to evaporate on his watch. The press bus would break down. The press plane actually broke down the day Rockefeller attacked the president's transportation policy. We always forgave Slote, a man unduly burdened by the futility of his job. He became a good friend of mine.

So Rocky's "727 Flying Circus" swept through the spring skies with its cargo of dreamers buoyed in the belief that somehow, when the delegates came to their senses, the GOP would turn one hundred eighty degrees from Barry Goldwater in 1964 to Nelson Rockefeller in 1968.

Hubert Humphrey came to the race that spring, still shackled to an unpopular lame-duck president.

Lyndon Johnson was in no hurry to surrender his influence and commit to empowering his ambitious vice president. At the same time, despite New Hampshire, Humphrey's camp continued to dismiss Gene McCarthy as a gallant irrelevancy. They were also convinced that Robert Kennedy's late entry was no more than a desperate gamble, a party-busting move that would destroy him politically.

But Kennedy, who'd given up on the inept Democratic Party regulars, was now campaigning with the formidable support of the Kennedys' own nationwide network. Humphrey was left to cobble together a campaign team from the ranks of the party's city hall backrooms and clubhouse-ridden state delegations. While

Kennedy played to television's love of spectacle and action — surging street crowds, impassioned sound bites, personal derring-do — Humphrey was dusting off faded slogans and aligning himself with icons of the past. Eleanor Roosevelt plugged his campaign. The younger Democrats gravitated to McCarthy and Kennedy.

The party's rank and file loved Hubert in a sentimental way. But too many of its influentials recoiled at his cravenness toward Johnson, his echoing the president's stance on Vietnam. Initially they withheld their pledges of support and kept their checkbooks closed. Undeterred, Humphrey plunged ahead. *Time* scheduled yet another cover story on him. This time, when I rejoined him on the road, I had a chance to study more closely the man who many came to believe personified the ultimate tragedy of presidential politics in the sixties.

All his life Humphrey had been trying to reach the top. He was still chasing the dream, pursuing it through the hurts and indignities of being Number Two: having to dance with old ladies at Polish-American picnics or turn a cheek to Lyndon Johnson's crude jokes at his expense. On the flight back from Martin Luther King Jr.'s funeral he'd shucked his sadness and bounced up the aisle, humming the Negro spirituals he'd sung in grief an hour before. He was as incapable of prolonging sorrow as he was incapable of exacting vengeance. Others might play the game that way; Humphrey's triumph was that he'd risen as far as he had without resorting to it.

He was too busy preaching good. The years had tempered his finger-wagging righteousness. On civil rights his tone was more forgiving as he campaigned through the South that spring. He even began to hedge a bit on Vietnam, questioning the infallibility of the administration's course, a first faint sign that he was becoming more his own man on the issue.

Occasionally amid the campaign whirl one could locate the stillness in Humphrey, his sweet vulnerability to the wrenching changes all around him. He thought he understood the students, and why they were rebelling. Part of it was the increasing sterility of campus life. He hated the new computerized report cards, the mechanizing and dehumanizing of so much of modern life. He agonized over the dying of family farms, the threat of small towns and their values going the way of the dodo.

When I joined the Kennedy campaign late that spring it was storming through the countryside, seeking to implant among voters the idea of Bobby's inevitability.

Kennedy had already trashed the Humphrey and McCarthy forces in two midwestern primaries. He was building momentum for the big prize, California. He was running, and winning, in every post-New Hampshire primary despite the fact that the Democratic establishment and large chunks of Middle America abhorred him and that Humphrey was still far ahead in overall delegate strength.

Kennedy was riding the winds of the Camelot phenomenon, the public's still potent veneration of his martyred brother. His campaign message — reaching out to touch the nation's heart and bind its wounds — inspired a deep-seated fervor in the crowds besieging him everywhere. Still, the young, mostly white elite shunned him. Their hearts belonged to McCarthy.

Robert Francis Kennedy had evolved by degrees into his role as spokesman for the poor and dispossessed. He was a Washington outsider who had come to identify with society's outsiders. He was a moralist with little tolerance for human frailty. I'd seen him first in the late fifties when he was staff counsel for a Senate committee probing corruption in the Teamsters Union. He'd sat hunched and accusing in the Senate hearing room, firing questions in the harsh flat accents of his native Boston at the Teamsters' defiant boss, Jimmy Hoffa.

Later, visiting Appalachia, Kennedy had come face-to-face with a miner's family living in a dirt-floor shack, and had viscerally felt their despair. He grew angry with those unable or unwilling to share his emotions for the impoverished.

He viewed the world in black and white, though his own character was intensely complex. He was a serious, if intellectually limited, man awash in paradoxes: blunt but often inarticulate; star-crossed romantic and cold-eyed existentialist. Half of him dreamed of better things; half of him operated with pitiless realism. Norman Mailer said RFK was a sheriff who could have been an outlaw. He was compulsive and driven, at times sophomoric, saturated with irony and a dogged fatalism.

Part of Kennedy's magnetism was his role as a hotspur always tempting the third rail, an impulsive thrill seeker. He scaled steep mountains, kayaked white-water rapids, dove into piranha-infested lakes. His attraction to danger was as unsettling as his seeming need to polarize large swatches of the electorate. I found it remarkable that so abrasive a man could be so appealing. I was also persuaded that something unfulfilled kept driving him to test his manhood in myriad and public ways.

As a matter of course he came to be the most electrifying politician of his time. Everything about his quest for the nomination in 1968 was played at full throttle. In the annals of presidential campaigns, wrote one observer, there may never have been another like the last campaign of Robert Kennedy.

It raced hell-bent across the landscape and emotions of America, a riotous carnival exuding passion, tingling oratory, and kleig-lit hoopla. It brought excitement to the small towns up-country, to the crowds everywhere engulfing his motorcade. They kept coming, swept up in the delirium of the bands and wailing police sirens, aroused by the frisson of sighting beautiful people and famous television faces in the Kennedy entourage, galvanized by the screams of their neighbors and children, by the roar of the press buses and, when the motorcade finally reached the speakers platform, the frenzied clacking of a hundred typewriters as newsmen recorded the dateline of their town above dispatches soon to be read by millions across the nation.

In Omaha, Nebraska, I watched as the crowds seemed to

explode on cue from storefronts and schoolhouse doors, rushing toward Kennedy, trying to touch his slight frame or run their hands by his tousled hair. In the city's black district, the motorcade swung past dingy bars and tenements as scores of young men raced alongside his car. Kennedy and his aides reached out and placed some of the youths on the hood. By the time it reached the rally site his convertible was submerged in a swirl of black faces.

In Columbus, Ohio, where radio spots had urged crowds out to the airport for a moonlight reception to meet the candidate, a huge traffic jam occurred. Unable to reach the airport, people parked their cars on the side of the highway to await Kennedy. As his entourage proceeded toward town, a bumper-to-bumper procession of glowing headlights massed behind it.

In city after city Kennedy's arrival signaled pandemonium, people tumbling down like rubber dolls as they mobbed the motorcade. A young man leaped on the candidate's car and clasped RFK in a bearhug; a mother tossed her baby into the car where it landed on Ethel's lap. His bodyguard put a hammerlock on Bobby to keep him from being swept away. The candidate grabbed a bullhorn and tried to calm the crowd. It was useless. He stood there swaying on the car's hood, his hair flying, shirttails and cuffs aflap, begging someone for a spare tie clip or cuff link, checking to see if the mob had at least left him his socks and shoes.

I wondered how much punishment Kennedy could take. The physical toll showed: his face was worn, his eyes bleary, his hands puffy and bleeding at night. Amid the pandemonium his campaign message was in danger of getting lost. At times it simply failed to penetrate the tumult. It was then that Kennedy moved quickly to wind up the show, flinging out a ritual Shavian quote that cued the reporters to reboard their busses, and the motorcade would depart in a flurry of cheers.

In the last days of May, Kennedy turned westward to focus on two major primary hurdles: Oregon and California.

By now his campaign, buoyed by successive victories in the Midwest, had become a cyclonic force. These last two primaries, though, would be his toughest; in both states the polls showed him barely ahead of McCarthy.

Kennedy applied a full-court press. The bold-faced names, the big-foot journalists, and the beautiful people poured into Oregon. Mother Rose held press conferences and teas. JFK's old press secretary, Pierre Salinger, lobbied the local Rotarians and Shriners. The historian Arthur Schlesinger Jr. fired up student rallies across the state. The coiffed and peppy "Kennedy Girls" handed out RFK fortune cookies.

The candidate barnstormed across the state in a chartered DC-4, swooping down to bedazzle the denizens of countless farming communities. Each stop was like a Second Coming. When I caught up with Bobby he'd switched to the rails, the Southern Pacific's *Beaver State Special,* and was whistle-stopping through Oregon's lush and vote-fertile Willamette Valley. The train was packed with friends, reporters, advance men, and a strolling Dixieland band. For all the merriment, the spectre of a setback in the making hovered.

A lot of Oregon folks thought the Kennedys a bit much. Bobby's offhand remarks seemed condescending at times toward the farmers and their families who swarmed about his train when it rolled into Tillamook or some other crossroads village. His disrobing in front of reporters and plunging into the ocean on a whim struck them as undignified for a U.S. Senator. They inclined toward the less intense McCarthy who talked to them quietly about issues and treated them like grown-ups, not extras in a made-for-TV moment.

On May 28 McCarthy won a stunning victory in the Oregon primary, jarring the calculus on Bobby's inevitability.

Oregon was an unexpected windfall for Hubert Humphrey. He was already leading the delegate race in nonprimary states. Now he saw himself less pressured by the stalled Kennedy juggernaut. Oregon raised doubts anew among Democratic leaders that Kennedy was the party's best vote getter. Even a Kennedy victory in California might not fully restore his earlier momentum.

What Kennedy needed desperately was the road-clearing elimination of Eugene McCarthy. For if McCarthy was still in the race at the nominating convention two months hence, Kennedy would be denied any realistic chance of overtaking Humphrey on the first ballot; McCarthy would drain away too many delegate votes. Without a first-ballot victory, Kennedy would be forced to wage a backroom brawl with Humphre,y whose backers controlled the convention machinery. California was therefore crucial, the must-win battle.

The Kennedys threw everything into it. One bone-crushing day followed another as RFK's caravan dashed across some twelve hundred miles of the state from Eureka in the north to San Diego in the south. In Los Angeles there were triumphal passages through the black and Hispanic ghettos with mariachi bands and stampeding Bobby fans who left the streets heaped with broken placards, crushed roses, and sunglasses; in San Francisco tens of thousands in the city's Chinatown district showered the motorcade with tickertape, a crush so enormous that shoes went flying, their owners trampled trying to retrieve them.

As primary day neared, the delegate counts across the country for the first time inched toward Kennedy. His defeat in Oregon had made him, ironically, seem more vulnerable, more likable; it had taken some of the edge off people's hostility toward him.

Kennedy had given the Vietnam issue a timely jolt with a speech lambasting the Johnson administration for prolonging the war. He'd also made a ringing commitment to Israel during a little noted televised appearance at a synagogue. Watching Kennedy on the screen, hearing his words, had so agitated a young Jordanian living in Pasadena, one Sirhan Sirhan, that he'd broken down and left the room in tears.

On June 4 Kennedy won the California primary, crushing the

Humphrey slate and effectively ending Gene McCarthy's quixotic quest for the presidency.

That night, when the last of the polls had closed, I joined the celebration in the ballroom of Los Angeles's Ambassador Hotel, a grand rococo pile long past its prime. Some eighteen hundred of Bobby's supporters uncorked the bubbly and partied joyously till shortly before midnight, when Kennedy's triumph was sealed and the candidate entered the ballroom to give a short victory speech.

A bright blue balloon floated by his face as he stood under the hot television lights and let the cheers wash over him. He spoke gracefully about ending the divisions in the country, the violence. They were among his last words. "On to Chicago and let's win there!" he shouted. Then he left the stage and the cheering celebrants and ducked through a partition of gold curtains into a kitchen passageway where the gunman waited.

I remember walking back from the podium where Kennedy had just spoken, along the fringe of the crowd, chatting with the Washington columnist Joe Kraft, asking what he made of the primary returns and, before he could respond, hearing the screams.

Anyone hearing screams at a Kennedy event tended to dismiss them as the norm. Only this screaming sounded unhinged and intensifying. I peeled away from Kraft and started running toward the noise. The crowd had surged back from the door Bobby had just exited through, like a mass recoiling from some unimagined horror. The exit door slammed in my face and two anguished Kennedy aides blocked my way, shouting at everyone to keep back. I pushed forward with my press credentials. One of the aides grabbed me round the neck and put a knee to my groin. I broke loose and bolted through the door.

On the other side it was a charnel house. In the semidarkness of the hotel pantry there was no one in charge, only a herd of raging, terrified men tripping over a handful of figures lying motionless on the cement floor. One of them was Kennedy. Sirhan had been four feet from him when he fired, the .22-caliber slugs popping in rapid succession, the sounds like dry wood snapping. Kennedy had crumpled quietly to the floor. Five others had gone down with him in the fusillade. I stumbled over one of them as I burst through the door, a labor union official who'd taken a shot in the forehead.

The scene was eerily bathed by television lights. Ashy cordite-smelling particles hung in the air, and aides were wiping the blood from Robert Kennedy's face. He lay on his back a foot or two from the union official, his eyes open and staring, his stockinged feet spread apart; a shocked aide sat nearby holding his shoes. Kennedy's tie had been undone to aid his breathing. Someone had folded his suitcoat and placed it under his head, and beneath the coat had placed a newspaper. The newspaper had begun to absorb a dark pool of blood oozing from two wounds to his head and neck. The wound behind his right ear, impacting his brain, would prove mortal.

Ethel Kennedy, who'd been several steps behind her husband when the firing started, knelt by his side and implored the photographers to back up and give him air. Jean Kennedy Smith in a white evening dress rushed into the melee to get to her brother. Tempers flared, fistfights broke out as aides tried to disperse the panicked onlookers. A TV cameraman lost control and charged, raging, at the reporters surrounding Ethel who was holding Bobby in her arms, a Pieta-like tableau amid the bedlam.

Down the passageway a knot of Kennedy aides were still trying to subdue Sirhan and wrest the gun from him. They pinned Sirhan against the stainless-steel counter he'd stood on to shoot Kennedy. He was still flailing, trying to squeeze off more shots. The three-hundred-pound pro footballer Rosy Grier put a hammerlock on him, and Rafer Johnson, the decathlon champ, finally forced the gun down, banging it against the countertop. It took eight men to quell Sirhan.

It seemed an age before help came; no police, no medics. Kennedy lay there, his life draining away. A priest scurried in to administer last rites. "He needs a doctor, not a priest, for God's sake!" someone yelled. Moments later the cry went up again as a hotel security guard ran in with his handgun drawn. We thought the world had gone mad.

The cops and ambulances arrived at last. They lifted Kennedy onto a stretcher, a pack of ice cubes secured to his right temple. They wheeled him down the corridor and into a freight elevator that malfunctioned and took the group to the wrong level. They got him finally to the ambulance where an empty police car was blocking the way, the driver nowhere in sight. The ambulance attendants tried to bar Kennedy's aides from riding with him. More angry words, more starts and stops. The ambulance with its police escort sped off at last in a bawl of sirens.

I attached myself to several Kennedy friends on the scene. We piled into a car and took off behind the ambulance headed for L.A.'s Central Receiving Hospital. In the emergency room a photographer tried to barge in and Kennedy's enraged bodyguard knocked him to the floor. Central Receiving was not up to operating on the stricken senator, so they transferred him to another hospital, Good Samaritan. Again the driver of the police escort car couldn't be found. The chaos began to smell almost like a conspiracy on the L.A.P.D.'s part.

In the intensive care unit at Good Samaritan, Kennedy lay near death. His face, so sunburned hours earlier, had turned fog gray. His bared chest rose and fell evenly with his breathing, a sign, one observer thought, that connoted an aura of power not yet extinguished.

In the early hours of June 6th, four and a half years after his brother's assassination, Robert Kennedy died. At the funeral in New York's St. Patrick's Cathedral the matriarch, Rose Kennedy, sat with a worn smile of resignation.

People reacted varyingly to RFK's assassination. Lyndon Johnson, fearing a new outbreak of Kennedy mania, spluttered, "My God, how could he do this to me?" Some of Bobby's Senate colleagues took precautions; Peter Dominick of Colorado, our Spring Valley neighbor, bought a pistol for his bedside. Rosemary Clooney, who was close to Bobby, suffered a breakdown. The sad-faced Kennedy men packed up their fallen leader's Senate office. Once again a pall settled over the Capital.

We watched the summer stutter from one violent happening to the next. People wondered whether, and how, presidential campaigning in America would have to rearrange itself to accommodate the awful reality of politics by the gun.

The mood suggested reactionary times ahead. Editorials called for more stringent police measures. George Wallace saw his stock improve dramatically. The electorate showed unmistakable signs of turning hard right. No one was better poised to exploit the mood than Richard Nixon. He was already putting the final lock on Republican delegates when I arrived with the *Time* team in Miami for the opening of the GOP convention early that August.

The three thousand delegates descending on Miami were anxious to shed the scars from their ideological bloodfest in 1964. That convention had belonged to Goldwater's revolutionaries; this one would be run by the professional pols. It would focus on party unity and paper over the cracks of dissent.

Before the convention was barely underway it was declared a flop. The Broadway producer David Merrick said he'd have closed it after the first night, and added, "There's a morticians' convention in town that's livelier."

It had come down to Nelson Rockefeller trying to shore up endorsements from the likes of the AFL-CIO's Glass Bottle Blowers Association. He took his seat in the family box as the balloting began, still aglow from the cheers when his name had been presented in nomination and a sea of balloons had cascaded down from the ceiling. Then he watched as the whole ceiling figuratively collapsed on him. Midway through the count Mississippi threw its votes to Nixon. New Jersey split for Nixon, then Wisconsin put Nixon over the top, and that was it.

The Republicans had given the back of their hand again to Rockefeller, but they hadn't exactly traded up for a fresh face. Nixon promptly selected as his running mate Spiro Agnew, the governor of Maryland, a summer moderate who had turned hard-line on the race issue. He was a man with a face like a Buddha and his hand in the cookie jar.

The outcome of the Republican convention virtually guaranteed that the Democrats, heading for their convention in Chicago, would choose a nominee sympathetic to the nation's urban voters: its poor, its ethnic and people of color, its young and alienated. Except no one dreamed the young and alienated would turn Chicago into the bloodiest political free-for-all yet.

Certainly not those of us in the press who'd gathered on the shore of Lake Michigan with the Democratic delegates and their favored candidate, Hubert Humphrey.

The Democrats convened, shaken and diminished by the deaths of Robert Kennedy and Martin Luther King Jr. Their loss, and that of the president's credibility on the war, had eroded the party's spirit. Lyndon Johnson had become such a divisive force that he'd declined to attend the convention. Even in absentia, his was still a commanding presence. He no longer had the delegates' hearts, but he still controlled the nominating machinery and, by extension, the candidate-to-be.

The other commanding presence on the scene was Richard Daley, the outsized mayor of Chicago. "King Richard," as he was known, was right out of central casting: built like a bull, jowly visaged, the personification of entrenched bossism. The Democratic National Convention of 1968 was to be his and his city's crowning moment. The gleaming downtown office towers, the grand curving lakefront, the verdant parks, and bold expressways all would be on display for the world's media. Daley would occupy center stage at the convention, his lieutenants helping him hustle things along, his police enforcing order on the streets.

For there was this one annoyance: a core of noisy out-of-towners who'd come to Chicago to tear the place apart. They'd forced Daley to put his police on around-the-clock alert, to string barbed wire around the convention site, and place the state's National Guard on call. The troublemakers included the radical Students for a Democratic Society whose Weather Underground faction boasted scores of seasoned street fighters; the notorious Black Panthers; and the Youth International Party, an absurdist collection of pot-smoking, obscenity-mouthing kids. The yippies had vowed to put LSD in the city's drinking water and had warned that Chicago would become "a festival of blood."

Lincoln Park on the city's northern lakefront was where the first trouble started. On Sunday evening I left the Hilton Hotel where *Time's* team was quartered and strolled up to the park. It was already jammed with hundreds of yippies and antiwar protesters decked out in bells, beads, and sandals. They sported beards and granny glasses; the women wore flowers in their hair. The beat of bongo drums punctuated the chatter among the park's groves and grassy knobs; the scent of weed hung in the air.

The word was that Daley's cops would enforce a city ordinance and shut down the park at 11:00 P.M. The crowd was already setting up barricades using overturned picnic tables and trash baskets. It was scrounging bricks and bottles for a field arsenal that would also include (the cops later claimed) Molotov cocktails, ice picks, knives, bamboo spears, sharpened clay tiles, and golf balls embedded with tiny spikes. A little after eleven the first skirmish line of blue-helmeted cops appeared from behind one of the knobs and advanced toward the crowd. Behind them came a street sweeper, its water tanks converted to hold tear gas.

A police bullhorn sounded a warning. The crowd responded with jeers and clenched fists. The cops waded into their ranks while the street sweeper spewed clouds of gas. The crowd, enraged and choking, responded with a volley of missiles. An officer took a brick square in his chest and went down. The cops retaliated, charging through the park, pulling protesters out of trees, flailing away at any Medusa-haired hippie within reach of their nightsticks. That's when I started running with the rest of the newsmen, dozens of us trying to record the melee, pencils jabbing through our shirt pockets or cameras swinging wildly around our necks.

Arc lights in the park caught the surreal scene: the cops pursuing the protesters who were yelling curses, tossing rocks, and flaunting Viet Cong flags, the cops bludgeoning the protesters to the ground while the gray tear gas swirled around everyone's legs. The cops went after everybody including reporters, smashing their cameras and other equipment. In the darkness people stumbled and went down screaming under the clubs. Even when the park was finally cleared, the cops chased the kids as they scattered through the streets and alleys of the nearby Old Town section. That's where I came to a halt at last, out of breath and quite lost.

The second evening I dropped by Hugh Hefner's Playboy mansion that was party central for a lot of the press and visiting celebrities. Elia Kazan, the film director, was there and captured the scene in a piece for *New York* magazine: "Here they all were," he wrote . . . "Arthur Schlesinger . . . Teddy White bristling with curiosity . . . Art Buchwald sharp as a tack behind his innocent cigar . . . Ted Sorensen, the Kennedy biographer . . . the *Life* people . . . the *Newsweek* people . . . Lansing Lamont of *Time* — everybody was 'somebody' and everybody was being asked what they thought and showing off their points. It was great fun."

The shoptalk at the mansion was political and focused on what was happening on the convention floor of the International Amphitheater out by the old stockyards.

There, inside the red-and-blue carpeted hall, things seemed initially in control. The Humphrey cause advanced inexorably. Blacks took their seats for the first time in every state delegation from the

Deep South. But tensions were building. An emotional tribute to the slain RFK, coupled with an aborning Ted Kennedy boomlet, threatened to stall the Humphrey steamroller. A fight erupted when McCarthy and Kennedy backers tried to insert a peace plank in the party platform, replacing one that affirmed the president's Vietnam policies; the president's surrogates torpedoed the move amid catcalls.

Shortly, any semblance of comity evaporated. People turned from raucous to insulting. The air was rent with charges of bullying and bigotry. Delegates shouted each other down. Dick Daley's security goons began manhandling the unruliest ones, then turned on the newsmen. Mike Wallace of CBS took a punch to the jaw. People started exiting the hall in disgust. Outside on the streets it was getting worse.

A protest rally in Grant Park on the third day began in a mellow enough mood. Hundreds of veterans of two nights of fighting, many in bandages or arm casts, strummed their guitars and sang along. Then some kid lowered the Stars and Stripes flying near the bandshell, and that tore it for the watching cops. The kid went down under a rain of billy clubs. The crowd hurled rocks and bottles. Tear gas canisters were tossed. The cops withdrew.

By late afternoon the protesters had begun forming for an unauthorized march to the convention center four miles away. In the gathering darkness they moved out of the park, eight abreast, arms linked. In front of and behind them the police and National Guard fanned out, the guardsmen blockading selected streets, the cops smacking their clubs against their palms in anticipation. The demonstrators spilled onto Michigan Avenue that runs past the Hilton. They came face-to-face with the guardsmen holding fixed bayonets and with cops lined up holster to holster on both sides of the avenue.

That evening, as the delegates began balloting for the nomination and the tide began sweeping Humphrey toward an expected first-ballot victory, the air outside the Hilton rang with shouts of "Dump the Hump!" and angry curses at the cops blocking the protest march. On every floor of the Hilton people peered from windows at the spectacle below. Television lights flared and the protesters, sensing what was to come, chanted, "The whole world is watching!"

I'd returned to the hotel from the convention hall to file a long piece. I peered out my window shortly after midnight just as the Battle of Michigan Avenue began.

There must have been more than three thousand people below, taunting and mooning the police, burning draft cards, booing the news of Humphrey's nomination, booing the busloads of delegates returning to the hotel, spitting in the faces of the officers, yelling, "Pigs eat shit!" Some in the crowd hurled bags of urine and condoms filled with feces. They sprayed the cops with mixtures containing lye and pelted them with missiles made of fence slats. At some point Daley's cops had had enough.

One of them gunned his motorcycle onto the curb while others lunged into the crowd, clubbing with abandon. Demonstrators and bystanders were swept up in the rampage, many dragged down the avenue and tossed into police vans. Those who didn't move fast enough were bloodied on the spot; a clergyman was struck on the head, a cripple shoved and whacked. The cops beat the hippies to the ground, then rapped their genitals for good measure. They maced ordinary onlookers. "My God, help us," an older woman pleaded, struggling to raise herself from the ground, blood pouring from a head wound.

Police discipline had broken as surely as protesters' skulls. In the Hilton's Haymarket Lounge, a ground-floor bar named for an 1886 Chicago riot, the front window collapsed under the weight of bystanders outside. The cops charged in, pursuing several youths and scattering the guests like chaff. Fifteen floors above, in McCarthy's staff headquarters, nine young volunteers were brought up from the street, bruised and bleeding.

When the cops' rage was spent and the last demonstrators had limped off into the night, they took a damage count. Michigan

Avenue was a mash of broken glass and drying blood. There were no deaths, but hundreds had been injured, including cops and newsmen; hundreds had been arrested. A large portion of the police injuries were to hands, leading one newspaper wit to deduce that a lot of culpable citizens had gone around smashing their faces on cops' knuckles.

The battle in the streets echoed on the floor of the convention hall. When word of the police's handiwork reached the delegates as they prepared to crown their nominee, it ignited an uproar. It subjected Dick Daley to the worst humiliation of his career. It ruined the celebration for Humphrey.

One leading Democrat after another rose to condemn the Chicago police. Gene McCarthy was so angered he refused Humphrey's invitation to join the nominee at the podium in a show of party unity. When Connecticut Senator Abraham Ribicoff interrupted his nominating speech to decry the cops' "Gestapo tactics," Daley blew his stack. The mayor shouted an obscenity at Ribicoff. Then he struck a *Life* photographer and shoved the camera in his face.

The postmortems on Chicago painted a grim picture: a nation irretrievably fractured; a major political party's convention wrecked before a watching TV audience of millions. The Democrats would be remembered, my colleague John Steele wrote, "as the party that commissioned Dick Daley to keep the peace, then sat back and watched while he did it with appalling — and unnecessary — brutality." An official report later concluded the cops had participated in an organized police riot.

Daley issued his own report claiming his city had been beset by "terrorists," and many Americans, fed up with protest marches and hippies, agreed. Among them, my sainted mother. I could barely hide my astonishment when she told me the kids had it coming to them, that my concern for a few cracked heads and assaults on law-abiding citizens was misplaced. If my mother, a peaceable and tolerant sort, had joined the swelling law-and-order crowd it boded ill for the Democrats. Right then I reckoned their election goose was probably cooked.

Chicago stamped its seal on an ugly political year. Afterward few had much heart for the election campaign. The polls that September had Nixon cruising to a possible landslide victory. Humphrey, loyal to his party and the president but growingly doubtful about the war, was caught between a rock and a hard place. As if his shambles of a campaign organization wasn't already in trouble, he would have to perform a miraculous balancing act to have even a chance in November.

THE GREAT AMERICAN TRAGEDY: ELECTION '68. The sign on the fringe of the crowd in Springfield, Ohio, said it all.

I was aboard the Republican nominee's campaign train, the *Nixon Victory Special*, whistle-stopping through the Midwest in late October. A supremely confident Nixon had refused to debate Humphrey or seriously engage on the issues as he stumped the country. His campaign was conducted like a coronation processional.

It was a carefully scripted show designed to appeal to the Republican base: white suburbia, white southerners, mostly white workers in the midwestern rust belt, and all those well-salaried white professionals dubbed the "affluentials." Nixon gave short shrift to the have-nots; he avoided the urban ghettos. When a lone black was spotted at a Nixon rally in Cincinnati, someone cracked it was a white guy wearing three coats of Man-Tan.

I remember the beauty of those Ohio mornings, the sun rising over the cornfields, white clouds floating above the lofty grain elevators, and the first hints of a fall chill as our train wound across the state. We'd pull into some lunch-bucket steel town at noon, the factories belching smoke, the ladies in curlers plunking down their camp chairs by the tracks, then standing on them to get a better glimpse of the candidate as his train wheezed to a stop. In the evening, sprinkled through the crowds, were all those flash attachments on Brownie cameras winking merrily like fireflies. Then Nixon, in his dark suit and sonorous tones, would turn the festivities to stone.

He'd wind himself up for the big rhetorical moment, eyes closed, lips pursed. "We're gonna sock it to 'em!" he'd declare to perfunctory cheers. Then he was off, arms pumping out of sync with his speech rhythms, his eyes blinking a bit too fast, like an impaired metronome. He'd praise America's military strength, his chest thrust out and fists clenched; crack a joke at Humphrey's expense with a gloating grin; then finish off by raising his arms above his head in his trademark V-for-victory salute.

People talked about the new Nixon, smoother, less vindictive, more voter friendly. Not everyone bought it. A sign at one shopping mall read, A NEW NIXON? ONLY HIS HAIRDRESSER KNOWS FOR SURE.

By October Humphrey's campaign had moved from disarray to despair. He was chewing up valuable time trying to explain away the convention debacle and placating the warring wings of his party. He was frantic to prove his independence without seeming to desert his sponsor, the president, even as Johnson remained sulkily aloof from the race.

Humphrey soldiered on, his voice hoarse and pleading, a good man lost in memories, offering no new road map for the future, only, as Nixon jibed, "a scrapbook of his clippings." He couldn't help himself. The garrulousness and tears came too easily when he was bone tired near day's end. He bared his soul while his opponent's remained shrouded. He lacked the cold reserve of the ruthless. He had no instinct for the jugular.

The last time I saw him was in Chicago, the site of his party's August woes. There was a torchlight parade through the city's black and Mexican-American districts. Humphrey's motorcade inched through the detritus of the Fourth Ward, past the derelicts on West

Madison Street's skid row and the seedy hotels with their tattered awnings and dejected residents. Bobby Kennedy had come into this same ward and ignited the crowds. This time the electricity was missing.

Instead of jubilant mothers and kids, Humphrey was met by people who lifted their brown-bagged beers in tired salute as he passed. On the speakers platform at Chicago Stadium the city aldermen in their baggy suits waited impassively for the nominee. The mayor was there, glowering in blue serge. Hundreds of seats were empty. When Humphrey spoke, rousingly, the party hacks sat on their hands. When Humphrey finished, Dick Daley clapped dutifully. Humphrey turned his back on him. You knew how it would all end.

But not without a last dramatic spasm.

Late in October the polls began breaking for Humphrey. Nixon's campaign was perceived to have peaked. The Democrats' coffers reopened; money again flowed to a buoyed Humphrey. The nominee came sprinting down the home stretch with a second wind. This flattest of presidential campaigns was pointing toward a photo finish.

Five days before the election Johnson ordered a halt to the U.S. bombing in Vietnam. The respite came too late to save Humphrey. Nixon edged him out by barely five hundred thousand votes, less than 1 percent of all those cast for the two men.

Nixon had ridden into office on a tide of resentment, the voters' bellyful of the anything-goes counterculture and its amen crowd in the media and academe. The conservative backlash would continue spreading and Nixon would ride it back into office again four years later in the biggest landslide in U.S. electoral history.

Humphrey's fate was to have stayed too long on stage, the ever hopeful stand-by. In the end, he was unable to divest himself from a president mired in a hopeless war. So he was denied the office he'd sought for so long and would have, I believed, singularly honored.

In Hubert we'd have gotten the bright sunny music of a humane reformer. Instead we got dissonance and a prince of darkness.

The last time I saw Nixon he was waving stiffly to a crowd of admirers on Broad Street in Manhattan's financial district, standing on the running board of a new bubbletop, bulletproof limousine ordered up by the White House Secret Service detail.

Lyndon Johnson did not go quietly into the good night. He clung as long as he could to the spotlight of the presidency.

I saw him last at a small dinner party in Manhattan. The party in a West Side apartment was to honor Lady Bird Johnson. The two dozen or so guests included people like the actor Douglas Fairbanks Jr., the aging playwright Marc Connelly, and the Gardner Cowleses of *Look* magazine. Johnson lumbered in after dinner, plopped himself in an armchair and began grousing, a bit disingenuously, about life in the White House fishbowl. Just to get himself across town from the Pierre Hotel had required a laborious production to keep his whereabouts secret.

The president removed his gold-rimmed glasses and rubbed his eyes. He hadn't been sleeping well lately. The war, the protesters, the election outcome. He looked forward to passing on the pressures and the insomnia to his successor. Let *him* deal with the relentless exposure, the busybody Secret Service, and the press. Nixon, too, had chosen the Pierre for his Manhattan visits. "He has good judgment about hotels," Johnson mused. "I hope his judgment is as good about running the country."

I wanted the year to end. There'd been too much Sturm und Drang, too much sadness.

My beloved Uncle Ranny had died that August. He'd savored a decade of Maine summers with his elegant second wife, Diana, in the old Metcalfe Cottage below Sky Farm before the throat cancer struck. He'd withered away this last summer. One night, exhausted, he'd asked Diana to help him to their bedroom on the second floor.

She'd carried his wasted body up the stairs and laid him gently in the bed where he died a few hours later.

Ranny and I had had a special rapport. My father's and my relationship had been more formal; we wrote each other affectionate, thoughtful letters, but we weren't pals. Ranny and I seldom exchanged letters; we didn't have to. We were so on the same wavelength we could effortlessly pick up and reconnect on issues and people over a long drink whenever we happened to meet. He treated me like an equal, as my father couldn't afford to; he accepted and advised me on my own terms.

Ranny sensed my unsureness growing up in a competitive family that aspired to the highest standards. He was my release valve when things got wound too tightly. Slow down, he'd signal, don't accept everything your elders tell you. Be true to yourself and your own dreams, not others'. Face life squarely and enjoy it. Things usually work out.

We knew, as the cancer worsened, he'd be forced to bow out bravely. And he did. Mencken was one of his favorites and Mencken's words were more than a fitting epitaph. *Say a prayer for some poor sinner and wink your eye at a homely girl.*

A few gleams appeared in that otherwise dark year.

The Paris Concorde made its transatlantic debut, a flight so swift that passengers barely had time to down a Merlot before landing in New York. Jackie's remarriage, albeit to no one's idea of Lochinvar, lifted hearts. The Harvard-Yale game ended in an epic 29–29 "victory" for the underdog Crimson. Three Apollo astronauts reached the vicinity of the moon and became the first humans to orbit it.

Time threw an especially nice gleam my way: deputy chief of its London bureau starting the first of the new year.

I was delighted to be a foreign correspondent in the magazine's most prestigious overseas bureau. Still, it was wrenching for the family. We were leaving our home of the past decade, leaving behind fast friends. But I knew it was time. Too long covering the Washington scene and you became part of the scenery. You took to thinking of yourself as, and thinking like, an insider. Not wise for a reporter.

Time itself was changing course. The Fuerbringer era had expired. The new regime, led by Fuerbringer's successor, Henry Grunwald, was shedding the Stalinist mentality of old. It was moving to cure the antipathy in the reportorial ranks. For the correspondents, frustrated at having their best work ground up by the editorial mill in New York and given little say in the finished product, help was on the way. Grunwald instituted reforms. New York would continue to have ultimate control, but the correspondents would henceforth play a more decisive role.

Heralding our new status, Dick Clurman, *Time*'s chief of correspondents, summoned to Paris more than a score of European bureau chiefs and correspondents for a sit-down with the new managing editor to discuss *Time*'s international coverage.

On a December day, I took a seat with my new colleagues around a triangular conference table in a high-ceilinged room of the Trianon Palace at Versailles. A massive chandelier illuminated the eighteenth-century art adorning the cream white walls with their gold filigree. The talk was good — the cigars and wine even better — a combination perfectly suited to Grunwald's Continental tastes. Henry declared we correspondents would no longer be treated as second-class citizens, but I recall little else of the occasion. I was absorbed in daydreams, the grandeur of the setting, wondering if my grandfather had sat in this same room a half century before when he'd attended the First World War peace talks and treaty signing.

Clurman, aware of Henry's fondness for *l'affaire éclat*, arranged a boat trip one evening up the Seine. Several score-journalists and the cream of Paris officialdom boarded a *bateau mouche* complete with orchestra and enough paté and stuffed quail to feed the entire Quai d'Orsay. As we glided up the Seine, floodlights illuminated on cue the passing landmarks like Nôtre Dame. I was seated beside a soignée blonde, a top aide to Premier Pompidou, who couldn't wait for dinner to end to escape my execrable French. "Rather a cold mackerel, that one," I remarked to one of the local journalists. "Of course," he said, "she's the most notorious lesbian in Paris."

I thought it all a splendid baptism of the new Grunwald era. Even the French, who know how to celebrate the passage of ancien regimes, seemed impressed.

When I left for England in early 1969, the decade was playing out its messy coda: Woodstock, Kent State, Chappaquiddick.

What I remember most of that last summer at home was the afternoon we sat with friends around the television set at Sky Farm, spellbound as Neil Armstrong took his first tentative step on the moon. We cheered and wept for everything that freighted moment meant.

Man's view of his place in the universe had been forever altered. America's moon landing came, like water to a parched man in the desert, as a welcome reaffirmation of the human spirit. This decade had been such a bitter, bloody hour in our history, begun with such optimism and become so intensely malign. It had encompassed war and great social upheaval while driving us to a loss of proportion and restraint.

Our public discourse at the beginning had been about visions and dreams and bold ideas. It had declined into a drumbeat of demands for this and that right, into meretricious twaddle about celebrities, fads, and cures for one's natural aging process. *I feel* had replaced *I believe*. Like the liberated youth of Cicero's Rome, too many of our privileged young had turned their backs on public service, living only for the moment in self-righteous rebellion.

We'd exhausted ourselves in the passions of violent change. We were out of breath and out of harmony. I couldn't wait for London.

10

Have Trench Coat, Will Travel

An asterisk in the local "celebrity" bulletin marked my arrival in London on a drizzly January day. Me and Tab Hunter and a touring British rock band.

I moved into temporary quarters to await my family, who would join me in six months after the children's school year ended. I was too busy to moon over this longest separation from them. I went over to Aquascutum's and bought a proper trench coat. Then I dug in and began familiarizing myself with the turf.

London had transformed itself dizzyingly from the city I recalled two decades earlier still digging out from the war. After years of grim austerity it had emerged in the sixties as the hip London of King's Road and Carnaby Street, funky Soho coffee bars, Mary Quant boutiques and, of course, the Beatles. The city's renaissance had been celebrated recently in a *Time* cover spread: "Swinging London."

Londoners must have been amused. All the wild trendiness couldn't make over this most tradition-bound of cities. From

Mayfair to Highgate, Londoners, however mod in miniskirts or bell-bottoms, still reverenced their queen, their queues, their cricket, and their high tea, their smoky pubs, thin beer, and the World Cup Chelsea Blues. Class still counted: Eton and Harrow still schooled the aristocracy; Ascot and Henley remained the purview of the royals and the Oxbridge set; the St. James Street clubs were still exclusively High Wasp. Long weekday lunches had so far not been abridged by anything as gauche as the work ethic.

Time's London office was the biggest and best staffed of its foreign bureaus. The chief and my immediate boss was a seasoned older journalist, Curt Prendergast, who'd run bureaus and covered big stories from Paris to South Korea. We became compadres.

The bureau also employed a bevy of smashing young Englishwomen as editorial assistants. I was assigned one named Ann with a bawdy wit and runny mascara. I occupied a commodious corner office overlooking the busy intersection of New Bond and Bruton streets, a stone's throw from The Guinea, which served cold prawns in pink mayonnaise, and a china shop that sold Picasso plates for a song.

The Time-Life Building, brimming with pulchritude, talent, and Henry Moore sculptures along its facade, thus proclaimed its own enviable corner of London's journalistic universe.

The greater part of that universe resided in the older City. Fleet Street housed the magisterial broadsheets and the spicy tabloids with their screaming headless-torso banners and photos of scantily clad bimbos. Despite their lumpish management and their supine deference to the Official Secrets Act, which served to outlaw aggressive probing of government malfeasance, Britain's newspapers compared favorably with those elsewhere. In no other country, my friend Louis Heren of the *Times of London* observed, was it possible to buy so many good-quality daily and Sunday papers at any corner shop.

While I missed the urgency of Washington, I found London boundlessly invigorating, the antithesis of the capital as a one-industry government town.

There was its visual history, the soaring Wren churches, the cobbled mews, the art museums with their telling portraits of Tudor court life, princes and ladies all pale with small mouths and fishy eyes. There were the fusty traditions — the hotel porters in their Prince Albert coats, the Parliamentary Lords buried in ermine, the red-uniformed Chelsea pensioners tending to the city's love of tidiness — that embodied the civilizing impulse and pride of the race.

I liked the Brits' understatement, their crisp slang, their "lifts" and "brollies." I liked the vigor of their lingual slugfests in Parliament, their disdain for euphemism. I liked their obstinate, peculiar ways.

They'd lost an empire, but not the power to cow outsiders with the perversity of their spoken language. Mispronounce Beauchamp ("Beecham") Place, and you became in an instant socially regrettable, un-Debrettable, in Noël Coward's words. At a Whitehall press briefing I volunteered a question, carefully enunciating the briefer's name Featherstonehaugh, only to be curtly told it was "Fanshaw."

British plumbing also baffled me. For no discernible reason my tub at the Grosvenor House overflowed one evening while I was readying for dinner. Frantic, I phoned the front desk, buzzed for the valet, then ventured half-naked into the hall, shouting alarums to no avail. I was on my knees with a towel, trying to sponge an inch-high layer of water off the floor when the valet finally appeared. He seemed put out at having to rescue a flooded guest.

I was better at pomp and circumstance.

Group Captain and Alderman the Honorable Peter Vanneck, my old Harvard chum, invited me to the annual white-tie-and-tails dinner of The Worshipful Company of Fishmongers. The seven-hundred-year-old Fishmongers Guild was one of the twelve great livery companies of the City of London, awash in charitable good works and tradition. The occasion required evening dress "with decorations." I summoned a renter of formal wear for a fitting and smartly pinned on my only two medals: an assistant sergeant at arms badge from the 1952 Republican convention and my infantry rifleman's badge from army days. Then I sallied forth to the ancient Fishmongers Hall hard by London Bridge.

I think I was expecting to dine with a bunch of cod merchants in something like a Kiwanis lodge. Instead, I entered a grand lobby whose every wall and niche was adorned with magnificent armor, porcelain vases, and Romney oils. In a glass case lay the dagger that a fishmonger had used in 1381 to slay the antiroyalist rebel Wat Tyler. The queen's own trumpeters summoned us to dinner. I sat beside Vanneck at an enormous semioval table with 120 other guests, all male, all richly bemedalled up to their wattles.

There were endless graces and toasts. At one point a procession of men marched in, shouldering oars, the winning crew of the Doggett's Coat and Badge Race on the Thames, an event sponsored annually by the Fishmongers since the early 1700s. Everyone passed around a loving cup from which we drank copiously. I thought it a most congenial affair, though Vanneck claimed the wine had been watered and the viscount to my right had trouble deciphering my decorations.

It took me a while to figure out the Brits' obsession with sex.

The celebrated Mrs. Patrick Campbell had supposedly set the standard. ("It doesn't matter what you do in the bedroom as long as you don't do it in the street and frighten the horses.") But here I was regularly exposed to front-page stories about kinky sex scandals usually involving members of the upper class. Every month, it seemed, some lord or cabinet minister was being splashed across the pages of the ha'penny press for having been caught *in flagrante embarrassimento*. Some blamed it on the public (private) schools, others on the weather and lack of central heating. The whole thing seemed passing strange and closer to home than I'd imagined.

After the tub fiasco at the Grosvenor, I'd rented a small flat on Montrose Place in Belgravia. I was in bed one night, reading, when the doorbell rang. It was my neighbor, the owner of a film studio in

Soho, inviting me down the hall to a party being given by the wife of our landlord who was off in the Bahamas. I couldn't refuse without seeming unfriendly. The guests were an odd assortment — a film director, a discothèque owner, a film producer accompanied by a statuesque black model, a female BBC staffer who was built like Marilyn Monroe, an unpublished novelist, and an abortionist — all tenants in the building.

The Monroe look-alike from flat No. 1 said she'd spotted me as "the new man hereabouts" while she was putting out the trash. The landlord's wife from flat No. 9 offered to fix my faulty plumbing anytime. I excused myself early and retreated to my flat, convinced I had rented my digs from a pimp. Immediately I had second thoughts about my bedroom, which had been done in bordello red, its king-sized bed outfitted with deep purple drapes. I grew chagrined having to sleep there and couldn't wait to chuck the whole arrangement.

In this land of eccentrics there were plenty of offbeat yarns to be reported. Witchcraft and murder most foul on this or that moor. The campaign to ban fox hunting and tree the tally-ho crowd. The mystery of the Loch Ness Monster.

I flushed out odd pieces like the Hermit Duck Hunter of the Norfolk Marshes; the League of Toy Soldier Warriors, and other curiosa. But the more staple fare of the London bureau leaned to national politics: Northern Ireland's sectarian strife, Britain's love-hate affair with Europe, and the continuing soap opera of the royal family.

In every interim between their wars on the Continent the British had retreated back across the Channel into their island shell. They regarded alliances with Europe as balefully as they did the Europeans' character and institutions. They might enjoy the Alps and Viennese opera, but they would not commit to a European army or a European currency if their last tuppence-and-ale depended on it. For perfectly sound reasons they thought the

Europeans a squally lot given to launching blitzkriegs every quarter century and acting feckless the rest of the time. Besides, Britain had its own Commonwealth obligations and internecine struggles.

Racism, John Bull's ugly little secret, had outed itself. Commonwealth immigrants of color had flooded into Britain by the thousands under newly relaxed immigration laws. Locals whispered that the wogs were taking over their jobs and neighborhoods. Demagogic politicians turned the whispers into racist rants. Violence followed Paki-bashing and other assaults by skinhead gangs.

Violence was already the way of life in the slums of Northern Ireland. The civil strife between working Catholics and Protestants had escalated from riots and rubber bullets to bombings, kneecappings, and random executions by the Irish Republican Army. Vengeful Protestant militants had added to the carnage. British troops, with little tolerance for the Paddys' vendettas, patrolled the mean streets of Belfast and Londonderry.

We had plenty on our plate in the London bureau.

One day a cherubic-faced young man marched into my office at the appointed time and plunked himself down behind my desk, leaving me to conduct the interview from a lower side chair. He'd sized up the terrain and cheekily commandeered the high ground. About par, I thought, for the grandson and namesake of Winston Churchill.

Young Winston had been covering the civil war in Nigeria, a Commonwealth member. The hard-line government there was trying to quell a spreading revolt by secessionist forces in the oil-rich Biafra region. Churchill's stories in the *Times of London*, depicting the barbarity of the conflict and the plight of Nigerian civilians, had shaken British readers. His reports had fueled public demand that Britain intervene in the stalemated two-year-old war to save Nigeria before it collapsed and became a ripe target for a Soviet takeover.

In late March, Prime Minister Harold Wilson flew to Nigeria to assess the crisis. I went along.

When we touched down at the airport outside Lagos, its perimeter ringed by nervous government troops, I walked into an immediate screw-up. The local welcoming committee had no record of me. My name had somehow not made it onto the correspondents' manifest. Worse, I'd misplaced my passport. The Nigerian authorities claimed my visa was a fraud and threatened to put me back on the plane. When I insisted on staying, they threatened to jail me. I was about to be frog-marched to the nearest pokey when a local press officer came to my rescue.

The next few days I trailed Wilson down shell-cratered roads, through squalid villages scarred by the fighting where the townsfolk in their colorful *rigas* scampered from their ruined homes to wave at our motorcade. At an overburdened refugee center swarms of starving Ibo children crowded the dank, putrid-smelling wards where their tubercular mothers lay near death next to ravaged victims of pneumonia and edema. The war had caused delay of adequate shipments of food; the number of Biafrans who had starved to death as a result was conservatively estimated at more than two million.

A Catholic missionary whose parish had been dispensing aid to the refugees described to me what had happened one morning not long before.

A federal artillery barrage had opened up at dawn. Everybody had started running, including the five hundred patients in the mission hospital. They fled, cripples hobbling off on their crutches, people on intravenous feeding dashing off with the drips still attached to their arms. Everyone was running, and the relief workers were running after them with food. The roads were black with people, wailing women and children, carrying their belongings, pots and pans, bits of food. "I could see the terror in their faces and I could do nothing," the missionary said. "They were running to their doom."

More than twenty thousand refugees in all fled the parish. Every few yards groups of them would pause to crouch in the shade of trees; some never got up again. Raked by shell fire, strafed by government jets, too weak from hunger to keep running, the refugees settled into a long slow death march.

The figure responsible for much of the mayhem was General Yakubu Gowon, the head of Nigeria's federal government. Raised by Scottish missionaries and a graduate of Sandhurst, the autocratic Gowon liked to dress up in uniform with a rakish Glengarry cap. He regarded himself a reluctant warrior forced to take stern measures in the face of tribal rebellion.

Learning that *Time* planned to do a sidebar on him as part of a larger piece on the war, Gowon began to defrost a bit toward the visiting press. I didn't like his war or the way his military was waging it, but I had a job to do and I needed quick entrée for an interview. I would use the Scots connection. I spruced myself up for a press reception Gowon was hosting in Lagos, prominently displaying my clan tie. In the middle of the reception Gowon spotted me, strolled over, and flicked my tie. "What tartan is that?" he asked. "Clan Lamont," I said. "Not as good as Clan McGowon," he deadpanned. My interview was arranged on the spot.

I flew to Northern Ireland the next month. The rioting between Catholics and Protestants had threatened to plunge the Connecticut-sized province into wholesale civil war. You could smell the trouble coming. It was a nasty business, rock-throwing bloody, and about to turn even more lethal.

Ulster's "troubles" were rooted in nearly three hundred years of sectarian bitterness ever since the Protestant King William of Orange had defeated the Catholic James II at the Battle of the Boyne in 1690. Catholic defiance against England had begun even before that. In the late 1500s, the Tudors had set out to crush the core of Gaelic resistance in Ulster; Cromwell's forces in the next century had sacked entire towns there and slaughtered the inhabitants.

It was "King Billy's" KO at the Boyne, however, that had secured Britain's domination of Northern Ireland. Protestant

Orangemen there annually celebrated the battle with noisy, taunting marches through Catholic neighborhoods. The granting to Ulster of its own Parliament in the 1920s, independent from Dublin's, further reinforced the Protestant hegemony. It fed the resentment of the Catholic minority who saw themselves as second-class citizens on the bottom rung of a desperately poor economy, the Protestant boot as always on their neck.

Ulster's Protestants, some the descendants of my people who'd originally emigrated to America, resented Catholics' obstinate allegiance to the pope rather than the crown, their fostering of religious distinctions and incendiary myths: some Catholic parents still taught their children that Cromwell's troops had rolled Catholic babies down the streets in nail-studded barrels.

By the mid-1960s, the lines had hardened irreparably. The Catholics had instituted their own civil rights movement with a twenty-one-year-old firebrand in miniskirts, Bernadette Devlin, as its latterday Joan of Arc. Her followers marched under the protective gaze of armed members of the Irish Republican Army. The Protestants' leader was a hulking, thunderous demagogue, the Reverend Ian Paisley. His followers were abetted by the notoriously brutal Ulster constabulary.

In Belfast, a decaying nineteenth-century industrial city with rows of small brick houses, the odor of charred wood permeated the chilling drizzle. The blackened frames of shattered windows bore mute testimony to the fire bombing that had gutted shops and post offices and all but destroyed the city's reservoir. In Londonderry, epicenter of the violence, three hundred people had been injured in the rioting; many of those arrested were beaten up by the police. In Bogside, Derry's Catholic sector, the litter of overturned cars attested to the battle's fury. An armored police truck had mowed down and crushed a fourteen-year-old boy.

Protestant extremists talked of reactivating an armed force reminiscent of the feared Black and Tans of the twenties. Catholics talked of organizing their own vigilante groups within the IRA. The

Derrymen were fashioning more homemade fire bombs —
"Bogside doodlebugs" — gasoline mixed with soap powder and
paint in a milk bottle. A toothless old Bogsider warned: "I remember '21 when they were shooting people off the rooftops here. We're
edging toward that now. There's nothing for it but the gun."

During a chat with Lord Thomson of Fleet for a back-of-the-book
piece on the *Times of London*, the press lord seemed remarkably
sanguine about his financially floundering paper. "If you've got
money, Lamont, what better way to spend it than to own the *Times*?
Unless," he paused, "it's to own *Time* Magazine." He saw me shift
uneasily. "Of course, I don't think I can get it," he grinned, "but
would you mind asking what the selling price is?"

Time scheduled a cover story that summer to mark the investiture
of Charles, the royal heir apparent, as Prince of Wales.

The ceremony, which attracted an estimated five hundred million television viewers worldwide, was one of the last historic pag-
eants of the twentieth century.

It marked not only a milestone in the apprenticeship of the
twenty-year-old Charles, the queen's eldest son. It reaffirmed the
symbolic link between England and one of the United Kingdom's
restive member states. The event, held in Wales's thirteenth-
century Caernarvon Castle, was set against the backdrop of diminished empire and nationalist stirrings among a growing number of
the queens' subjects including the Welsh. In its grandeur and
panoply the occasion would serve as a showy reminder that the
Crown, despite its vicissitudes, believed it still had a significant role
to play.

The Crown's sway as symbolic master of 650 million subjects,
dispersed over a quarter of the globe, had shrunk in time to a mere
whisper. Still the Crown retained a disproportionate influence as
the one indissoluble link in the Commonwealth chain; and the
Commonwealth itself remained an international presence to be

reckoned with. Moreover, no royalty came close to Britain's in sheer eminence and mystique. For all their ribbon-cutting mummeries, the Windsors knew how to celebrate with flair when the occasion demanded. The Crown's relevance might be increasingly questioned, but its cool steadfastness suited the British temperament. In a very unstable world it reassured people.

The dowdy and dutiful queen was still in the spring of her rule. Elizabeth II had worked hard to ensure the monarchy's survival in a time of turbulent change. Persevering, she'd acquired near iconic status. Britons and much of the world saw her as a reservoir of starchy good sense even as she doted on Hollywood westerns and her corgis. She was beloved.

Less so were her next of kin. Elizabeth's husband, aka Philip the Sharp-Tongued, suffered from what he quaintly called "dontopedalogy," excessive foot-in-mouth disease. Younger sister Margaret excelled at gaucheries: dancing with the nude cast of a West End musical and listening to the prizefights on her transistor radio during formal dinner parties. Charles, with his Toby-jug ears, was likeable enough.

Painfully earnest, his Royal Highness Prince Charles Phillip Arthur George, Earl of Chester, Duke of Cornwall, Duke of Rothesay, Earl of Carrack and Baron of Renfrew, Lord of the Isles and Great Steward of Scotland, would not be mistaken for his great-uncle David, Edward VIII, who had raised royal dalliance with commoners to a new level. At least not for the time being.

Following a stint at Cambridge University, Charles was now studying Welsh at the University of Aberystwyth to prepare for his investiture. I decided to prepare for my end of the cover story by immersing myself in the Welsh landscape and lore. I set out for the northwest, driving through a hauntingly beautiful countryside of dark crags, towering waterfalls, and roads mantled with yellow gorse.

The green of the Welsh valleys softened the starkness of the summits with their ghostly cairns and ruined fortresses. The primeval forests conjured up the history of a phantom land where, someone had written, an ancient wind was ceaselessly remembering the clash of battles past — "a gleam of spears, a murmur of arrows, a shout of victory, a scream of torture," insurgent warriors defying the hated oppressors from the English east. The road to Aberystwyth wound through a silken mist, past heifers grazing by languid rivers. A traveler could still lose himself between Cwm and Plwmp.

On Wales's northern coast, literary legend drifted through the streets of Llandudno where Lewis Carroll had beguiled the local minister's daughter, Alice. Pockets of snow still clung to the crevices of Snowdonia's peaks above which flashed the silvery underwings of circling hawks. At Caernarvon, readying for the great event, the sunsets turned golden beyond the Menai Straits where the breeze blows in from the Irish Sea. The city looked a cross between armed camp and festival.

There'd been threats of sabotage, rooted in unforgotten humiliations from Wales's past. Caernarvon, like much of the land, was overhung with the specter of violence from English-hating extremists. On the eve of the ceremony, a gelignite blast had killed two men trying to place their time bomb in a Cardiff office building. The ragtag Free Wales Army had promised more explosions to mar the occasion. Navy minesweepers lurked in Caernarvon's harbor; frogmen searched for explosives in the river bed below the castle. Security forces numbered in the thousands.

The chief concern of the event's planners, however, was more prosaic: how to protect the royal family in case of rain. Garter Arms insisted a tent be thrown over the castle. Lord Snowden objected. They conferred with the queen. The people must be able to see the ceremony, she said; there will be no tent. "But ma'am," Garter Arms persisted, "what if it rains?" "I'll get wet, you ass," snapped the queen.

Investiture day dawned bright. The town's shops and houses were spruced up, the hourglass-shaped castle scrubbed clean, everything looking loverly. At mid-morning the castle gates opened to admit a stream of privileged guests and reporters. We took our seats under the battlements. The gates closed and the spectacle began, an operatic procession of the British aristocracy at its peacock finest.

Preening peers in toppers and doublets, ladies in umbrella-sized hats of every hue, mustachioed guardsmen, feeble old courtiers in Gilbert and Sullivanish uniforms, scarlet-cloaked beefeaters, the Queen's Mistress of the Robes, Gold and Silver Sticks in Waiting, a dashing equerry or two, all shuffling down the castle nave toward a patch of greensward at the far end where a makeshift throne stood. The Archdruid of Wales wore a gold head-dress; the mayor of Cardiff was done up like a chocolate eclair in a black and silver mantle. Lord Snowden had personally designed his rig, a figure-hugging tunic of green with tails and silk sash. I hadn't seen such finery since the Ascot scene in *My Fair Lady*.

To a trumpet fanfare and thunder of kettledrums, Prince Charles entered and proceeded to the throne. There, beneath heraldic banners snapping in the wind, the queen laid the ceremonial sword of his new office on her kneeling son and placed a coronet on his head. The kettledrums rolled again, a last trumpet fanfare echoed off the ancient walls, and it was over. Few guests heard the muffled blast of a time bomb at the city's post office a half mile away.

Time's cover story was its second largest selling issue on the newsstands that year. The cover headline read, "Is Prince Charles Necessary?" Readers responded by asking, "Is *Time* necessary?" The publisher's letter ran a photo of me in my trench coat standing in front of Buckingham Palace.

Britain's cherished pubs were in trouble, I reported.

Once, they were invitingly intimate places with sawdust on the floors and game rooms in the back; some of them hadn't been aired out since Waterloo. They flaunted their history. Curler's in Glasgow had been granted its open-seven-days-a-week license by Charles I in a royal fit of pique after the king had dropped by one Sunday and been unable to get a dram. The pubs offered darts, dominoes, cards, and boisterous singing in an all-male atmosphere. They were neighborly retreats stamped with the eccentricities of their region.

Now the giant brewers were taking over, catering to a younger generation — including women — with different tastes. The pubs were becoming models of plasticized blandness, fitted out with black leather seats and indirect lighting, serving beer so weak you could brush your teeth with it. Soft carpets had replaced the sawdust; Formica-topped bars the old brass-railed ones. You could still get Scotch pies, whitebait, and bangers, but they had to vie with fancier French and Italian dishes. The new pubs with their swizzle-stick decor offered talent contests and nude ballet.

The Dear Boy in Knightsbridge and some others held on to their past, with their warm bitters and staircases too narrow for a drunk to fall down. The old Lion and Lamb in Manchester forbade Muzak and still kept its gilded cage with a stuffed finch that chirped when you wound it up. But it was downhill elsewhere. Curler's was now serving Florida cocktails and filet of sole mornay. The Bubble 'n' Squeak in Bedfordshire, where highwaymen used to consort, had been remodeled in a Treasure Island motif complete with plaster trees and a faux Spanish galleon.

It wasn't far off, I concluded, before the bartender's closing cry would be, "Time, gentlemen. This is a recorded message."

That August my family rejoined me. I brought them back from the U.S. on the *Queen Elizabeth II*, the remodeled dowager of the Cunard fleet. The children, four dazzling towheads, plus their dishy mother, were the toast of the ship. In London, too, they turned heads. A few days after we'd moved into our new home on Walton Place, Ada took the girls to Harrod's. At the food counter she noticed a man staring wide-eyed at them; it was the actor Christopher Plummer. Douglas meanwhile was approached on the street by some lowlife offering him a modeling job. I thought it best we get everyone into the countryside pronto.

We chartered one of those little bare-bones boats that ply the Thames. It was called the *Mary Tudor II* and had a motor so simple even I could handle it. For five days we chugged up the Thames toward Oxford, the children savoring the sights while I deftly maneuvered our craft through the queue lines at every lock. It was a sparkling introduction to the riverside glories of England.

The children were trundled off to new schools. Virginia, a coltish ten-year-old, entered Lady Eaton's where the girls were required to wear dresses and straw boaters, a wardrobe that all but guaranteed she would end up one day in flip-flops, living in a Central American rain forest. Lisa was admitted to the marginally less buttoned-up Queensgate School where her classmates sported monickers like Xenia Graham-Dixon or Vanessa Twittlesley. Tommy, eight, was enrolled at Hill House where on his first day he was sent home by the headmaster to brush his teeth. Dougie, fourteen, entered Milton Academy back in the States and took up residence in my old house there.

Our new digs, amid a row of whitewashed Regency homes with tiny back yards, lay halfway between Harrod's and a small Anglican church where on any given Sunday the eight-member choir outnumbered the congregation. Despite the challenges of basement damp and a structure that was scarcely wider than a London cab, Ada ensured that 5 Walton Place became the most inviting home on the block.

The situation in Northern Ireland was worsening.

Belfast had been torn by three days of rioting, shooting, and burning in mid-August, the worst violence yet. The British army, called in to quell the fighting, had for the first time since the latest "troubles" began, fired on British subjects. Eight persons had died; more than two hundred fifty had been injured.

On my return, I found Belfast wracked by fear and rage. Royal Marines and paratroopers, toting submachine guns in their armored Saracen trucks, patrolled the streets that crisscrossed the

Protestant Shankill Road and Catholic Falls Road districts. Angry mobs, fortified with whiskey, surged behind barricades, hurling epithets at the troops and police. Children stood behind their parents and hurled stones, bolts, and iron bars. "Kill them! Kill them!" they screamed. The sounds of sniper fire pierced the night air.

The dead were mostly Protestants. Catholics cursed the troops for not killing more "Prods." Both sides cursed the army for having intervened. The soldiers grew testier. Two of them with loaded carbines burst into a house where I was interviewing a Catholic woman, Miss Davey. They forced me to terminate the interview, claiming I'd no authorization, then escorted me to the nearest police station.

Miss Davey had lived for forty-nine years in her two-story home on Percy Street chockablock with her Protestant neighbors. It was a few score yards, about a one-minute walk, to the house where Mrs. McCullough, a Protestant, had lived for the last thirty-five years. The two women could look down the street to one another's doorstep; they could have shared tea and gossip together. In fact, they'd never met, nor likely ever would. The sectarian divide was fiercely personal.

They buried young George Dickey and Herbert Hawe in a Shankill cemetery just before dusk. Dickey had fallen in the street amid gun fire so intense it took a priest ten minutes to pick his way to Dickey's body. The same day they'd held a funeral for a twenty-nine-year-old policeman, Victor Arbuckle, who'd left a widow and an infant son. A sniper had killed Arbuckle with a bullet to the temple. The soldiers and police had then fired into the mob, killing Dickey and Hawe, killing them as the mob waved Union Jacks while hurling bricks and defiance at the queen's troops. Such was the madness of Belfast.

Under sullen skies I watched the funerals. Fifteen thousand Shankillites turned out. Members of the Orange Order carried the two men's coffins. The undertakers wore black silk toppers, and

Dickey's sad-eyed father walked behind his coffin. The cortege passed a Presbyterian church with a sign on it reading, "Jesus said, 'Love your enemies.' " The people of the Shankill had long since rejected that advice.

Happily, I accepted a week's R&R in Scandinavia, part of the London bureau's beat.

The Finns were holding elections and I watched the returns in Helsinki's main hotel. The pressroom was jammed, journalists, diplomats, and pols all schmoozing and imbibing freely. The election outcome had produced a sharp swing to the right from the Finns' normally left-wing leadership, which naturally upset the Soviets. The *Pravda* man was deep into the vodka. He sidled up to me and whispered mysteriously, "The color is changing." The local stringer for the *Chicago Tribune* was on her fifteenth Scotch and weeping hysterically because the editors would give her only two paragraphs for the story. I thought she was lucky at that.

The Danes were having a sex fair, Sexpo '69, under a vast tent in Copenhagen. Most of the customers who'd poured into town from all across Europe seemed bored by the offerings: endless peep shows and phallic doodads on display. But my editors in New York were captivated by the novelty of the event — an open skin bazaar that wasn't locked away in some dark Times Square "adult shop." They urged me, grandson of a Presbyterian bluestocking, to file away.

The Brits, I concluded, went over the top when it came to their pets, an irresistible story.

Ten million British households harbored more than five million dogs and as many cats, along with incalculable numbers of finches, hamsters, hedgehogs, budgerigars, titmice, and baboons. The Royal Society for the Prevention of Cruelty to Animals was almost as venerated as the queen herself. Churchill had disclosed secrets "I could tell no man" to his favorite poodle. Nothing was too good for the little furry ones. Londoners even bought camel's hair maxicoats for their dogs, which offended the RSPCA, which said it was demeaning to the canines.

When Gina Lollobrigida hit town wearing a tiger skin maxicoat, the Society went ballistic. The film star was wearing one-sixtieth of the world's tiger population, it thundered. La Lollo purred back with irrefutable logic, "The tigers in my coat were already dead. I didn't kill a thing."

"Life is a gamble at terrible odds," lamented a character in *Rosencrantz and Guildenstern Are Dead*, the hit play of the London theatre season. The Brits lived that quote to the full, spending much of their lives gambling at atrocious odds. I set out to investigate the craze.

England's history had been one long series of odds-off bets, like taking on the Spanish Armada in 1588 or the Luftwaffe in 1940. Its historical figures celebrated gambling. Boadicea and Cymbeline were accomplished dice rollers. Henry I's win over Louis I of France in a heavily wagered chess match so enraged Louis that their subsequent enmity led to war. Shakespeare infused his Elizabethan dramas with references to the joys of gambling. After a while the toll in broken homes and crippling debts became all too evident. It was said of Crockford's, the tony London gaming club dating from the 1700s, that a generation of upper-class English youth had been ruined at its tables.

By 1969, Britain had become the gamblingest nation in Europe. Legalized betting was almost its largest industry. One out of every two Brits "took a flutter" at some form of gaming from horse races to the slots. The millions who patronized casinos, betting shops, and bingo clubs consumed — and wasted — much of the nation's energy. The addiction was more to blame for parents' neglect of jobs and children than any other cause, including alcohol. It was particularly rampant in the industrial north, a once dismal sector of the country, now swept up in a frenzy of modernizing and reconstruction.

In a crowded betting parlor in Manchester, the touts were pushing a nag called Shandy and the stale air rang with shouts of wagers and odds. Outside, amid the construction cranes and jackhammers, the city's blighted guts were being torn out to make way for new civic structures and parks. It was the same in Birmingham and Liverpool where the football pool, Britain's mother of jackpots, operated side by side with the city's spanking new repertory theatre said to rival London's Old Vic.

I left the Midlands with enough reportage to carry *Time*'s piece on "The Floating Casino." I'd sampled the gambler's numbing pastime and gained a clearer perception of the England beyond London. I'd even found myself more forgiving of the Englishman's fancy for a flutter, though I still gave Crockford's a wide berth.

I thought 1970 would usher in a decade free of the excesses of the sixties. I thought the old hatreds might abate along with the shrillness. I was deluded.

Some good things happened. The Vietnam war would end. We landed a spacecraft on Mars. America celebrated its bicentennial. But there was too much other stuff: My Lai, Jonestown, Kent State, the Iran hostage crisis, Watergate. The divorce rate kept climbing, the ozone layer kept depleting.

We tried to sweeten unpleasant truths. The aged became "senior citizens"; the poor became "the disadvantaged." It sounded like a kinder, more sensitized America, but the reality was something else. The new mantra was, *Take care of Number One.* The relentless competitiveness and cold calculation of professional life — personified by the hard-faced White House crew around Nixon — persuaded a few thousand Americans to leave their country for a spell and move to Britain.

Here, the newly arrived composer André Previn observed, "You could read the newspapers without going into shock before break-fast." The new expats included academics and writers, filmmakers and businessmen — some taking advantage of special U.K. tax breaks — plus a handful of draft evaders. In interview after inter-view they poured out their disillusionment.

America had become "an uncomfortable place, unloving and unreal," complained the film writer Reginald Rose. He and his fel-low dissidents preferred their new environment: safer, slower-paced, without the spleen and elbow shoving. The Brits confined their violent protests to the mistreatment of small animals. They prized civility. Artists got respect here. And so on. Over kippers at the Connaught, S. J. Perelman lauded the intellectual camaraderie of his new home.

The gush was a bit overdone. My pal Slote, who'd forsaken pol-itics and was now a London-based executive with RCA, had taken to his new environment in a Lambeth walk. But even he acknowl-edged imperfections in the local scene: the aggravating smugness and the plumbing (Slote said he'd had to take lessons in flushing the toilet). And the queues. You could polish off Gibbon's *Decline and Fall* waiting for the salesgirls in Selfridges. The cab drivers were chattier but no less homicidal than the ones in Manhattan. At least they didn't lean on their horns as they ran you down.

Otherwise, from where I sat under a British sky, 1970 was shap-ing up as a pretty good year. Laurence Olivier was made a lord; Margaret Court, a Brit, became the first woman to win a tennis Grand Slam in two decades. The skiing in Europe was unsurpassed.

After months of keeping his Tory opponents on edge, Harold Wilson decided to leverage his rising polls and Britons' summery mood by calling elections in June. Our London bureau geared up.

I thought the prime minister had made a rash call, given his Labour Party's disarray and the volatility of the British electorate. But the old balming influences were at work on his behalf. Britons basked under the spring sun. The looming newspaper strike, the doctors' threats to close up shop over their low pay, warnings of economic calamity ahead — all seemed to fall on deaf ears.

Brits were deep into the World Cup matches. Or else they disported at the shore, thronging the quays at St. Ives, rigging their sailboats that bobbed on the tides of Penzance Harbor. They jammed the Royal Shakespeare Theatre at Stratford and went wading in the gentle waters of the Avon. Couples punted dreamily on the Cam or puttered in their gardens. Families picnicked in fields of buttercup. Hikers tramped through the blooming purple thistle of Argyllshire. Even Northern Ireland managed to put a brief smile on its "troubles." The riots hadn't scared off the tourists. Quite the opposite. "They've put us on the map," the prime minister told me.

The languor worked fine for Harold Wilson, that least charismatic of leaders. Britons had always preferred prime ministers of the pedestrian Wilson stripe. For every Disraeli or Churchill they'd voted in a host of nondescript Asquiths and Wilsons. The national complacency was understandable: Britons well remembered the pain of war, the blitz, and rationing. They'd long given up dwelling on the glories of empire. "They never want to be top dog," an editor in Sheffield told me, "facing the responsibilities you blokes have now."

When I cornered Wilson's Tory opponent, the equally undazzling Edward Heath, on the campaign trail, he mused on America's newly inherited role as the free world's dominant power: "If you exercise it, you'll be accused of bullying. If you don't exercise it, they'll say you lack leadership. It's the sort of thing we British have had to put up with for the past three hundred years."

Heath seemed a poor bet for the rough and tumble of an election race. He was ill at ease with his mechanical smile and face like a smallmouth bass. Ordinary Brits found it hard to warm up to him, a bachelor who raced yachts, played the classical organ, and spoke in plummy, high-Anglican tones — an acquired accent. Neither candidate set hearts aflutter.

Wilson was as hard to engage as quicksilver, masterful at evading reporters' questions and the quotable bon mot. He was a stolid spokesman for the Middle England consumed by issues like butter prices and widows' pensions. After five years in office, he'd become Harold the Avuncular — as comfortable as an old shoe. He and Labour, seeking to shed their cloth-cap image, had moved to upgrade Britain's backward industries and to effect an unprecedented restructuring of the nation's social services. Banking on the assumption that Brits had irrevocably accepted the welfare state, Wilson's Labourites were poised to become the permanent majority in Parliament.

Days before the election, bookmakers' odds favored Wilson six to one. A lot of Labour backers, figuring Wilson had bagged the race, planned to stay home. That was inviting a lower electoral turnout that would favor the better organized Tories. The race came down to the wire. By midnight on election day it was clear that Harold Wilson had lost in one of the great political upsets of modern British history.

The outcome confounded bookies and pundits alike. Only one pollster got it right, my friend Humphrey Taylor. While Britain's political establishment slumbered through the balmy weekend before election day, Taylor went out and repolled a sample of undecided voters, his findings foretelling the dramatic outcome.

Time went to a crash cover on the new prime minister, one of a dwindling number of cover stories it would henceforth devote to foreign statesmen and political leaders. Reading tastes back home were changing. Vietnam, the assassinations, and upheavals of the sixties had soured Americans on political and foreign news. *Time*'s main domestic edition would increasingly pander to readers' obsession with lifestyle trends, rock stars, and television entertainers. In the decades ahead, overseas news, unless it importantly touched the lives of Americans, would get shorter shrift in the pages of the weekly newsmagazine.

In the first post-election months the new prime minister played the wraith. He was variously reported to be piloting his racing sloop at

Cowes or rippling through Handel on his Steinway at 10 Downing. The press compared him to the Loch Ness Monster, shy and inert in the vast deeps of Whitehall.

Ted Heath, in fact, was submersed in his job. He was bringing administrative order to the amiable chaos his predecessor had bequeathed him. He and his corps of bright Cabinet aides were working overtime to accelerate Britain's modernization, to propel it forward with cooler, businesslike efficiency.

The nation's hoariest institutions — its monarchy, church, and class system — would persevere unaltered. But elsewhere the forces of rude change were on the march. Private investment and industrial expansion were increasing, the City of London's financial sinews expanding. At the same time, suburbia was spreading across Britain's green expanses; more cars were jamming its woefully lagging highway system. Mini-skyscrapers had begun to mar the graceful London skyline; glassy hotels and office structures were shoving their way onto the quiet side streets and historic little squares. It was a different world coming, and not all Britons welcomed it.

One world that defied change was Northern Ireland.

When I flew back to Belfast that July, pools of blood were drying on the streets amid still smoking ruins. A weekend of rioting had left seven dead and at least two hundred fifty people injured; more than a hundred homes, pubs and stores had been leveled by firebombs. The renewed violence bore the earmarks of a guerilla-style conflict designed to destroy the fabric of order in Ulster. The run-up to this latest outrage had been fueled by the extremists on both sides.

The Reverend Ian Paisley, armored in Old Testament righteousness, stumped across the province, roaring his antipapist invective in a voice that could shatter Waterford crystal. When he led his followers in a march to the wail of flutes and the beat of Lambeg drums, the cry went up everywhere, "Remember the Boyne!" IRA toughs, meanwhile, had been arming for months, their arsenals updated from the vintage revolvers and breech-bolt rifles of Easter Rebellion days to automatic weapons and deadly bombs.

When the fighting began, the firepower and arson erupted almost on cue. While teenage mobs overturned buses and rained bottles and stones on the outmanned police, snipers roamed the rooftops, pinning down the British troops crouched on street corners. Rival gunmen burst from doorways, firing haphazardly at each other. Young boys, their slingshots filled with ball bearings, took aim at solitary troopers; they cheered wildly when a soldier crumpled in agony. Women looted abandoned ice-cream parlors and soft-drink arcades, then watched the shops go up in flames as they licked their cones and swilled lemonade, like so many Madame Dufarges savoring the havoc.

The only thing holding Ulster together was the army, an occupying force of eleven thousand rattled Tommies besieged on all sides. I'd never seen a peacetime city more at war's edge than Belfast that summer. When I walked into the army's headquarters with a *Time* photographer, a nervous trooper raised his automatic rifle to firing position as we approached. At a checkpoint outside Armagh to the south, troops stopped our car marked PRESS and, despite our protests, turned it upside down searching for weapons.

We were issued gas masks. Television crews (but not the pen-and-notebook guys) were outfitted with flak vests and special bullet-proof breastplates. It seemed a bit much, but you never knew with these Ulster crazies. One noon in the bar of the Royal Avenue Hotel where the press was staying, someone discovered a firebomb inside a floral bouquet. The frightened barmaid showed it to the *Daily Express* man who was having a quiet nooner by himself. "Yes," he nodded, "call the bomb squad," and went back to his cups.

In Westminster's eyes Ulster had become incorrigible, but no one seemed to know how to handle the errant child. The hatreds had reached untenable levels; both sides despised the puppet masters in London. When Home Secretary Reggie Maudling rushed to Belfast on the heels of the latest bloodbath, angry protesters greeted him on the streets. In the Shankill, women screamed for tougher action against the rioting "Caths." "Shoot them down! We'll give you a nice big tea!" they yelled at Maudling.

In the next two years the death toll would rise exponentially.

That August I took my family to the top of Norway. In Oslo we loaded up our rented Peugot station wagon and set out for Bergen on the west coast where we boarded a cruise ship, the *Nordstjernen* (North Star). On a brilliant starry evening, our Peugot secured in the hold, we glided out of Bergen Harbor past the Hanseatic merchant houses lining the waterfront, and set course for the Arctic Circle.

We skirted the Norwegian coast, popping into snug fishing villages that reeked of dried skate and herring. We passed lovely moist green islands with silver birches and purple phlox along the roads. Beyond the towering fjords, snowcapped mountains shimmered in the distance. Each time we docked to unload cargo the townspeople flocked to the quay. The *Nordstjernen* carried everything — chickens, cars, the living and the dead. At Alesund we dropped off a fully laden funeral casket.

On the ninth day we reached our destination, Kirkenes, a mining community on Norway's far northeastern border with Russia. We debarked with the Peugot and started driving south over crude dirt roads, dodging potholes, deer, and foxes. I'd misgauged a few things like the size of my traveling wardrobe and the distances between towns or pit stops. The children, packed in the back like sardines, grew squirmy. Still, I told myself, it was a grand adventure, and if the locals thought us a bit odd it was only because we appeared to be the sole Americans swanning about this Nordic wilderness.

At Lonsdal we were the talk of the Polarcirkell Motel. I'd run low on shirts and was wearing my pajama top till we reached a decent laundry facility. Tommy, weaned on toy soldiers, was conducting his own nightly war games complete with sound effects; in addition, he'd locked Douglas in their room by mistake. Ada had loudly expressed her longing to see some exotic wildlife.

Next morning I overheard two of the locals talking. "Sven," said the first, "you seen the Americans that arrived last evening?" "Did I see them!" said the other. "The man wore his pajamas to dinner and the little boy kept running through the lobby, shouting to himself." "That's nothing," said the first. "The older boy was in his room pounding on the door for hours while the mother was pestering the clerks about where she could find a moose. Then they all started chasing a rubber ball around, using one of the sun chairs for a goal. Mad, the lot of them."

At some point between stops, picking our way through fog clouds along the Peer Gynt Road, we veered east toward Stockholm, where we turned the Peugot in. Sturdy, if cramped, it had carried us from the roof of Norway to our terminus in Sweden's capital, nearly 2,300 miles.

London drew a constant procession of debonair Americans. Some merely passed through, others stayed on, like our new sidekick Stanley Flink.

A former Hollywood correspondent for *Life*, Flink had found London the curative for a bad divorce back home. As publisher of *Playbill* for the city's West End theaters, he knew everyone in the entertainment world. At one time he'd briefly squired Marilyn Monroe and secured the last known interview with Marian Davies, the ill-fated paramour of William Randolph Hearst.

Flink was an irrepressible raconteur and so anglophilic it was rumored he'd upgraded his middle name from Edgar to Edgerton (which I thought rather commendable). He proved perceptive enough to take a shine to Ada and attend to her and the children during my frequent absences. He escorted Ada to a performance of *Oh, Calcutta*, the raunchy hit musical of the season, thoughtfully covering her eyes with a *Playbill* during the nude chorus scene. He procured center-court seats at Wimbledon for the kids.

Through Flink we met the Broadway composer Arthur Schwartz, a recent emigre who'd moved in down the street. Arthur began showing up evenings at 5 Walton Place where he commandeered our Steinway, performing works from his classic shows like *The Bandwagon*, *A Tree Grows in Brooklyn*, and others. He brightened our home like the Great White Way itself. As did Flink.

Enoch Powell, the renegade Tory MP and race-baiter, proved a compelling interview. Powell on race was like General Lemay on the bomb; both men dreamed of a final solution. In our session Powell was in full xenophobic mode over Britain's hot-button issue: to join or not to join the European Community.

Most Britons opposed joining while fearing its inevitability. Powell tapped into that fear. Might as well talk of the unity of Asia or Africa, he argued. "The fact is, you can't ask us to think of ourselves as Franco-Germans anymore than you can ask the Swiss to feel like Italians."

A millennium spent refining their island civilization had ingrained in Britons' psyches a deep resistance to conforming to others' ways. It had taken them centuries, for example, just to sort out their peculiar currency; the idea of cashing that in for something called the eurodollar was unnerving. Then there was their general distaste for Continentals — all those garlic-scented Florentines in their varooming Alfa Romeos, those beefy Germans with their Brunhilde wives and mania for efficiency. Why chum up such folks? Heaven was home with Alfie and Brenda in a rose-bordered Sussex garden.

It was a destructively insular view. Sooner or later Britain would have to make the crossing and become one with the European Community; she could not afford to stay out. But Powell, with his fiercely contrarian logic, articulated the feelings of millions of ordinary Brits.

The new prime minister had bought himself the briefest of honey-moons.

Shortly, Britain was embroiled in a series of massive strikes and protest marches. Ten thousand dock workers struck, idling scores of ships, many about to discharge eagerly awaited Christmas cargo. In Glasgow twenty-five thousand auto and shipbuilding workers walked off their jobs. The worst was a slowdown of 125,000 electrical workers that plunged the nation into a blackout and deprived millions of homes of hot water and warmth on one of the year's coldest days.

In Covent Garden, Bizet's *Carmen* was performed in darkness. In Soho the owner of a strip club supplied his customers with flashlights to keep the show going. At Buckingham Palace the queen sipped her tea in candlelit gloom. I was in a West End bistro interviewing Bernadette Devlin, the Ulster revolutionary, when the lights went out. Devlin lit a candle and carried it to a table where a chap was dining alone. "Here," she said, "my contribution to the brotherhood of man."

When no one thought it could get any worse, the postal workers struck, shutting down the mail.

Britons' customary shrugs turned to snarls. The year was ending on an awful downer. Amid the dismay there was one cheerful blip on our homeland horizon: Manhattan's twin World Trade towers, in the last stages of construction, were about to become the tallest pair of buildings on earth.

In early 1971, I flew to Singapore to cover the Commonwealth prime ministers conference.

The modern Commonwealth, no longer exclusively British, had come under increasing strain. Once an extension of the Empire, viewed by many as a privileged white man's club, it was now a racially mixed hybrid — neither political union nor federation, neither military alliance nor economic bloc, but having elements of all four. Prime Minister Heath had put the institution at risk by appearing to tolerate apartheid in South Africa, a Commonwealth member. It was a posture that deeply angered South Africa's black neighbors, some of them, like Uganda and Zambia, also members of the Commonwealth.

When I interviewed Kenneth Kaunda, the president of Zambia, one of the largest independent states in Africa, he spoke to the issue eloquently. To him there was a clear difference between the sectarian racism of states like India, Northern Ireland, or the Balkans and the racism of South Africa and America. "One can change his ideology, his faith, or religion," he said. "One cannot change his color. If you persecute a man for that, what chance has he?"

Singapore was a thriving modern city-state ruled by the iron-handed Lee Kuan Yew; its economic core was run by its Chinese merchant class. I was quickly baptized in the city's mores: a gin sling at Raffles; a tour of the Chinese quarter. I inhaled the pungent odors from food stalls, the gabble of street cries. On a back lane I happened onto a "death house" where families brought their deceased before burial; a corpse lay under a brightly colored blanket while the family milled about, offering cups of sake to visitors, an oriental wake. At prayer time in an Indian temple half-naked priests waved censers and pounded bongo drums. One of them propositioned my female guide while I was inspecting a shrine.

With a letter of introduction, I drove across the causeway separating Singapore from the southern tip of Malaysia to call on His Highness Tungkun Mahmoud ibni Sultan Ismail, the Rajamuda, or prince, of Johore, one of the largest of Malaysia's nine states. At the villa the prince walked out with his pet cheetah on a leash to meet me. He was candid about his nation's problems, namely, too many destitute Malays working the profitable rubber and palm oil plantations so that members of the constitutional monarchy, like him, could live the good life.

Next day, at the prince's invitation, I brought a group of my colleagues over for a Sunday cruise up the Johore Strait. The prince had put his navy — a forty-foot yacht and six-man crew — at our disposal. The excursion did wonders for my standing with the foreign press corps.

Our charter flight back to London was pure Evelyn Waugh. The Reuters man had been in charge of arrangements and had signed up a shadowy duo to handle the details, a Singaporean Indian named Asithayam and a silky travel agent named Yeoh. Mr. Yeoh had brought along his associate, Miss Khoo, a shapely Singaporean Chinese who sported aviator shades and red-lacquered fingernails.

No sooner had the doors closed on our bus to the Singapore airport than Miss Khoo announced our flight had been delayed in Karachi due to engine trouble. At the airport Mr. Yeoh tried without success to book us all back to London via Aeroflot. Having pocketed our money in advance, he took off alone on the first Aeroflot flight available; when his flight was detoured to Moscow, he deplaned without a visa and was promptly clapped in jail.

With Mr. Yeoh out of the picture and Mr. Athisayam sidelined for incompetence, Miss Khoo was left to deal with the mess and forty angry journalists. She managed to get us as far as Kuala Lumpur where things unraveled further. The word from Karachi was that spare parts for our plane had arrived from London, but the Pakistani authorities wouldn't let them through customs.

That ripped it for the Danes who abandoned our group on the spot, threatening to sue Miss Khoo in the process. Then the Swedes exploded, upbraiding the British reporters for not taking charge of the mess. The *Evening Standard* man lashed back and asked where "the bloody Swedes" were in the last war. The Reuters man started shouting at Miss Khoo. Miss Khoo dissolved in tears. The *Guardian* man stepped in, gallantly claiming she was the victim of circumstance and not to be blamed. Personally, I wouldn't have trusted Miss Khoo to call me a cab.

Three days later our plane was repaired and ready for departure from Kuala Lumpur. Mr. Yeoh had been sprung from jail; Miss

Khoo vowed she was leaving his employ anyhow. Mr. Athisayam had recovered his confidence and was making little command noises again. At our last dinner in Kuala Lumpur, the *Evening Standard* man in his thick Scots' burr recited verse by Robert Burns. It being the poet's two hundred twelfth birthday, we celebrated by draining a fifth of Glenlivet.

A dull glow hung in the skies over Belfast the evening I returned on my fourth tour.

There'd been a huge fire near the city docks, the work of arsonists. The glow, visible from the airport, had an almost apocalyptic tinge. The latest violence had been the worst in more than a year. I drove down darkened streets past groups of police huddled in doorways and hard-looking men lounging in front of pubs, all watching, waiting for something to happen. In the rock-littered streets that had echoed to gunshots only hours before, there was a sense of spent force and energy; but only for the moment.

Belfast was a city rocked by nightly explosions, its residents sunk in black despondency. By night they cowered in their homes while street battles raged outside; by day they trooped to the funerals of the victims. The shopping crowds had thinned; housewives no longer ventured downtown for fear of bombings. Bus service was virtually halted after sundown, the drivers fearful of hijackings; the buses made effective street barricades.

The weaponry had acquired further refinement: ammonia bombs that could blind a person; nail bombs that could perforate an army Scout car or shred a man's legs at twenty yards. Children now comprised nearly a quarter of the police arrests and a horrifying portion of the casualties. The week I was in Belfast a fourteen-year-old Catholic boy had his hand blown off as he set to hurl a gelignite bomb; a five-year-old girl was killed by a Scout car pursuing bands of rock throwers.

The IRA had stepped up its vigilante justice against suspected informers or "touts." The penalty was no longer just kneecapping, but a bullet through the mouth. More chilling was the vengeance directed at the troops who were increasingly viewed as brutal occupiers. The IRA issued a vow: two soldiers dead for every one Irishman killed. Both sides had upped the ante.

By now I'd developed sources beyond the officials and politicians on both sides. I'd begun approaching the IRA leaders in their lair.

In the garage behind his tiny Dublin home the IRA's chain-smoking chief of staff, Cathal Goulding, boasted of his power — five thousand armed regulars — and warned that things would get worse ("British soldiers are going to get killed.") And so they did. The week I reached Belfast, three Royal Highland Fusiliers, unarmed and in mufti, were lured away from their downtown pub crawl and brought to a lonely country road where they were shot. The body of one of the soldiers was propped against a tree, still holding a glass of beer. The killings unleashed fresh outrage among Protestants.

Seventy-five miles west of Dublin, in a stucco house in Roscommon, I found Rory Brady, a seasoned IRA terrorist, in his slippers and tattered sweater. Brady, commander of the breakaway IRA Provisionals, had masterminded much of the guerilla violence in the north. The authorities had tapped his phone, so he spoke to his associates in a Gaelic patois. The phone rang in the middle of our interview. A voice on the other end whispered the news that the British commander in Belfast had just collapsed from a heart attack. Brady laughed and hung up.

I was put in touch with a high-ranking officer of the IRA's Belfast Brigade. He used a fake name, Quinn. His men escorted a photographer and me to the Catholic Falls Road neighborhood. As we approached a row of shabby red brick homes, a stranger appeared, pointed silently toward Quinn's door, then melted back into the shadows. Inside, Quinn, a heavyset man with a shock of gray hair, motioned us to follow him upstairs. In his bedroom he and his aides donned masks to shield their identities in the photographs.

Quinn spoke to the feelings of militant Catholics on both sides of Ireland's borders. Partition was the root of the evil, a cruel injustice. The British troops had to go. They'd broken and entered Catholic homes, ordered families evicted and put out on the streets. "They've slept in our beds and pilfered our ornaments." There was no solution but counterforce. And, eventually, the sheer exhaustion from mutual slaughter.

The Cold War was still with us.

Britain had two early-warning systems against nuclear attack. One was a network of sophisticated electronic detectors like the radar dishes swivelling round the clock at the RAF Flyingdales Base in Yorkshire. The other was a network of civilian volunteers known as the Royal Observer Corps. The ROC manned its own alert systems from John o' Groat's to Land's End. I took it on myself to inspect one of the key links in the ROC's early-warning network: Joe Elwen of Boon Hill Farm, Cumberland.

Elwen's farm sat high on a hill miles from nowhere. Joe, a ruddy-faced man with smoke-stained teeth, explained how he'd gotten to be such a vital cog in his nation's nuclear defense system. The police had come by and asked if he'd object to "their puttin' an early-warning system in me house." He said no, and an inspector drove out to install it.

The system comprised a tinny box shaped like a cash register with a red volume-control wheel that emitted a series of bleeps when switched on. The box was attached to the phone in Joe's living room. It was linked directly to the ROC's regional headquarters in Carlisle, twenty miles away, and from there to both the main RAF operations in High Wycombe and the Ministry of Defense in London.

Joe had been left a set of written instructions that were quite explicit. If the bleeper issued a warbling note followed by a spoken message — "Attack Warning Red" — it meant nukes were on the way. Joe then had to sound his siren for a full minute. Siren? Joe lugged it into the living room, a clunky World War II device that had arrived in pieces in a crate and been assembled by Joe and his son. Joe began cranking the siren by hand. A low wail filled the room. A cow outside answered.

On a good day when the cows were quiet the siren could be heard for two miles. Except that Joe had never gotten around to testing it. Mrs. Elwen explained. "They told us to start cranking the moment we had an attack warning, but that we'd only have three minutes to take cover ourselves. Who's going to take the time cranking?" The instructions also stated that Joe should activate the system once a week to check that the bleeps were getting through. This, too, he'd disregarded. "What good would it do? If the bombs come, where would everyone go? Down a rabbit hole?" Besides, the bleeping would get on his nerves.

Mr. Elwen apparently didn't truckle to the awesomeness of his responsibility. He'd never for a moment entertained the notion of a missile attack that might vaporize all the RAF's fancy radar dishes, leaving only the Boon Hill bleeper intact. In fact, they'd had a hard time finding Joe during the last practice alert. The local weekly had bannered the story, STOP THAT BOMB — JOE'S IN THE PUB. His neighbors continued to pray that no attack would come while Joe was hoisting a few at the Blacksmith's Arms. "At least it'd be a fine way to go," Joe said.

Time's new chief of correspondents, Murray Gart, flew into town one summer's day to warn us that the magazine faced drastic cost-cutting, staff-shrinking days ahead. In London the staff shrinking would begin on the spot. Gart made me an offer I couldn't refuse: chief correspondent in Canada and Ottawa bureau chief. I would make the move in a month.

Ada was devastated and hurled one or two household furnishings my way. The kids reacted with equanimity, even pleased at the thought of moving nearer home. We'd have welcomed another year in London, but I knew professionally the move was a step up. Besides, the big stories had assumed a predictable pattern — election campaigns every year or so, the metronomic labor strikes, the ritual royal soap operas. I was ready to go. But not before one last investigative jaunt.

Long before the Harry Potter craze, the Loch Ness Monster had captured the world's imagination. Nessie was everyone's favorite mystery, the subject of countless "sightings," the darling of Scotland's tourist industry. Said to be lurking in the depths of an ancient Highland lake, she had defied all attempts to verify her existence. I headed north to Inverness.

Of all the legendary serpents thought to inhabit Scotland's lochs since the dawn of time, none was more storied than the Loch Ness Monster. She was variously described as a humpbacked creature, forty to fifty feet long, with a serpentine neck, large flippers, and an absurdly small head. Her habitat, a murky freshwater lake five hundred miles north of London, had begun to challenge Big Ben and the Eiffel Tower as a prime tourist destination.

"Nessie" was said to be an evolved form of plesiosaur, part of a family of marine reptiles that had become extinct some seventy million years ago. Her forebears may have been survivors of a breeding herd of these giant amphibians, cut off from the sea at the end of the last ice age when melting glaciers had puddled hundreds of fjords and sounds throughout the valleys of northern Britain.

The Roman scholar Pliny and the early Norsemen had heard of the monsters. St. Columba, the great monk of Iona, had encountered one in the Loch Ness region in A.D. 565, according to the saint's biographer. In Cromwell's time, ministers in their Inverness parishes referred to Nessie's forebears as evil omens of death. Sea captains in the seventeenth century acknowledged the "floating islands" in the Loch. Even so reputable a local as Lord Malmesbury claimed in 1857 that his game stalker had sighted Nessie.

On the heels of the latest reported sightings in 1971, the narrow road encircling the twenty-four-mile-long loch had become clogged with trailers, land rovers, autos, and motor bikes, all conveying hordes of the curious. Inns and lodges were booked solid, every available lochside parking spot taken by camera and binocular-toting visitors intently studying the unfathomable waters.

I stopped by the field headquarters of the Loch Ness Investigation Bureau (LNI). Its honchos were a reputable lot and included the head of the Academy of Applied Science in Boston; the eminent British naturalist Peter Scott; and a former aeronautical engineer named Tim Dinsdale. They had been probing Loch Ness for years with mixed success. "I've seen the bloody thing," Dinsdale insisted. In 1960 he'd filmed the suspect from a roadside vantage point; now he screened the film for me. What I saw was a humpish blob moving through the water, creating a distinct V-wake. The Royal Air Force, after studying the film, had concluded only that the blob was some form of animate object.

The Nessie sighters were not easily discouraged, least of all the local Chamber of Commerce. For Loch Ness in summer, nestled amid hills abloom with yellow primrose, was an inviting spot. The sheer size of the loch, the largest cubic volume of fresh water in the kingdom, argued the case it might indeed harbor a monster or two. Besides, the hunters' technology was improving: digital sonar, high-tech miniature subs, hydrophone buoys to detect Nessie's grunts and thrashings. The excitement quickened.

A Hollywood film crew arrived to shoot a monster movie. They spent weeks preparing a mechanically controlled monster that was set afloat on the loch and promptly sank. The tourists kept coming along with the sharpies and promoters. The Cutty Sark whiskey people offered two million dollars to whoever captured Nessie alive and unharmed. The response was immediate. Hundreds of bounty hunters from as far away as Florida and Nigeria embarked for the Highlands, although a Mississippi housewife scoffed at the offer.

"Capture the monster?" she said. "I've been living with him for twenty-seven years."

I persuaded the prior of the Benedictine abbey at the loch's far end to row me to the spot where he claimed to have spotted Nessie on a halcyon July morning thirty years earlier. The prior was quite persuasive. Still, I had my doubts, given the brisk little trade the abbey's tourist shop was doing and what I detected was the prior's affinity for the liqueur bearing the name of his order.

Most of the serious press dismissed the idea of Nessie. The respected *Economist* observed, however, that just because monster spotting had become a big time sport, "it does not follow that monsters don't exist." I agreed. After a week circumventing the loch with my high-powered binocs, poring over sonograms and detailed LNI reports, plus interviewing the pillars of the local gentry, I was ready to accept that *something* lurked in the bowels of Loch Ness.

Accordingly I wired New York: "Have just filled out Cutty Sark registration form. Stop. Have secured collapsible rubber raft and blow darts. Stop. Plan to donate reward money to favorite charity. Colon. Small Aberdeen distillery run by one of my forebears." I judged from the lack of response that the editors were just as glad I was on my way to Ottawa.

We decided to make our way to Canada circuitously. En route we would pay homage to the shrines of my ancestors — the memorial at Dunoon, the ruins of Toward Castle, what remained of Ardlamont House. We'd have a taste of the Emerald Isle, too, leprechauns and all. Scotland worked out fine. Ireland was another story.

A sopping rain dogged us throughout. The windshield wipers on our car malfunctioned; we lost our way from the Belfast airport to Ballygally on the Antrim coast. Our first night in Ballygally Castle a spotlight beamed into our bedroom. At Bunkeg the hotel band kept us up till dawn; the same in Sligo where the amplified guitars could be heard in the next county. At the inn near Ballyrougham two women in the next room caroused through the night; each time Ada banged on the wall, the women got louder. I'd have joined Yeats in the Dumfries graveyard just for relief. When I spotted the bartender bringing the women drinks at breakfast the next morning, I lost my temper.

Dingle, with its sublime bay and curving beach, offered a balm of sorts. Still, the Irish have a curious way with their beaches. They cover them with litter and gallop horses up and down them. The beach was scattered with picnic leavings, horse dung, and the trash from vanfuls of tinkers, or gypsies. The hotel was a lunatic asylum. Three valets broke down our bedroom door after we'd entrapped ourselves due to a faulty lock. The girls' toilet overflowed. At dinner I found a large worm disporting in my salad. Our nights were given over to a barking dog and, when he gave up at dawn, to a barnyard symphony of pigs and sheep.

"Romantic Ireland's dead and gone," Yeats wrote. "It's with O'Leary in the grave." He had a point.

Not that Canada was exactly a romantic notion.

Nanook of the North, Nelson Eddy, Jeanette MacDonald, and the singing Mounties had done their best, but history and clime had teamed against the place. There was little romantic about its long indenture to the redcoats and Jesuit black robes, its struggles to tame a cold and unforgiving land. Winter came early and ran into summer. Canadians spent much of their lives in earmuffs and galoshes, resentfully tolerating their neighbors to the south who tended to regard them, patronizingly, as an extension of Nebraska.

In the fall of 1971 we reached Ottawa and settled in within sight of the Gothic spires of Canada's Parliament buildings. Our new home in Rockcliffe Park was across the road from an outdoor hockey rink. The children were enrolled in neighborhood schools within walking distance. We finished unpacking just as the October snows arrived.

Our first winter in Ottawa was one of the coldest and longest on record. We bundled up like Inuits each time we ventured out. (By May the snowdrifts were still head-high outside the house.) Weekends we joined the fur-hatted multitudes skating along the boundless reaches of the Rideau Canal. The bond between ice and Canadians is metaphysical, like wine and the French. I remember the sheer delirium in the Toronto Arena at the opener of the historic hockey series between Canada and the Soviet Union. When Canada triumphed in the final game, the nation's business came to a virtual halt.

Shortly after our arrival, thieves broke in while we were sleeping and made off with the television set and record player. The police up the road acted swiftly. They impounded several of our most valued furnishings in their search for forensic evidence and urged us to bolt our doors more securely. Word spread that the nice new Americans had gotten a rum welcome. Soon a few of the neighbors came calling with words of sympathy. Our social schedule took a bump up.

It helped that in Ottawa, a tenth the size of Washington, I was something of a player in the foreign community. As *Time*'s chief correspondent, I was nominally in charge of a half dozen other staff correspondents in Montreal, Toronto, Vancouver, plus the Ottawa bureau. We serviced our weekly Canadian edition of *Time*, which carried several pages of domestic news. Our stories, assembled by a team of Montreal-based editors, were read by a million or more Canadians, though they seldom appeared in the magazine's U.S. edition. Too many editors in New York thought Canada a great white waste of time.

In fact, the country was a splendid training ground for journalists. Many of the most successful had gravitated south and burnished their reputations with the *New York Times* or the major TV networks. Canadian-born publishers would, in the Baron Beaverbrook tradition, stamp their imprimatur on the British and U.S. news industries. Canada's intelligentsia boasted a disproportionately high number of world-class scholars, writers, and states-men — from Margaret Atwood to Lester Pearson. Its cities, like Montreal and Toronto, possessed cultural and corporate sophistica-tion. Vancouver with its shimmering skyline and mountain views was a sensualist's dream.

Ottawa, a company town like Washington, was political hub to a nation of twenty-seven million people. The city felt small, perched on a high plain above the Ottawa River, facing the empty Gatineau Hills that stretched north into the vastnesses of Quebec. Like most capitals it had its incestuous overtones, too many power-driven bureaucrats and mandarins bathing in each other's bath-water. The city served as dateline for most of the big stories affect-ing Canadians' destiny: Quebec separatism, the fractious regional-ism of the English-speaking provinces, the love-hate relationship with America.

Covering Ottawa was measurably simpler than covering Lon-don or Washington. In Ottawa, shoe-leather reporting amounted to a short walk from our office to Parliament Hill where all federal power was concentrated. I quickly established contact with key party leaders among the ruling Liberals, the opposition Progres-sive Conservatives, and Canada's third party, the socialist New Democrats.

The prime minister's office adjoined the main Parliament building and was tougher to penetrate than Loch Ness. Its occu-pant, Pierre Elliott Trudeau, had vaulted to power in the wake of a 1968 riot in Montreal. In the final throes of his campaign for the prime ministership, Trudeau had faced down a mob of rock-throwing separatists. His coolness under fire, his offbeat flair and erudition set off nationwide Trudeaumania. The electorate gave him and the Liberals a thumping victory at the polls that year.

Two years later, Trudeau had emerged from Canada's worst terrorist crisis as a hero, albeit a controversial one. When Quebec militants kidnapped and murdered a provincial government official, Trudeau had called out federal troops and imposed martial law. After that he was seen not only as an uncompromising foe of separatism but as a steely authoritarian. The role belied Trudeau's foppish persona: he dressed like a Bohemian, quoted Racine, and squired beautiful women about town.

When I first met Trudeau all my preconceptions of him as a Kennedyesque figure vanished. He was far more understated and opaque, anything but the dynamic statesman his press had led me to expect. He lacked the gravitas that distinguished a Lester Pearson or a John Diefenbaker, prime ministers whom American presidents took seriously even in disagreement. Yet his fiercely independent streak, his quintessentially Canadian reserve, attracted voters. Trudeau would persevere through three more elections over another decade before retiring, the most remarkable Canadian of his generation.

However bonded to America as ally and neighbor, Canada in foreign affairs increasingly followed its own star. It cozied up to suspect Third World governments and slashed its once respected armed forces to the bone. It instituted unfriendly moves against U.S. firms seeking to invest in Canada. Its political center shifted markedly to the left, away from Nixon's assertively conservative America. Trudeau kept his distance from Washington. As Lyndon Johnson had roughed up Pearson for opposing the Vietnam War, so Nixon abominated Trudeau, seeing him as a feckless meddler in the peace negotiations and, worse, an unrepentant swinger.

Ada and I sensed a certain coolness toward Americans in Ottawa. But one day a Rockcliffe Park neighbor invited us over for tea. He was an engaging fellow, a rising Liberal star in Canada's House of Commons, a former Rhodes Scholar at Oxford; he read *Time*. His name was John Turner and eventually he'd become prime minister. We made more contacts after that, other young comers in Canada's government and journalistic circles, some of whom would remain friends for life.

Marshall McLuhan, the prophet of electronic communications, spun his concepts about the global village from a cubbyhole office at the University of Toronto. His book *The Medium Is the Message* had become the new age's bible while catapulting him to global celebrity. McLuhan forecast that television and the computer would radically transform the old linear communications like newspapers and news magazines. He'd even singled out *Time* and its sister publications for their "glossy mediocrity and stereotypical order."

I thought my bosses in New York might profit from McLuhan's insights and arranged for a sit-down with him. The meeting in Toronto went off well, though the more earthbound types like me could decipher only a few odd bytes of the conversation. McLuhan was at his wildly brilliant best, offering breathtaking assertions about what the cybernetic future held for us mortals, "throwing up ideas as effortlessly as a wet dog throws off drops of water," in Henry Grunwald's words. It was easily the most stimulating encounter I'd had since that long-ago afternoon in Princeton with Robert Oppenheimer.

On a maiden trip to Canada's far northwest I got to know a personable young French Canadian politician, Jean Chrétien. He was Trudeau's minister of Indian affairs, responsible for the welfare of the native peoples of the vast Yukon and Northwest Territories. Chrétien, too, would one day become prime minister.

The trip was an eye-opener for him and for the reporters accompanying him across the once pristine Yukon subtundra. Man had intruded on this part of the world in callous ways.

The single-gauge railway from Skagway, British Columbia to Whitehorse in the Yukon passed mining sites where whole mountains of virgin pine and spruce had been denuded, replaced by a slate gray mush yielding tons of lucrative copper and asbestos. Miners had gouged open-pit wounds amid the hills and dumped acres of unsightly tailings near once translucent streams and lakes.

Flying north from Whitehorse, we could see everywhere piles of abandoned oil drums and oil surveyors' seismic lines knifing through the green fir forests. As we approached the Beaufort Sea at the northern edge of the Yukon, the land below was cluttered with portable housing units, huge graders, and trucks. The vehicles' tracks had scratched their way across the fragile permafrost, leaving a crisscross of scars, like Martian canals, on the natural tapestry of the landscape.

Canada's native peoples, forced to adapt to the extractive intruders, hung on barely. Mutual resentment lay heavy in the air like the summer heat. Pressured to abandon their villages, younger Indians had fled to the urban centers of the south, leaving their elders to cope with the white man's machine culture, his patronizing, and his liquor. In the Klondike, we cruised the Yukon River on a paddlewheeler, past deserted villages with names like Old Crow and Moosehide, their log cabins and schoolhouses slowly, sadly disintegrating.

In Dawson, the ghosts of Jack London and Robert Service flitted through the boarded-up buildings where swallows now tenanted. There, a decade ago, the authorities had whipped Indian children for bringing native food to school or for conversing in their tribal language. Once Dawson had been a prosperous mining center. Now its only income stream came from Diamond-Tooth Gertie's saloon, a tourist joint. The night we looked in, "Boom-Boom" Montana, a character who carried dynamite caps in his pants, was celebrating his release from jail for blowing up Gertie's the previous New Year's eve.

At a crowded bar in Inuvik one evening the tensions spilled over. A drunken Inuit was demanding another whiskey. The barmaid's response carried clear across the room. "If you can't behave like a white man when you're in a white man's place, then get out!" I watched the Inuit stifle a cry of rage, turn on his heel, and lurch out the door.

The natives of the Yukon had become part of the detritus of

industrialization. They mourned the squalor in their lives, their degraded status in a white man's world. The Chief of the Yukon Natives Brotherhood sat by my side on the plane next day, gazing out the window at the landscape below. "The Indian still thinks of that land as his," he said, "and no white man's laws can change his mind."

At the northernmost point of our trip we landed on tiny Herschel Island off the Yukon coast. It was a desolate, abandoned place speckled with reminders of the brutish life endured by its few inhabitants. A pair of whitewashed rocks marked the remains of two Inuits who had dug their own graves before being hanged for murder early in the century.

On a hilly field I came across a small plot enclosed by a picket fence. Inside was a single headstone that read: "CST. A. Lamont, RNWMP, d. 14 February 1918." I had found a kinsman. A constable who had died in the service of the Royal Northwest Mounted Police. Much later I learned how he'd come to this lonely interment.

Alexander Lamont had been born a Scot in Invernesshire. Fatherless at thirteen, he'd had to leave school and shift for himself. He had emigrated to the U.S. in 1910, and found his way to Alberta where he'd joined the Mounties. He had been transferred to the RNWMP outpost on Herschel Island. There in January 1918, the explorer Vilhjalmur Stefansson had come calling. Stefansson was suffering from what he thought was a severe cold; Constable Lamont helped nurse him back to health. In the course of his succoring, Lamont had contracted a fatal case of typhoid fever.

In the bitter Watergate year of 1972 my mother died.

Back from a trip abroad, and exhausted, she'd flown to Boston to watch her Milton grandson, our Dougie, play football against Groton. On a damp November afternoon she'd stood on a ridge above the gridiron, letting the fall chill envelop her. That evening she'd complained of a terrific headache and was rushed to the hospital. It was a massive stroke from which she never regained consciousness.

Growing up, I'd remained close to my mother. She was always of two minds about the wayfaring profession I'd chosen. Through my tears I recalled a passage from a John McNulty piece about his youth and his mother's doubts about his yen for playing jazz piano. "But it's all right, John," she'd said, holding him closely. "It's what you want to do. I don't understand it, but it's what is in your heart. And I gave you your heart."

Mother had lived a life outwardly that expressed her inner spirit and grace. She had a laugh like crystal bells. They'd have tinkled merrily had she seen how the spoils were divided after her death. Things went well till someone discovered a cache of old FAO Schwarz toy soldiers in an upstairs closet of the Long Island house. My brother, my brother-in-law, and I laid equal claim to the cache. The squabbling grew heated, three adult males intent on recapturing a piece of their childhood — several-score West Point cadets molded in lead, remnants of an infamous trade made more than three decades before. It was a defining moment in the annals of property-right disputes.

The weeks flew by.

I reported political developments, monitored the government's efforts to reduce *Time*'s presence in Canada (we were a competitive threat to their own news magazine industry), and periodically visited our bureaus across the country where I got a taste of the personnel problems that went with my posting: a correspondent with a near-fatal booze addiction; another, a Canadian, who resented having to answer to a U.S. superior. Our lonely Vancouver correspondent welcomed salmon dinners with me whenever I dropped into town. He was a Swiss who filed on deadline with clockwork precision and would one day become the magazine's managing editor.

On all my wanderings I never ceased to marvel that such a heterogeneous people, separated by such vast distances, could maintain even a semblance of unity. However proud of their nation, they fought among themselves like a coven of fishwives. I listened to oil men in Alberta excoriate the bankers on Toronto's Bay Street. On Newfoundland's barren rock, over a blinding rum drink called "screech," I heard the natives call down maledictions on the far-away Feds in Ottawa; the Newfies had more in common with Greenlanders. As for the fire-breathing separatists of northern Quebec, they habitually referred to anglophones in terms unfit for print.

From time to time I escaped work to join the family bobsledding under the icicled turrets of the Château Frontenac during Quebec City's winter carnival or to cheer the bronco busters at the Calgary rodeo or sample the snows of British Columbia's serried peaks. We heli-skied the Bugaboos and took the children on a summer trip, horsebacking across the heights of the Selkirk Range. I watched my daughters and youngest son bloom in the invigorating Canadian frost.

Hidden among the self-important bureaucrats and journalists who populated Ottawa was an unpretentious Canadian, a cultural treasure named Yousuf Karsh. An Armenian who'd emigrated to Canada decades earlier, he had become the world's preeminent portrait photographer. Karsh could transform the drabbest hausfrau into a Garbo. He kept his studio up the street from our office in the Château Laurier Hotel. To be photographed by him — to be "Karshed" — was like buying a piece of immortality. One day, when business was a bit slow, I visited his studio. He sat me down before a large unwieldy contraption mounted on a tripod, and I got "Karshed."

In the summer of 1972 Canada's incumbent Liberals fought the Progressive Conservatives in a telling election. By then the bloom was off Trudeau, the one-time wunderkind of Canadian politics. His profligate spending, much of it on costly welfare programs, had angered the business community; conservative westerners recoiled at his lifestyle and his bilingualism policies, forcing French down their throats; he was anathema to the separatist Quebecois. He won the election by only a narrow margin.

People said his opponent, a former premier of Nova Scotia, who lost the next election as well, was "the best prime minister Canada never had." I thought otherwise. Trudeau, for all his faults, was the last world-class prime minister Canada would have in my time.

A year later, one June day, the Lamonts drove across the border for the last time, reentering the U.S. amid the green hills of Vermont. I would miss Canada and my Canadian friends.

As we were waved through customs, an old Noël Coward line came to mind, something about loving America, "every scrap of it/all the sentimental crap of it." So we high-fived each other and stomped the floor in glee as we belted out a nearly on-key version of "God Bless America." We were home.

11

The Road to Autumn

My whirlwind life took a more measured turn, slowed from Force Six to a steady northerly. I mothballed my trench coat.

The New York I returned to as *Time*'s United Nations bureau chief was a city under siege.

After nearly thirty years I was back for good in the city of my birth and it was as though my time machine had locked gears. Nothing had changed, everything had changed.

Manhattan's unspoken landmarks remained in place, the old racial and class dividing lines. The Upper East Side's 96th Street still separated the luxury apartment buildings of the white upper class from the squalor of Spanish Harlem. Real estate brokers still didn't show certain buildings to blacks; when we moved into a co-op on 80th Street and Lexington Avenue, it had only recently admitted its first Jewish tenants. Except for a handful of new corporate structures enhancing the downtown skyline, little had changed architecturally. The natives still spoke with hard "t"s.

What had changed was the quality of life. New York under a succession of feeble mayors had become a wreck. Bankruptcy and lawlessness threatened. Bulging garbage bags clotted the cross-streets. The parks were infested with drug dealers, panhandlers, and punks with ghetto blasters. The homeless helped themselves to the sidewalks, park benches, and any available subway seat. The "squeegee" men with their soap and rags would ambush your car. On our litter-strewn street a mugger relieved me of all my cash one evening. "What a mess! This town's in tatters," Mick Jagger sang.

Our building, a handsome Rosario Candela creation with leaky walls and leakier security, was run by people we suspected of being as corrupt as they were inept. Shortly after we moved in, a jewel thief invaded our apartment and made off with Ada's engagement ring and other pieces. It took the building more than a year to rid itself of the culpable doorman. Faced with recurring leaks and faulty repair work, we were defenseless against the reassuring words of our building agent who turned out to be as indictably crooked as we'd first imagined.

Within months things came to a scorching head. I awoke at midnight, smelling smoke, and hurried to the window. Waves of soot were pouring from windows in the duplex directly beneath us. We gathered the children and rushed down the back stairs in our bathrobes. The lobby was empty, a single fire truck idling on the street outside. No one knew yet the horror that was enveloping the duplex. Its owner, the estranged wife of a prominent designer, had fallen asleep by a log fire in her paneled library; a spark had landed on the rug, igniting it.

The blaze became a fireball trapping and killing the woman and her two daughters as they tried to escape up the stairs. The son, a little boy Tommy knew, pounded on the walls and was rescued by firemen at the last moment. Outside on the avenue we watched the inferno consume the duplex, sure that our apartment would go next. It didn't, thanks to old-fashioned buttressing of reinforced steel and cement between the floors. We returned to the lobby: three body bags had just been brought down from the eleventh floor.

This was our reentry to the city I loved. We mourned the neighbors' tragedy and thanked our stars for having survived. Then I fired off a long-delayed letter of outrage to our building realtor. I was quickly becoming, once again, a New Yorker down to my last surly capillary.

It took a while to readjust to a place whose fixation was money, not politics.

New York was, disconcertingly, a city unlike London, Washington, or Ottawa. It reveled in the white-hot glare of big lucre. The city's social, political, and cultural forces depended on it. People gave dinners not for the pleasure of conversation, but to plug special causes and charities. Our mailbox overflowed with invitations to events benefiting everything from down-at-the-heel opera groups to Jesuit day schools in the Bronx. I thought briefly of Oscar Wilde's remark that philanthropy had become "the refuge of people who wish to annoy their fellow creatures," then joined the crowd.

Among our new friends was an owlish looking fellow in Savile Row threads who worked undercover at the United Nations for Britain's Secret Intelligence Service (SIS), better known as MI6. He looked about as much like a spy as my dentist. But then the Brits played the game more suavely, kept their covers better.

Alastair Rellie had earned his spurs in watering spots like Cairo and Kinshasha, turning Soviet agents, ferreting out their secrets, rising steadily within "The Firm." He professed a yen for American jazz and mobsters, which suited me fine. He was considerably vague about the details of his job as an obscure third secretary at the U.K. Mission. It was my fate to fall into Rellie's orbit. He and his antic wife admitted Ada and me to their exclusive Friday Night Club: membership, four.

After a late dinner we'd sally forth in Rellie's Maserati, headed downtown for the jazz spots. He favored a place under the Brooklyn Bridge called the Ali Baba. It was run by Cypriot gangsters (Rellie palmed himself off as "Al Asterelli", an East London wiseguy) and featured obliging women at the bar. It stayed open till 4 A.M. and we stayed open with it. Occasionally we might venture farther south to the Village for a predawn nightcap at Umberto's where Joey Gallo had been rubbed out in mid-linguini. It occurred to me and my exhausted wife that we'd taken up company with the busiest nighthawk since Hamlet's ghost, the Spy Who Never Slept.

Years later, when Rellie had retired after a distinguished career that earned him a C.M.G. ("Call Me God") from the queen, he asked me to be toastmaster at his sixtieth birthday party in London. We walked through the entrance of Brooks's that evening and the club was wall to wall with black-tied 007s, a reunion of Rellie's SIS mates. They seemed puzzled by my presence, trying to place me as perhaps a lost member of their tribe. Rellie by then was selling missiles at an arms emporium from somewhere in the Cotswolds. He missed the old days chasing KGB types. The game was now all gray and bottom-line. "Industrial espionage, that sort of crap, nothing to whet the appetite," he groused.

I didn't trust him, though. He was a deceiver, probably back in the Congo on weekends buying off rebel tribesman. Maybe up to some hugger-muggery in Kabul or Khirgizstan. Had me fooled for a while. One of the few spooks I knew who genuinely classed up the business.

North Haven kept to its own revivifying pace.

On a summer morn the island ferry, horn blaring, gunnels jammed with vacationers, would sweep down the Thoroughfare, its wash rocking the dinghies and lobster boats at their moorings. The windjammers with their boisterous cargos might shatter the quiet of our harbors from time to time; the mail plane or occasional chopper jolt our beach-and-hammock reveries. But there was always, too, the osprey's cry, the croak of the heron feeding along our farm pond, the waves lapping on our stony beach. High above us the transatlantic jets carved vapor trails across a cerulean sky. One or two freighters skulked like alligators far across the bay in the shadow of the Camden hills. We doted on our isolation, our serenity.

For more than half a century our island had resisted the intrusions of "progress." It had defied conventional summering on the grand scale, preferring the small incremental changes that fit its character. In the village, of a fresh July, you might hear the thonk of hammer on iron as a lone carpenter went about renovating the old saltbox next to the Legion Hall, or stop to admire the modest stock of new books and pewterware June Hopkins was laying out in her gift shop. Change was on a human scale: David Cooper, the mailman, tuning up his chops, training for a side career on the local stage; Bill Hamlen finally tying the knot.

One by one, our kinfolk passed and left us poorer. Ada's sainted mother, Alma Jung, collapsed in her Sheboygan home before Christmas, wise and strong of heart to the last. And one spring afternoon we buried Corliss's second wife, Helen, in the family plot at Englewood. We stood in a little knot, the sun streaming through an overhang of elms, as Corliss read from Santayana. I thought his voice would break, but it held.

We'd seen Helen last at a family lunch at Ossining, where she and Corliss had a weekend retreat by the Hudson. The cancer had etched pain lines on her face; the chemo had wasted her digestive tract. She was too weak to carve the lamb she'd cooked. Afterward we played tennis, Corliss leaping for balls, furiously defying his years. I sensed the anger in each lunge, his knowing Helen was back in the bedroom, exhausted, and slipping from him.

When the reading and prayers were done, I looked down and saw that I was standing on my parents' grave. Move softly, I thought. We're here again, the clan. The way we were a few short years ago when we'd buried Mother in a driving rain. We'll be here again another spring.

Time was the best of employers and I loved being a correspondent. But another tour abroad seemed less alluring, one more disruption for my family. The magazine, too, had changed.

Reflecting the changes in popular culture, *Time* no longer devoted as much space to serious stories and serious newsmakers. It was yielding more and more of its limited linage to frothy pieces geared to self-absorbed younger readers. Time Inc., the parent body, had evolved from Luce's fraternity of print journalists to a widely diversified communications conglomerate en route to becoming an even larger entertainment empire. Its magazines, once the polestars of the enterprise, now shared space with other profit-making equals like movies, records, books, and videos. The company's founding ideals and purpose had become diluted.

After a year at the U.N., reporting on international crises in the Middle East and elsewhere, I signed on as a writer in the magazine's foreign affairs section, a misjudgment. *Time*'s writers, like the U.N.'s cosseted bureaucrats, seldom exposed themselves to the world beyond their rarefied patch in the Time-Life building.

The typical writer, one of their own observed, spent his days "crouching in the blue-tinted horror of his writing hutch like an incorrigible solitary, fumbling with paper and hating himself." Correspondents, undeskbound and unused to the discipline of writing complex stories into a tight-fitting mold, had difficulty adjusting to this environment — especially those of us who compiled books on the side.

Late one evening in my twenty-third-floor hutch I watched as another writer I knew carefully arranged his office across the aisle in preparation for an all-night vigil, waiting for his copy to emerge from the laborious editing process. I remember him watering his window plant and adjusting his chair to the reclining position. In that moment, contemplating this as my future, I decided reluctantly to part ways with *Time*.

For the first time I felt professionally unmoored. But I was at work on two book projects. Freelance magazine assignments spiced my work schedule. Life opened up in other ways.

We bought a weekend house in Connecticut up the road from jazz legend Dave Brubeck and down the road from a spread once owned by the impressionist painter J. Alden Weir. Our town, fifty miles northeast of the asphalt jungle, was a bucolic holdout against the encroach of suburbia. It was a place Grandma Moses had overlooked, barely recognized on maps, ignored by the directional signs on the highways that bypassed it. The inhabitants were supremely indifferent to outsiders, given to whimsies like partying on Sunday nights and displaying their Christmas wreaths well into spring. They made the cheerfulest of friends.

Our house sat atop a rise called Nod Hill and our back meadow ran down to deep woods bordering a lake. In the spring we swam in the frog-infested pool we'd inherited from the previous owner. A mockingbird in the meadow summoned us to breakfast each morning. In the fall, the ashes and maples along the old stone walls threading our land turned to gold.

On July 4, 1976, the nation's two hundredth birthday, Americans staged an historic blowout. It was as though God had decreed one surpassing day of deliverance from the heat and thunderstorms, the wars and scandals and other woes that had been our lot of late.

On a hillside in Ada's hometown, Sheboygan, the locals whirled 1,776 Frisbees through the air; and off Manhattan a cavalcade of Tall Ships sailed up the bay, cheered on by a million spectators. We boarded a chartered fishing boat to join the celebration.

New York Harbor rocked with every variety of craft: ferry boats and weekend cruisers, Newport yachts and Brooklyn stinkpots, their rails and rigging decked with bunting. There were faux Spanish galleons and Viking ships, plus a pride of Annapolis yawls, their candy-striped spinnakers bellying before the wind. Beflagged barks and brigantines of every nationality crowded the waves.

Fireboats shot watery streamers into the blue. At the head of the parade, the carrier *Forrestal* readied to greet the president with a thunderous salute.

When the lead ship, *American Eagle*, swept under the Verrazano Bridge, the whole waterway erupted in a riot of jubilation. The *Forrestal's* guns boomed across the waters at the skyscrapers shimmering in the noon glare. The party continued that evening, fireworks bursting over the Statue of Liberty. Then it was over. The Tall Ships passed on, receding into memory. For a few glorious hours we'd felt ourselves lifted above their tallest spars.

No Harvard twenty-fifth reunion proves unrewarding.

No other college organizes reunions with such panache and egalité. The lowliest bean counter may find himself housed in palatial quarters near the president's office, while the mightiest board chairman is relegated to digs above the Dudley Hall laundromat.

The class of '52 had outdone itself living up to the popular notion that Harvard produces only future megastars. We'd turned out a Nobelist; a U.S. senator; a film star; an Olympic skating champion; two university presidents, and the world's finest harpsichordist; plus the usual array of corporate and legal whizbangs, medical geniuses, and a best-selling author or two. We'd given the country the man who unearthed the Pentagon Papers.

The rest of us needed to be reassured there were those among us who had *not* claimed (on the class questionnaire) lives of immaculateness, careers triumphant, wives and offspring worthy of sainthood. We needed to discover and console those who had married lemons, reared idiot children, and filed for Chapter 11. We needed to buy drinks all around for those unfortunates who had slid from grace.

So when we convened beneath the Cambridge elms that June of 1977, I sought out the beamish boy from Dunster F-14 whom I'd last seen passed out in a display window of Macy's. I never found him or the classmate who'd stuffed my mailbox over the years with reams of loopy handwritten letters. I did find the chap whose bio-sketch in our class report had noted, without further explanation, the abrupt end of his career in counterintelligence; also, the bank-rupt who'd ended up driving a taxicab.

After three decades under Mao, during which the country shut itself off from the West, China in 1978 opened its doors a crack to Western visitors, Ada and I among them.

Mao's cultural revolution had decimated China's urban profes-sional and intellectual class. Now, following his death two years earlier, the nation was trying to detoxify itself of its worst Maoist sins. The year we visited China was the year of its Great Thaw.

We flew in via Iran, a country also on the verge of upheaval. The pro-western Shah faced a revolution led by Iran's powerful theocrats who resented his efforts to wrest the Islamic nation from its backward religious past and propel it into the modern world.

The evening we reached Tehran, rioting was reported in Isfahan to the south, a city we planned to visit en route home. Just before our scheduled tour of the Shah's palace, army tanks rolled into its courtyard to seal off the premises. On that uneasy note our jet lifted off the next night, headed east across Afghanistan and the Hindu Kush, on over the Himalayas and the deserts of western China, to Beijing.

My first contact with the Chinese was not auspicious. I'd mis-placed my vaccination card. I was escorted to an anteroom in the airport terminal where guards and nurses from the People's Liberation Army swarmed about me, demanding proof of my small-pox shot and probing my arms for needle scars. To my rescue came a member of our group, the redoubtable Mrs. Alexander Morgan. Her vaccination card was also missing, but she had wiles to equal the Dowager Empress's. With one disdainful sweep of her arm, she hoisted her Halston skirt to thigh level to show the shocked officials what she insisted was her latest vaccination scar. In the ensuing tur-moil, we were both released.

The decimation of China's mandarinate and intelligentsia, the architectural atrocities of Mao's socialist planners, had for a time left its cities like Beijing bereft of elegance, lifeless centers whose arid boulevards were home to mute and guarded crowds, the silence broken only by the tinkle of bicycle bells. Now everything was in motion as though China's millions were racing to make up for lost time.

Beijing's boulevards were aswirl with bikers in uniform white shirts and black trousers. Everywhere carts, trucks, and tractors, packed with workers, were headed for the factories and crop fields. Ordinary Chinese, for the first time, emerged from the curbside crowds to talk with westerners without fear of police harassment. They approached us shyly, speaking softly, telling sad tales of their shattered lives under the cultural revolution: a teacher, her career cut short by mandatory labor in a farm commune; a bright young man who'd been ordered to spend his university years in a shoe factory.

The government, realizing the folly of trying to block out the nation's imperial past, was restoring its monuments to their former luster. The Forbidden City, once off limits, now beckoned foreigners with its exalted courts and palaces. The first tourists were swarming over the newly repaired Great Wall. On the grounds of the Summer Palace, where the late Empress Dowager had once ordered eunuchs beaten to death, families paddled about on an enormous man-made lake, one of the last relics of imperial indulgence.

In the countryside the odor of night soil (human excrement) wafted through our bus windows. One day I poked my head out and the sharp edge of the window sash opened up my scalp. A "barefoot doctor" at the next stop applied first aid, then checked me into the local clinic for a tetanus shot in my rump. When I started to disrobe, the nurse screamed and ran for a translator. By the time we reached Tienanmen Square, my bandaged head throbbed and I felt like a casualty from a police riot. I almost envied Mao lying in his mausoleum, serenely embalmed under a crystal shroud.

In Hangchow, favored resort of China's early emperors, the street lights were cut off at night to save electricity. We strolled its downtown under a gibbous moon, kibitzing the sidewalk card games, listening to the murmur of couples gliding in and out of the shadows. I'd heard the city hid an even older quarter untouched by time, and set out next day with a colleague to find it. We taxied to the outskirts of a rundown complex, crossed a footbridge over a canal, and entered another world.

There, amid twisting lanes overhung with medieval looking houses, the earthy sweating face of ur-China rushed up to meet us. Peasants, harnessed to their carts like plow horses, strained under loads of scrap iron and hemp. Old men, yoked to buckets of pig swill, trotted by. Women, some with their feet bound, fanned themselves in doorways. The air was suffused with the cackle of fowl and market smells. We were aware of faces crowding the windows, of whole families pouring from their homes to stare at us. By the time we emerged from the quarter a crowd was waiting, six deep along the curb, jostling for a closer look at us — the first westerners many of them had ever seen.

Let China sleep, Napoleon had warned, *because when she awakes, the world will tremble*. China had woken at last, still bone-poor and yoked to a decrepit Communist state, but pulsating at the prospect of rejuvenation. That would come in time, haltingly.

In a park in Hangchow we'd met one Ma Kung Que and his daughter Ping-Ping. I'd offered to exchange addresses so we could correspond. We'd invited them back to the hotel for tea. Ma had smiled and apologized: he could not accept our invitation; he could not disclose his address. He and Ping-Ping said good-bye, then melted back into the faceless crowd. Ma must have suspected the Great Thaw wouldn't last. Indeed, within eight months of our encounter it would end. Beijing would reimpose its freeze on contacts with the West. Ma and his countrymen would endure another long period of isolation from the outside world.

When we reentered Iran, en route home, the country was in a state of siege. By the time we reached our hotel, the spreading revolt had consumed the country for a fortnight. Scores of Iranians had died at the hands of the army, many more in an arson attack blamed on Savak, the shah's notorious secret police. The windows in our hotel lobby had been demolished by rioters.

We would be among the last American visitors before the collapse of the shah's regime, the sack of the U.S. Embassy and the long night of America's hostage ordeal.

Some believed that the autocratic shah, having survived a quarter century in power, would weather the latest storm. The mullahs were simply jamming a lot of wind. Our traveling companions were less sure; most wished to leave as soon as possible. I thought of the great monuments of Iran's imperial past, which we might never again see, and with Ada elected to stay. We rented a car and drove south into the desert kingdom of ancient Persia.

From our room in Isfahan's El Abas Hotel I could spy army tanks moving past the turquoise mosques into the bazaar where we'd shopped just hours before. We drove on, along nearly deserted roads, past magnificent necropolises carved in sandstone cliffs, till we reached Shiraz, the former capital of Persia. From there we drove east one dawn onto a windswept plain to view the tomb of Cyrus the Great, an elevated sepulcher, solitary and commanding under a sapphire sky.

Nearby were the ruins of Persepolis, Persia's royal seat under Darius and Xerxes. It was there that the body of the slain Darius, under orders from his victorious rival, Alexander the Great, had been borne in state and given a kingly burial beside his Achaemenid forebears. The wondrous imperial gateways of Persepolis, the columns, sculptured beasts, and sublime bas-reliefs stood atop an immense limestone platform. We wandered among them, unhurried and undisturbed, the only callers in evidence.

The shah had staged an extraordinarily lavish party on the site to commemorate the twenty-five-hundredth anniversary of Persia's birth. The huge caravansary tents that had housed a coterie of privileged guests feasting on roast peacocks and foie gras were still there, spread across an acre or more, testament to the shah's last willful gesture of profligacy. Our guide spat in their direction.

I published two more books, one that reviewers hailed as "compelling," the other that sank without a trace. Then, overnight as it were, I became a public affairs executive or, more precisely, a junior impresario.

Friends persuaded me to found a Canada–United States forum at the Americas Society, a non-profit group run by the banker David Rockefeller. Throughout the eighties, the forum became the best known in New York for airing bilateral issues that impacted the frequently fractious Canada–United States relationship. Leading Canadian politicians, journalists, writers, economists, and filmmakers beat a path to our door. The barefaced discourse drew headlines in Canada and, occasionally, the wrath of its officialdom.

Once a year I took Rockefeller up to Canada on a well-choreographed tour. He was the leading private-sector statesman of his day, networking on a global scale, eagerly welcomed by kings and presidents. Aboard his private Learjet, David would crack a bottle of Chablis and begin thumbing a worn black address book that contained almost as many names and addresses as the Manhattan phone directory. I'd brief him on the current political situation in Canada; I was never sure how much got through because politics wasn't his métier and he seldom asked questions.

It was hard not to like him. He treated the help with respect, said thank you to everyone, and made a point of carrying his own clothes bag through airline terminals. He spoke softly and was known as the Mozart of modulation. He was in fact so considerate and so cultivated, so well-intentioned, so Protestantly decent that one could almost forgive his consorting with a few too many reactionary Canadian oil barons and Latin American oligarchs with their frilly wives.

The eighties were one long made-for-TV drama, and no figure better suited it than the former actor we'd elected as our fortieth president.

Ronald Reagan bestrode the decade that brought the laptop into our lives and the end of the Cold War. He did so with the surety of a confidence man, which in some ways, he was. Trained in the arts of make-believe and brimming with Rooseveltian optimism, Reagan convinced millions of Americans that good times were about to roll again after the malaise of the Carter years. No one knew what to make of the man, whether he was Pied Pipering us to paradise or Star Warring us to Armageddon. But his sunny self-assurance captivated people.

Lo and behold, the therapy began to work. Morning in America under our massager-in-chief brought glimmers of relief. The hostages in Iran were freed. The Soviets showed a more reasonable face under Gorbachev. New York City displayed the first signs of revival. Prince Charles and Di wed. Our first grandson arrived on New Year's day 1984.

It wasn't all roses. The garbage still clogged New York streets, but change was on the way. The new wealth demanded it.

The city's grasping builders, developers, insurance magnates, and Wall Street dealmakers were already changing the cultural and political face of Manhattan, demanding more competence from City Hall, muscling their way onto the boards of the big galleries, museums, and other institutions. The newcomers raised and saw to the expending of extravagant funds, coarsening the cultural climate even as they made the arts more vibrant and accessible to average New Yorkers.

The random mugger was still around, but the chokehold of organized crime had been broken. The days of the Mob's hegemony, when hoods like "Ralphie Bones" and "Willie Blah-Blah" were filling up Sheepshead Bay with stiffs, had become distant memories. When the last Mob hit occurred in 1985, a gaudy rub-out in front of a steakhouse on Third Avenue, its very exception caused an uproar.

The times had become thin for crime reporters of the Damon Runyon stripe. Newspapers with their old-time flair for the gritty and sensational had succumbed to the marketing imperatives of the telecom era. The good gray *Times* was now so larded with style and food sections it had become a weight lifter's challenge. *Time* filled its pages with enough trivia to sate the dimmest baby boomer. TV's nightly newscasts were racing to fill their half hour with health-care bromides and pet dog stories.

We were approaching informational overload. We were awash in technology and statistics, our success measured, our lives evaluated by the size of our toys, the square footage of our homes, by ratings, stock prices, and quarterly profits.

I pulled jury duty like everyone else who was not a lawyer, a doctor, or otherwise engaged in indispensable work — and therefore exempt. Occasionally I actually got to sit on a jury.

A case I heard involved a woman who was suing a glassworks because one of their casserole dishes had broken in her hands and severed a tendon. In the jury room some of us began recounting similar accidents that had befallen us.

One guy had sliced open his knee with a chainsaw. I'd once put my hand through a windowpane and still carried the scar. A little man with a thick accent spoke up. "I got my cuts, too — at Auschwitz." He rolled up his shirtsleeve to show the ID number tattooed on his arm. Then another man displayed his arm with a similar tattoo from the same camp. A third juror stood up, a big hulking guy from the Bronx. He told the other two he'd been with the U.S. Seventh Division at Auschwitz. "Hell, I liberated the both of youse!"

The television journalist John Chancellor, whom I'd come to

know, was fond of saying that his mother had always urged him to cultivate his betters because something good might rub off. Chancellor had few betters, but in my case it was apt advice. Belatedly, I befriended a number of older and wiser men.

Bill Golden, my fellow trustee at the American Museum of Natural History, a self-made man, the grandson of Jewish immigrants from Lithuania, who had given scientific advice to a string of presidents starting with Truman, retaught me the virtues of modesty and a gentle wit while becoming the closest thing I had to a rabbi. Tom Watson Jr. of IBM, our North Haven neighbor and one-time ambassador to the Soviet Union, showed me the ways of living life fully and adventurously while serving good causes; he shared with me his world views and friends, once bringing former President Carter up to Sky Farm for bird-watching and coffee.

Robert Montgomery, another island friend, the film actor who'd at one time held in his arms Hollywood's most seductive actresses, reinforced an egalitarian spirit I admired, helping me appreciate that one could swap beer and ribaldries with lobstermen while fancying fine wines and Wyeths, that courtly grace was not necessarily divorced from macho. A local found Bob one night in a cabin, buried in poker chips with two visitors: James Cagney and George Raft.

Bill Beinecke, my Yale friend with the big lopsided smile, played golf around the world when he wasn't running the S&H Green Stamps empire. Beinecke's goal was to shoot par in every country and clime before he ascended to the heavenly links. One spring he persuaded me to accompany him to the North Pole.

I knew nothing about the Pole except it was a hostile place where a polar bear could decapitate you with one sweep of its paw and when you excreted, the turds froze before they hit the ground. Our tour leader, a promoter from Las Vegas named Wheeler, apparently knew even less. When we rendezvoused with him and the rest of the group in Edmonton, Alberta, he announced we'd be attempting the longest sustained encampment ever at the Pole.

I read up on the Pole on the flight north. It was a fixed point on the map, but on the ground it was something else: a point determined not only by compass readings, but by calculations on the speed of ice drift, elapsed time, and celestial fixes. You could make camp on it and wake up the next morning miles from your fixed position, stranded on an ice floe. So much for a sustained encampment.

Still we figured Wheeler must know something. He'd flown groups to the Pole before, high rollers from Vegas and little old ladies from Dubuque. This lot, though, was different. Except for Beinecke and me and another businessman, the group consisted of ham radio buffs plus a band of skydivers bent on freefalling over the Pole into the *Guinness Book of Records*. On hand to record their feat was an ABC television crew. I thought the whole scheme wacky enough to rate a story and called a magazine editor I knew who agreed.

At Resolute near the bottom of Ellesmere Island the outfitters and air charter people warned of heavy snows and refueling problems. The bush pilots had laid down an emergency cache of oil drums somewhere between our takeoff point and the Pole, only to find a few days later that, thanks to an ice shift, the entire cache had floated off without a trace. The head pilot took a dim view of Wheeler and his scheme; he was not about to risk leaving any of us alone at the Pole for some harebrained campout.

At Lake Hazen, our takeoff point on the northern tip of Ellesmere, we settled down in Quonset huts and waited for the weather to clear. The hams fiddled with their radios, the skydivers packed their chutes, I went fishing for char. I stood alone one morning near the top of the world, not far from where Peary had shoved off for the Pole seventy years before. I closed my eyes, held my breath, and experienced a transfigurative moment: no human sounds, no animal cries, no bird or wind song, no sigh of air, no crack of ice, only complete otherworldly silence. Emerson had described such a moment as being "part and parcel with God."

Early the third day we lifted off for the Pole. I was strapped in the front seat of a rickety DC-3 beside a stash of oil drums lashed to the forward bulkheads and containing three thousand pounds of extra fuel. The plane was christened "Air Napalm." A smaller Twin Otter with the skydivers and TV crew flew ahead of us. The Arctic Ocean stretched interminably, a vast penumbra of drifting ice whose glazed surface had been scraped raw by winds and lacerated by jagged pressure ridges. Three hours later we crossed the eighty-eighth parallel and saw ahead a gray impenetrable bank of fog. Some ninety-five miles from the Pole we were forced to turn back.

The DC-3 set down on a large ice floe south of the Pole so the skydivers could do their thing. I had a bad moment envisioning the plane sinking into old rotted ice and carrying me to a gurgling death, or landing so hard the fuel drums would jar loose and burst, incinerating us all. But the pilot, Hanlan, brought us down nicely on firm new ice about fifty feet thick. Everyone piled out and celebrated. The hams relayed phone patches to the lower forty-eight; I reached Ada. Beinecke planted a blue Yale pennon on an ice boulder the size of a house. Wheeler broke out champagne. The skydivers, in a profusion of colored chutes, dove into the record books.

The worst flash flood in a decade tore through a section of the Grand Canyon the day I hiked out with Ada and our youngest son after a week navigating the Colorado River in a dory.

Three miles up the trail to the canyon's rim a cannonade of thunder erupted, then sheets of rain sliced across the valley. Lightning, wind, and noise built in intensity. Crouched under a rocky overhang, we watched a fearful slide of loose earth and rock thunder down the slope, turning the hills on either side of us to torrents, the trail below to a seething wash of mud. A creek above us burst its course, uprooting trees and boulders that joined the avalanche. The scene was plunged in Biblical darkness.

The storm seemed a metaphor for the upheavals assailing much of the world.

The Russia we journeyed to in 1987 was engulfed in a reformist wave that would sweep away its moldered leadership and transform the country. From Moscow and the Caucasus to the Silk Road cities of Uzbekistan we caught the first stirrings of glasnost. At long last, Russians were about to grasp their yearned-for freedoms, open and unhindered religious worship among them. An image lingers: a perfectly proportioned twelfth-century basilica perched in grace above a mountain lake in Georgia, the pilgrims' offerings, scraps of cloth and paper, draped expansively over the surrounding scrub.

Aunt Wilma died, the ninety-nine-year-old matriarch of the Jung clan. She was followed a year later by her younger brother, my father-in-law, Wesley Jung

Wesley had nursed a single-minded passion: to preserve the legacy of his wagon-making forebears. Over the years he'd collected and restored more than a hundred old wagons and other vehicles from Sheboygan's past — horse-drawn milk trucks, sleighs, handsome four-in-hands, and trim buggies, even a circus calliope that was the pride of holiday parades in Sheboygan and Milwaukee. His craftsmanship was recognized throughout the state. The governor rode in one of Wesley's carriages before cheering crowds every Fourth of July; one of Wesley's carryalls had conveyed Ada's and my wedding party to the church. In due time, Wisconsin erected a museum in Wesley's name to house his remarkable collection.

We said good-bye, too, to Aunt Nancy, my favorite Philadelphia blueblood. In the rock garden below her Sky Farm cottage we drank to her gentle uneventful life. I began imagining ghosts, my mother floating on gusts across the West Meadow, Aunt Nancy tending her perennials in some eternal summer garden, Aunt Eleanor nursing a martini beneath an elm in Fuller's Cemetery. I walked up to the cemetery one of the last days in August. A southwest breeze played across the graves and a whitethroat sang in the branches above Aunt Eleanor. I said a prayer for them all.

Before the eighties were done, the Berlin Wall fell and we got a new president.

George Herbert Walker Bush was a Connecticut Yankee with Texas pretensions. I'd met him first in the sixties when he was a freshly minted congressman from Texas, his adopted state, and I was covering the House for *Time*. He was decent to his fingernails, but lacked the fire and vision of a Kennedy or Reagan.

When the Wall came down in late 1989, and the sound of Berliners hammering the hated concrete into pieces reverberated around the world, it was, as the journalist Harold Evans wrote, "the global triumph of liberal democracy over Communist totalitarianism." The Wall's collapse also signaled a future of doubt, a sobering uncertainty for a world no longer burdened with the irrefutable superpower rivalry.

In 1992, the voters traded in George H. W. Bush for Bill Clinton.

The Clinton years veered from the trivial to the embarrassing, with the occasional inspired turn. Later, some derided the era as sex between the Bushes. Americans fretted about globalization and their Social Security. They hissed stock villains like the tobacco industry and the ethnic cleansers in Serbia with unpronounceable names.

We were intrigued by laptops, Palm Pilots, virtual-reality computer games, and cell phones. Manhattan's streets ran riot with people wired from the neck up busily talking to themselves. On the cusp of the new age of hurry, we e-mailed, faxed, FedExed, instant-messaged, and multitasked. Cable TV's shouters began to shape our political attitudes; the young read fewer and fewer newspapers, then virtually gave up reading anything. We lived in what one essayist called "the delirious daydream" of the nineties.

Still, I applauded the resurrection of my city. Gone were the panhandlers and squeegee men. The streets almost sparkled, the parks were walkable again. Once blighted neighborhoods revived.

Violent crime subsided. People rediscovered their manners, offering the occasional bus or subway seat to the old and infirm, rationing their outbursts of obscenity. I found myself swept up in the reformation, walking blind men up the subway steps to the street, venturing apologies for the absentminded shove as I threaded my way through the Midtown throngs.

In the city of O. Henry and William Cullen Bryant I oriented my working schedule toward the world of books. I helped support the scholarly publications of the American Wing of the Metropolitan Museum of Art as a Bryant Fellow; directed a prominent archives foundation that preserved valuable troves of correspondence from leading figures in the growth of New York's literary arts; and presided over the American Trust for the British Library. Along the way Norton published my third book, *Breakup: The Coming End of Canada and the Stakes for America.*

The *New York Times* reviewer said it was "the best book on Canada by an American journalist" he had read. Despite the overheated title, I had hoped to alert American readers to the danger of Canada's imploding over the separatist crisis, the implications for those of us living next door below the 49th parallel. The trade magazine *Publishers Weekly* said the book was "a compelling wake-up call that should stir wide debate." So it did, but principally in Canada.

When my publisher introduced *Breakup* at our sales conference in Toronto, several of the sales reps became visibly distraught. The *Montreal Gazette* accused me of "big-stick Yankee arrogance." There was outrage at my Canadian distributor for peddling so subversive a work. One reviewer even urged the folks in Newfoundland to file a class action suit against me for belittling their province.

The phones began lighting up at my first talk show interview on a cross-country media tour. I looked around for a flak vest. To my relief, the calls were from Canadians across the country, eager to vent their spleen at one another over a host of regional grievances.

I sat there quietly, a bystander caught in the crossfire, marveling at how it all proved my book's thesis.

On the royalties from *Breakup*, about enough to cover dinner for two at Lutèce, I took a small flier on a Broadway musical that became a hit and actually repaid its investors.

Music seemed the one art immune to political pressure. The p.c. crowd tinkered with Berlin and Gershwin at their peril. Popular songs were the pulse of a nation's heart, Yip Harburg had said.

However I regretted the passing of the great American Songbook classics, the deconstruction of the Broadway musical from the joyous shows of my youth to the witless spectacles of the new age, a part of me kept hoping for salvation. Soon, out of the ashes, a new generation of pop singers would rise to dust off and burnish the old standards, those "little houses in which our hearts once lived," the songs that distilled our deepest aches and dreams.

There was still gorgeous music around if you listened for it. Beethoven in a taxicab. The trill of spring thrushes in Central Park. Violins and zithers in the subway stations. The occasional Broadway revival. A handful of veterans like Rosemary Clooney and Margaret Whiting from the big-band era kept the torch alight. Margaret sang one evening at a black-tie party in our apartment, the scene, she said, transporting her back to one of those Cole Porter nights, just one of those fabulous flights.

My piano playing had woven a melodic line through my life. I'd played from Aspen to Zürs: at a party with the legendary trumpeter Doc Cheatham; at the old Eddie Condon's in Greenwich Village when Joe Sullivan was taking a longer than usual refreshment break; at the correspondents' annual bash in Canada's House of Commons. It had helped leaven my hitch in the Army and break the ice with wary news sources.

I never kidded myself that I was more than a gifted amateur, that I could gig with the pros, those guys with the unerring base-lines and flatted fifths who, in the words of a character from

Corelli's Mandolin, made the music look "as though it's coming out by magic."

One day in the mid-nineties, following surgery for prostate cancer, I found myself standing alone on crutches in a hospital corridor. I was weak, unshaven, and trailing a snakelike catheter connected to my penis. I felt soiled and somehow shamed by my helplessness, unable for the first time in my life to control my bodily functions. I started to weep. A nurse saw me and led me to another patient, a young boy dying from an inoperable brain tumor. The boy greeted me with a wide smile and we chatted. I shuffled back to my room, profoundly ashamed, vowing never again to feel sorry for myself.

Corliss went out with gusto, aged ninety-two. The phone had rung one afternoon in his hospital room and a nurse, intercepting the call, had thought at first it was a Miss Epstein calling. "This. Is. Katherine. Hepburn," said the caller, all icy hauteur. She was inquiring after Corliss, her old hiking companion on the Palisades. Corliss's obituary noted among other things that he had left fifty step-grandchildren.

My Harvard pal Paul Murphy gave up the ghost in Switzerland. After graduation he'd vanished into the bohemian mists, playing piano in Scotland, composing jingles for an ad agency, and wandering through Europe with an Italian circus troupe. He'd come to ground finally in an Alpine chalet with the love of his life, a spirited Egyptian named Frances. We'd flown over for their wedding in a twelfth-century château. A while later Murphy had checked into a Geneva hospital with inoperable cancer.

It rained all afternoon the day he died. The sun broke through just before dusk, bathing his small room in light. A few sparrows hopped from the balcony through the open door. Frances, holding Paul's hand, turned to him a last time and said, "Look, darling, the birds have come for your soul."

The summer of 1995 we celebrated Sky Farm's Diamond Jubilee.

The world beyond had grown uglier. Rwanda's genocide had turned the commanding UN peacekeeper there, a Canadian general I'd once interviewed, into a broken man. Russia, liberated but adrift, had become an economic basket case. Washington was muck-deep in l'affaire Monica and the humiliation of a sitting president. But New York was still on a roll. Tourists were flocking back. The Yanks were winning the World Series.

Reluctantly we sold Loverly and said a final adieu to the Rappahannock Valley and Virginia. We'd settle for Nod Hill and the summer rhythms of North Haven. But even those were changing.

For many of the new summertimers the island was becoming just one more holiday option. The new breed was restless to change things, to modernize, accelerate the pace, build big, and build prodigally. They flew across the bay, bearing the toys and habits of their urban culture. Our summers became flush with good-works projects and fund-raising requests. Benefit events sprouted like liverwort. McMansions rose; the largest of them might have been erected by God himself if he could have afforded it.

A bitter rupture between the Haven's traditionalists and the new progressives — over a local school issue — rent the islanders' usual comity. There were vengeful acts of petty vandalism and mean-spirited letters in the local paper. Neighbors refused to speak to each other; family members became estranged. The island rode out the storm, the disputants sensing perhaps their deep communal tug to the place. For me, that feeling was always reinforced at summer's end.

The good-bye was wrenching, the end of a rapturous affair. It was especially hard when the weather had been kind, the sailing good, and the people around you sympatico. On those waning August days you could hear the sadness in the gull's mew or see it in the way the aspens bent sorrowfully to the northwesterlies signaling fall. If you happened to depart on a heaven-sent morning when the storm the night before had washed the skies clear and left the bay a panoply of white-capped blue, the air so crystalline you could reach out and almost touch the steeples of Camden — well, that was the hardest.

I came to think it better to bow out in a damp easterly. Made the going a little easier.

The last seasons of the millennium passed in laughter and nostalgia.

A friend brought Julia Child, the cooking guru, up to Sky Farm. She bustled into the kitchen to examine our ancient, faulty stove. She turned a knob and, whoosh, a spray of flame sent her reeling backward. "Nothing wrong with this stove," she burbled. "Just twist the knob and run like hell."

Anne Morrow Lindbergh, at ninety-four blind and beset with Alzheimer's, returned to the Haven for the first time in years. She crossed the bay in an open launch, headed for Pulpit Harbor and a last visit to the old Morrow homestead. She sat dozing, huddled against the wind as they neared the harbor, her back to the shore. No one alerted her, but as they passed the Morrow house on Deacon Brown Point something jarred her senses. She sat bolt upright. "Slow down," she said. "I'm home."

One August day I took my final sail on *Minuteman*.

She was the last wooden dinghy built on North Haven, carefully crafted by Ben Brown of the Y-Knot Boatyard. We'd launched her on the two-hundredth anniversary of the Declaration of Independence. She was a patriot's dream on water with her clean white hull, blue keel, and a red '76 stitched on her mainsail.

We'd raced her for some fifteen summers and she'd won a pennant or two. Then the fleet converted to fiberglass and the woodens gradually slipped into the wake of the newer boats; each year they became fewer, retired to the dark corners of their owners' boathouses or reconfigured as quaint little flower gardens. One summer we pulled *Minuteman* from the Thoroughfare and brought her to rest in the backwaters of the Pulpit. She lay there a few more years, moored quietly among a handful of old friends. Each winter we had her scraped and painted and recaulked. Each summer she got sailed less, an aging beauty with fewer suitors.

We sensed the time had come to retire her permanently. The cost of keeping up her appearances had become prohibitive. She dozed at her mooring, the gleam gone from her, the varnish flaking from her gaff. When Ada and I cast off for the last time, her rigging creaked, the tiller wobbled in the rudder hole, the centerboard jammed. You could feel her system shutting down. She had one good sail left in her that golden afternoon near summer's end.

She breezed by the few remaining summer cruisers in the harbor and tacked into the sharpening westerly that swept in from the bay. She beat sluggishly past Norton's Point, and somewhere under the lee of the Cabots on Minister's Creek we brought her about and headed for home. We tied her gently to the mooring, furled and stopped her tired mainsail, and left her there in the waning summer light. Even as the harbor slowly invaded her leaky timbers, *Minuteman* breathed a lovely defiance at the last.

No century chronicled as many milestones as the twentieth. Two world wars. The atomic bomb. Medical breakthroughs by the score. Men on the moon. The birth of the airplane, movies, television, pushbutton phones, and the Internet. The phenomenon of suburbia and the shopping mall. Just for starters.

The century's movers and shakers, the demigods of statecraft and revolution, had commanded the stage. But in the end, its seminal figure was a modest, Bavarian-born physicist named Albert Einstein. In crowning him Man of the Century, *Time* lauded Einstein as "the locksmith of the mysteries of the atom and the universe," the man whose work had transformed all the key fields in our age of science and technology. More than anyone, he had been the reluctant creator of that day of Trinity on the Alamogordo desert.

On New Year's Eve, 1999, we celebrated the millennium with friends under the glass dome of the new planetarium at the American Museum of Natural History. It was a gala affair with bands and bubbly, the best knees-up in town. With the rest of the world we toasted the new century ahead and the next one thousand years.

Little did we know what we were toasting, the horror just over the horizon.

12

Where Have You Gone, Cuddles Sakall?

The phone rang twice in our bedroom that September morning.

Twenty paces down the hall, behind the closed door of my office, deep into my writing, I was oblivious to the ringing. Ada was in Connecticut.

Two hours later, after the planes had slammed into the Twin Towers, I wandered back to the bedroom to fetch something and saw the message light blinking. It was my sons calling from Boston, wondering if their mother and I were okay, if we'd seen the television reports. "New York's burning," Douglas said.

I called the family, reaching them just as the jammed phone lines were shutting down across the city. I grabbed my camera and rushed out onto Lexington Avenue. Southward five miles or more a pall of smoke blotted out the lower reaches of Manhattan, spreading on the wind like some malevolent plague.

Thousands had stampeded from the World Trade Center area, fleeing the falling debris and smoke storm. Some fled to the nearest bridge spanning the East River; others slogged their way uptown trying to reach their homes. Crowds of people were walking north along Lexington Avenue, searching for bars or coffee shops where they could rest, call relatives, and follow news of the catastrophe on TV.

In Lower Manhattan, ambulances shrieked down the streets filled with terrified people. Hundreds of firefighters hurried toward the burning towers and, we'd later learn, their doom. The site was barred to all but emergency vehicles. The subways shut down, the airports shut down, the schools shut down. A thick white ash settled on the scene like a nuclear winter.

I joined a line of blood donors outside Lenox Hill Hospital. There was a five-hour wait and then it turned out there weren't enough injured to meet the response. In emergency rooms across the city medics waited in vain for the injured to arrive. Only the morgues filled up.

People turned to the churches and parks for relief. In nearby St. Jean de Baptiste I found the prayerbooks laid out, pages opened to the Twenty-second Psalm ("My God, my God, why hast thou forsaken me?"). I headed for Central Park. Hundreds of families already had gathered there, watching numbly as the pall to the south crept northward and the first acrid whiffs of the holocaust reached us.

In the days ahead, friends called and wrote — many from abroad. An old Canadian colleague phoned from Medicine Hat, Alberta; overcome, I lost it for a moment and must have deeply embarrassed him.

It was the young primarily, the starting bank clerks, brokers and traders, the paralegals and junior office managers, who had perished in the inferno. At our local Engine and Ladder Company on 85th Street, they mourned the deaths of nine of their young firefighters. Thornton Wilder in *The Bridge of San Luis Rey* tells of the collapse of the finest bridge in Peru in 1714, and of the five persons who were thrown to their death in the river below. A priest who saw them die says to himself, "Why did this happen to *those* five?" It was the same question the pastor of our Wilton church asked at Sunday services after he'd read the names of five young parishioners missing in the World Trade carnage. It was the question, for the total three thousand victims, we were all asking.

The trauma of 9/11 would haunt us for years. When the grieving was done, a terrible vengeance would assert itself.

On Thanksgiving Day we made a pilgrimage to Ground Zero.

The barricades were still up. Beyond them, some ten weeks after the attack, firefighters continued to pump great plumes of water on the still smoldering ruins. Around the gaping crater where the towers had stood lay piles of jumbled steel and girders, remnants of adjoining buildings that had been leveled in the blast. Structures of seven or eight stories had been pancaked into thin layers of metallic rubble. The scene was surreal, a vast junkyard of a tomb. I'd seen some of the remains of Berlin after World War II and this was near their equal.

Hundreds of families had come to pay their respects. They moved in a silent throng around the perimeter of the crater, people from all over. By the grille fence fronting St. Paul's Chapel near the site, people had placed masses of flowers, small flags, and other tokens of sympathy. Draped across the fence, as long as a block, were white sheets on which mourners had scrawled prayers, condolences, and personal messages in every language. We joined the crowds, waiting to add our own tribute.

We stopped at Trinity Church to offer prayers. In the graveyard, where Alexander Hamilton lies, a blanket of ash still covered the headstones.

I returned to Los Alamos one last time.

In a world where the terrible scale of death from wars had become the central moral fact of our time, the atomic bomb had been "the turn of the screw" that rendered the prospect of any future world wars unacceptable. It was, however, useless against the new terrorism.

The superpowers' decaying nuclear arsenals still posed a threat, but the weapons themselves seemed almost redundant, part of the wallpaper of the age. The scientists at Los Alamos had built no nuclear weapons since the mid-1990s. Once, they'd worried whether the Trinity test would blow up half of New Mexico; now they worried about forest fires destroying their homes and laboratories. They spent their days overseeing the diminishing weapons stockpile, living out unfulfilled careers.

I went back at the instigation of Richard Rhodes, whose Pulitzer Prize-winning book, *The Making of the Atomic Bomb*, had been published two decades after mine. The occasion was a weekend commemorating the Manhattan Project and promoting a campaign to preserve the historic wooden sheds where Oppie's team had fashioned the Bomb. "Save America's Treasures" was the artless title of the campaign.

For two days, in that haunted landscape with its ravishing vistas of the Sangre de Cristo peaks, Rhodes and I revisited the bombmakers' stamping grounds. We tried to sound scintillating in panel discussions and indulged in long reminiscing interviews for the local papers. I was not unhappy when the weekend came to a close.

Family and friends were one's refuge in those months of 9/11's aftershock. My imperishably lovely wife of nearly half a century remained my anchor against the winds of sorrow and setback. In Ada, I found the inner calm, the patient diplomacy that brought us through the tough patches. She ran three homes, our complex finances, and the grandchildren's education fund with the adroitness of a Schwab or a Buffett.

Our children had followed divergent paths, one son into the investment business, the other into teaching; both had married ladies of beauty with a talent for helping the less fortunate. Our daughters had married men in noncorporate lines of work, one a farmer-conservationist, the other a builder. All had settled in the Boston area, except for our maverick youngest daughter who'd opted to raise her brood in a remote Costa Rican villa, surrounded by toucans, high above a lake in the shadow of an ancient volcano.

The president had vowed to wage war on the terrorists who had done the unspeakable to us. First in Afghanistan, we struck back; then, less explicably, in Iraq.

One day in 2003, I sat before a TV with two of my grandsons and watched the opening salvo of the Iraq invasion. The images captured the night bombing of Baghdad, the incoming cruise missiles, the city's darkened skyline erupting in huge fireballs and showers of burning metal. From our living room a quarter of a world away, it seemed obscene watching so much death rain down on that ancient capital by the Tigris. Never before had such destruction been unleashed "live" on television and with such lethal precision. I found it deeply disturbing to watch, like a public execution.

Yet it was also a curiously reaffirming moment: America's ascendancy as the planet's prime enforcer, hopefully for the good.

In the months ahead it became clear that, however well intended, this was a dubious venture, incompetently managed in its post-invasion stage. For all our military prowess we were hard put to prevail, warring so far afield on alien soil amidst an alien culture, alone except for Britain and the meager "coalition of the willing." Things would get worse.

My old friend Cabot bought the farm, dead at seventy-three of a brain tumor.

His obituary noted the old saw about the Lowells speaking only to Cabots and the Cabots speaking only to God. I was never privy to Charlie's conversations with the Almighty, but I was certain he had done more than his share of God's work, all the good causes he'd led and fought for over the years.

From time to time I'd offered him advice on how to deal with his pedigree, especially after one newspaper ran a piece labeling the Cabots the first family of Boston.

"Your Highness," I wrote him, "this 'first family' business is rub-bish. Everyone knows the Fitzgeralds and Kennedys are the first families of Boston. The Cabots aren't 'first,' only the most fertile and exclusive. Still, this royalty game is a hard knock. My equerry and I admire the way you handle it, always playing it down. Let the commoners try coping with the pressures of being part of a first family, and see how they like it. I kiss your ring."

Charlie wasn't himself on our last *Echo* cruise the year before. Near the end I dropped by his house with Ada to say good-bye. He was giving the busybody nurse a hard time. Five days later he was gone. The church in Dover couldn't handle the overflow at his service.

I was sure the grim reaper was waiting in the wings for me, too. I would keep him an understudy as long as possible. I had books to write and twelve grandchildren to amuse as I pondered their future.

It was easy to distrust the world lying in wait for them. Some days I thought everything had been reduced to one long sound bite. The clutter of small commotions that filled each day moved at cyberspeed, flattening the warning emotional bumps that sug-gested serious pause and reflection.

Even if the rush-age technology confounded me, I knew our math-smart "grands" would master the bandwidth and the browsers. If they didn't become socially disconnected or develop carpal tunnel syndrome along the way, they would be the next Napoleons of the Google epoch. I would surely join Tyrannosaurus Rex, but they would ripple through life on their Apple keyboards.

I might go mad trying to unsheathe the plastic from my pill bottles or pushing ever more phone buttons trying to reach a live voice on the other end. But they would thrive. They would conquer the multipushbutton, 500-channel globalizing universe with all its lucrative trading and technology transfer. It would line their pock-ets with gold. Whether it would line their insides with humanity and vision, I was less certain.

I wished them lives free of the traumas that had scarred ours, that they would never feel the desolation of losing a father or brother in war, the shock of seeing public leaders cut down in their prime.

For all my Luddite ways I remain an optimist.

I rue the predicted demise of the printed word as we know it, a coming world bereft of tactile books and newspapers, the personal memoirs of our age reduced to surviving e-mail messages. But on the whole I'm hopeful.

We'll be okay if we start trimming our sails a bit, stop lording it around the world for a while, drive smaller cars, and curb our appetite for excess. We need to make more useful things and make them better so they last, as we once did. We'll do fine if we think as hard about the ideas we want to communicate as we do about the technology of communicating them. We'll do even better if we cool the fevers of our ideologies and zealotries.

I like growing old in New York, the city of my youth.

I used to take a detour on Madison Avenue and 84th Street to avoid passing the Campbell Funeral Home, a silly superstition.

Not long ago a woman on her way home from shopping on Madison felt the urge to relieve herself. There were no hotels or restaurants in sight, but she spotted the Campbell Funeral Home and ducked in. A service was in progress. The woman joined the few mourners, perfunctorily paid her respects to the deceased, signed the register, then scurried to the restroom. Months later she received a letter from an unfamiliar law firm. Attached was a check for five thousand dollars. A recently deceased heiress had before her death instructed her executors to make generous payments to all those friends who troubled themselves to attend her wake at the Campbell Funeral Home.

I've since stopped the detour business.

I have few regrets. I'm sorry they downgraded Pluto, pride of my birthday, to a dwarf planet. Sorry I never spent enough time with my children when they were children. Never got to a jazz funeral in the Big Easy before it went under. Never saw the Lord God Bird.

Never met Bogie. But I have those indelible memories of the moment, those small epiphanies:

Dawn among the colonnades of Palmyra . . . the smell of London's streets after a fresh spring rain . . . the mosques of Samarkand at dusk . . . the sounds of an a cappella male choir in an ancient Kazakhstan chapel . . . nighthawks wheeling over Sky Farm at summer's end.

The ways have been sweet to us, Ada and me. When I think of her in the autumn of our years, I think of the dialogue in a Yeats vignette. A neighbor asks another, "Did you pass an old woman walking by just now?" "No," he says, "but I saw a young girl, and she walked like a queen" . . . on that beach in Florida ages ago, last evening when we were young.

It still snows in Rochester on Christmas Eve, I'm told, and the candlelight service we once attended as kids is still packed.

Few if any Miners or Ranlets are left there, but their names, especially Ned's, are writ large in the annals of that city. The same with Tom Lamont in New York. His and Florence's home on 70th Street houses the Visiting Nurse Service, which dispatches ministering angels to the sick and infirm; and there's a marble plaque in Tom's memory at of the Metropolitan Museum of Art.

They say the more memories you cherish, the more of you endures. So well before the sweet bye-and-bye, before memory and muscles start to melt, I'll play and sing once more the songs that drifted away with a piece of our hearts. I'll laugh again with the too many ghosts of forgotten cruises and ski runs. In the wee small hours of the morning, when the bourbon has mellowed the soul, I'll drink to them all.

In the thin blue glow of the tube I'll go weepy when Judy returns from the Land of Oz for the millionth time. I'll get a lump in my throat for Scarlett and Rhett down among the magnolias. And I'll raise the rafters for Rick and his jowly headwaiter, Carl, as they flummox the bad guys in that faraway café in Casablanca.

Acknowledgments

I am first of all indebted to the oral and written remembrances of old friends, relatives, and colleagues who have reinforced my occasionally faulty memory:

Charles Bracelen Flood; Margot Lamont Heap; John D. Macomber and his late brother, William B. Macomber; Robert M. Pennoyer; and the late Anne Miner Richardson, to name a few. Also, Thomas Griffith (*Harry & Teddy*) and John Stacks (*Scotty*). Certain anecdotes, identifications, and atmospheric details are attributable to them.

The works of Hector McKechnie (*The Lamont Clan*), Edgar Berman (*Hubert*), Ogden Nash, Drew Pearson, and Jules Witcover, among others, further complemented my own recollections or added salt to my prose. Close readings of the *Boston Globe* and *Boston Herald*, as well as the *New York Times*, *Washington Post* and, of course, *Time* helped firm the historical accuracy of this memoir. Other contributing sources are quoted directly in the text.

I thank especially three persons who took the time and effort to

read the draft manuscript and offer their advice and encourage-
ment: Barbara Silber Lamont, my daughter-in-law, a one-time professional editor, now a teacher and mother of three; Simon
Michael Bessie, who published my first book and has remained a
good friend over the decades; and Lawrence Hughes, longtime
publisher and another old friend.

This project would not have borne fruit without the vision and
attentive nurturing of Eric Kampmann, president of Beaufort
Books; David C. Nelson, former vice president and publisher at
Beaufort; and Margot Atwell, Beaufort's associate publisher and
managing editor. I am grateful to all three. For copyeditng the manuscript with such scrupulously informed care, I also extend plaudits
to Susan Hayes.

Tom Wallace, my friend and agent, took an early shine to this
work and has supported it with verve and enthusiasm from cradle
to bookstore. My deep thanks.